LIKE A TWO-EDG

Like a Two-Edged Sword

The Word of God in Liturgy and History

Essays in Honour of Canon Donald Gray

Edited by
MARTIN R. DUDLEY

The Canterbury Press
Norwich

First published 1995 by The Canterbury Press Norwich
(a publishing imprint of Hymns Ancient & Modern Limited
a registered charity)
St Mary's Works, St Mary's Plain,
Norwich, Norfolk NE3 3BH

A catalogue record for this book is available
from the British Library

ISBN I-85311-115-5

*Typeset by Waveney Studios
Diss, Norfolk
and printed in Great Britain by
St Edmundsbury Press Limited
Bury St Edmunds, Suffolk*

CONTENTS

PREFACE

IN HIS Presidential Address to the 1989 Congress of Societas Liturgica, Donald Gray addressed the question of liturgical inculturation from an unexpected angle. He examined the liturgical and ritual response to the Hillsborough football disaster of April 15th, 1989, in which ninety-five fans were killed. In doing so he combined two things: a finely-honed perception of the nature of liturgy and a down-to-earth grasp of human need. It is not for nothing that his study of the social and political dimension in the renewal of Anglican worship, published in 1986 as Alcuin Club Collection 68, is entitled *Earth and Altar*. Liturgy needs particular skills; it is neither pure scholarship nor pure practice. The good liturgist has a feel for what will work and an understanding, based on historical research and on the study of texts, of what is consonant with the Church's tradition of worship. By these criteria Donald Gray is amply qualified for the significant role he has played in the development of liturgy and liturgical studies both in England and abroad.

It was with a good deal of pleasure that I accepted the invitation to edit this *Festschrift*. Such collections are all too rare in ecclesiastical circles. Time was short and though the volme had from its very conception an overall theme and focus on the Word of God it was clear that its content would depend a great deal on what the contributors were already thinking about and working through. Perhaps it is the more remarkable that this is not merely a *Festschrift* made up of somewhat disparate contributions by distinguished scholars but, if I may change languages, a *mélange harmonieuse* in which the essays really do complement one another. The centre is the Word of God but, as befits a volume in Donald Gray's honour, other themes important to him cluster here: Alcuin and the Club that bears his name, Westminster Abbey, lectionaries, psalmody and hymnody, the history of the Church and the history of the liturgy.

This volume honours Donald Gray on his sixty-fifth birthday – July 21st, 1995. I am glad that it does not mark his retirement. It marks his contribution to liturgy. I am very grateful to the contributors who worked very hard to meet a demanding schedule.

Various aspects of Donald's liturgical activities are represented by the contributors, though the Alcuin Cub, of which he has been Chairman since 1987, is probably the major link – half of the contributors have served with him on the Committee. If there had been more time it might have been possible to have a broader spread both internationally and ecumenically. I hope that Donald's friends will understand that this was not ultimately possible if this *Festschrift* was going to be ready for his birthday. I am enormously grateful to Gordon Knights and Kenneth Baker at The Canterbury Press Norwich for so willingly accepting this volume and for encouraging me to proceed with it.

MARTIN R. DUDLEY

AN APPRCIATION BY
THE DEAN OF WESTMINSTER
THE VERY REVD MICHAEL MAYNE

THE TWO factors that most help a great abbey or a cathedral to be
true to its heritage are the emphasis placed on worship and liturgy,
and the chemistry of those who minister at its centre. I am no
historian, nor am I a liturgical scholar; but I care greatly about the
centrality of eucharistic worship and how it is ordered, and I place
the loyalty and companionship of friends very high on the list of
essentials. Which is why I have so much valued Donald and his
presence as a colleague at Westminster for the past eight years.

Donald has brought to the Abbey community certain invaluable
gifts. Warmth for a start, a no-nonsense, open-hearted northern
kind of warmth and hospitality; and a great sense of humanity and
plain speaking, though always with charity and restraint. He can be
stubborn sometimes, but that's no bad thing; and surprisingly
vulnerable, but that I find an attractive quality. We have a shared
love of novels, theatre and poetry, and a similar eye for the absurd.
There's enough of the old 'pro' in him to enjoy the razzmatazz of
the Commons, the buzz of excitement in the Tea Room, the
processing and dressing-up; but rather more of the pastor in a
ministry to politicians of all persuasions.

As a member of Chapter Donald can be courteously forthright:
essentially a simplifier rather than complicator, he sees the consensus view not as a weak compromise but as the expression of a
proper collegiality. In the somewhat wider context of the Committee that plans our worship his liturgical expertise can be
maddening, for he is usually right; and when he is defeated he
accepts with the gently amused air of the man who has learned that
to give way graciously is to live to fight another day.

Donald is the only man I know who deliberately wears a hat in
order to preserve the old-style courtesy of raising it to all those he
meets, but this odd passion for preserving the customs of the past
does not extend as far as Cranmer and the Book of Common
Prayer. As Rector of St Margaret's he has worked very slowly at

changing the main thrust of the worshipping life from Prayer Book Matins to a weekly sung Eucharist, and over the years he has attracted to the church a succession of college chaplains and non-stipendiary clergy to assist him on a Sunday who clearly feel a great affection for him and Joyce.

Ah, Joyce! Will she be mentioned in this book of historical and liturgical essays? I hope so, for Joyce has made it all possible by being the most loving, supporting and affirming of wives, a natural home-maker whose kindness is evident to all. She and Donald have just bought their retirement home in Stamford, and I suspect that in a few years there will be those who will come (as so many have in the past) to warm their hands at the fire of this particular marriage.

In short, while Donald may not be the paragon I seem to be describing – we are all a bit more complex than our obituaries will make us – nevertheless I could not wish for a more loyal and dependable colleague, and I am proud to have him as a friend.

AN APPRECIATION BY THE SPEAKER OF THE HOUSE OF COMMONS THE RT HON. BETTY BOOTHROYD, M.P.

Donald Gray is the 77th Speaker's Chaplain since 1660. If his predecessors carried out their duties with the commitment and enthusiasm which Donald has shown over the last eight years, the House of Commons has been remarkably fortunate. His learning, his sense of humour, the power of his preaching and his Christian kindness are legendary in the Palace of Westminster where he has acquired many friends across the political and religious spectrum. His 65th birthday is an occasion for celebration and is well marked by this collection of essays; but it is also a moment of regret for me in that it brings nearer the day when I must lose his services.

CANON DONALD GRAY
BIOGRAPHY AND BIBLIOGRAPHY

DONALD CLIFFORD GRAY was born in Manchester, England, on 21st July, 1930. He studied Theology at King's College, London, became an Associate of King's College in 1955 and was ordained Deacon in the Diocese of Manchester in 1956 and Priest the following year. His title was Leigh Parish Church. In 1960 he became Vicar of St Peter, Westleigh, and in 1967 Vicar of All Saints', Elton. For ten years, from 1964 until his move to Liverpool in 1974, he was a member of the Church Assembly, and was a member of the General Synod of the Church of England, 1980–87. The Church of our Lady with St Nicholas and St Anne, Liverpool, was the focus of his ministry from 1974 until 1987 when he was made a Canon of Westminster, Rector of St Margaret's, and Chaplain to the Speaker of the House of Commons. An Honorary Chaplain to the Queen, 1975–81, he became Chaplain in 1982. In 1980 he received the degree of Master of Philosophy from Liverpool University and in 1985 the degree of Doctor of Philosophy (under the supervision of Richard Buxton) from the University of Manchester for the research which became the volume *Earth and Altar*. In 1988 he was elected a Fellow of the Royal Historical Society.

The primary purpose of this brief biographical summary is to point to Donald Gray's service to the liturgy and much else that he has done must, therefore, be set to one side. His membership of the Church of England Liturgical Commission began in 1968, during the final stages of Series 2. It continued through Series 3 and the preparation of *The Alternative Service Book 1980* and ended in 1986, when he became an Official Observer. During this time it fell to him to present the new liturgies as the Commission's spokesman in the Northern Convocation. In 1971 we find his name on the list of members of the Commission as it presented Holy Communion Series 3 to the Archbishops of Canterbury and York. Among the better known members at that time were Ronald Jasper (Chairman), Colin Buchanan, Geoffrey Cuming,

David Frost, D. E. W. Harrison, Leslie Houlden, Peter Moore, and E. C. Whitaker; Leslie Brown was among the corresponding members. Nine years later the Commission, still under Jasper's chairmanship, and with Buchanan, Cuming, Frost and Whitaker remaining as members, included David Hope (soon to become Archbishop of York) and David Silk (now Bishop of Ballarat).

Liturgy today is an ecumenical and international enterprise and Donald Gray has been involved in both these wider dimensions of liturgical renewal. In 1969 he became a member of the Joint Liturgical Group, an ecumenical body drawn from various Churches in Great Britain. He became its Secretary in 1980 and was its chairman, 1989–94. Also in 1969 he joined the international Societas Liturgica. He has served on the Council since 1977 and was President 1987–90. A member of the Alcuin Club since 1970. He joined the Committee in 1980. The world of liturgical scholarship remains a small one and there were familiar faces around the table including Ronald Jasper and David Silk, together with the younger scholars, Paul Bradshaw and Kenneth Stevenson. Donald Gray succeeded George Timms as Chairman in 1987. The heady days of new liturgies had passed and it became increasingly difficult to find a British publisher willing to publish scholarly liturgical writing, yet under Donald Gray's chairmanship, with first Michael Perham and then Martin Dudley as Secretary, the Alcuin Club has regained its position in liturgical scholarship. From 1978 until 1984 he was Founder Chairman of the Society for Liturgical Study created by the initiative of Geoffrey Cuming to promote the work of younger liturgists. In 1985 he was appointed to the English Language Liturgical Consultation and was one of its representatives on the Task Force that prepared the *Revised Common Lectionary*.

The following, in chronological order, are his publications (excluding journalism and reviews of books, which have appeared in *News of Liturgy*, *Alcuin Journal*, *Music and Liturgy*, *Worship* and the *Church Times*):

1967

1. *Notes on the Celebration of Alternative Services Second series: An Order for Holy Communion* (with John T. Martin), Paines 1967.

1968

2. 'The Furthest Station West', in *Journal of the Royal Army Chaplains Department*, vol. 21, no. 109 (May 1968).

1973–74

3. 'A Disciple of Discipline', Leigh Local History Society Lectures, 1973–74.

1975

4. 'An Anglican Point of View' in R. C. D. Jasper, ed., *Worship and the Child: Essays by the Joint Liturgical Group*, SPCK 1975.

1976

5. Contributions to R. S. Matthew, ed., *The Story of the People of God: a basis for Christian education in the Church Community*, British Lessons Council 19756.

1980

6. 'The Society for Liturgical Study', in K. W. Stevenson, ed., *Symbolism and the Liturgy I* (Grove Liturgical Study 23), Grove Books, Nottingham 1980.

1982

7. 'The Work of Geoffrey Cuming', in K. W. Stevenson, ed., *Liturgy Reshaped*, SPCK 1982.

8. 'The Setting of Worship', in R. C. D. Jasper, ed., *Getting the Liturgy Right*, SPCK 1983.

1983

9. 'Worship' in J. Mills and J. Nelson, eds., *Exploration into Parish Ministry*, Liverpool Diocese 1983.

10. Editor of *Holy Week Services: Joint Liturgical Group*, revised and expanded ed., SPCK 1983.

1984

11. 'The Influence of Tractarian Principles on Parish Worship 1839–49', in *Alcuin Journal*, 1984.

1985

12. 'Pushing at the Door', in C. O. Buchanan, ed., *Nurturing Children in Communion* (Grove Liturgical Study 44), Grove Books, Nottingham 1985.

1986

13. *Earth and Altar: The Evolution of the Parish Communion in the Church of England to 1945*, (Alcuin Club Collection 68), The Canterbury Press Norwich 1986.
14. 'The Area Writes the Agenda', in G. Nairn-Briggs, ed., *Love in Action – The Human Face of Faith in the City*, Church Literature Association 1986.

1988

15. Editor of *The Word in Season: Essays by Members of the Joint Liturgical Group on the use of the Bible in liturgy*, The Canterbury Press Norwich 1988.
16. 'Introduction to a debate' in no. 15 above.
17. *Ite, Missa Est*: Liturgy and the Church in Mission', in T. J. Talley, ed., *A Kingdom of Priests: Liturgical Formation of the People of God*, (Alcuin/GROW Joint Liturgical Study 5) Grove Books, Nottingham 1988.
18. 'Sends us out into the word: Worship with political and social action', in *The Church Service Society Record*, no. 18, Autumn 1988.
19. 'Towards an Ecumenical Eucharistic Lectionary', in *Liturgy*, vol. 12 no. 4, April–May 1988.
20. 'The Revision of Canon Law and Its Application to Liturgical Revision in the recent history of the Church of England', in *The Jurist*, vol. 48, no. 2, 1988.

1989

21. 'Preparing the Way' and 'Postscript' in M. Perham, ed., *Towards Liturgy 2000*, (Alcuin Club Collection 69) SPCK 1989.
22. 'Societas Liturgica: Its 1989 Congress on the Inculturation of the Liturgy: An Introduction to a theme', in *Studia Liturgica*, vol. 19, no. 1, 1989.

1990

23. 'The Use of Hymns in the Churches: The Church of England', in C. Robertson, ed., *Singing the Faith: Essays by Members of the Joint Liturgical Group on the use of hymns in the liturgy*, The Canterbury Press Norwich 1990.

24. 'Bridging the Gap', in *Studia Liturgica*, vol. 20, no. 1, 1990.
25. 'Liturgy and Evangelism: The Church Revealed and Proclaimed', in *Living Stones*, vol. 4, no. 2, December 1990.

1991
26. 'Eucharistic Inflation', in M. Perham, ed., *Liturgy for a New Century*, (Alcuin Club Collection 70) SPCK 1991.
27. 'Liturgy and Society', in K. Stevenson and B. Spinks, eds., *The Identity of Anglican Worship*, Mowbray 1991.
28. *Chaplain to Mr Speaker: The Religious Life of the House of Commons*, House of Commons Library Document No. 19, HMSO 1991.
29. 'The Contribution of the Joint Liturgical Group to the Search for an Ecumenical Lectionary', in *Studia Liturgia*, vol. 21, no. 1, 1991.

1993
30. *St Margaret's Westminster: A concise guide*, Beric Tempest 1993.
31. Preface to Philip Holland, *St Margaret's Wesminster: The Commons Church within a Royal Peculiar*, Aidan Ellis 1993.
32. 'Baptising the Nation: The Problems of Baptism in an Established Church', in D. Holeton, ed., *Growing in Newness of Life*, Anglican Book Centre, Toronto 1993.
33. 'The Ecumenical Approach to Common Prayer', in M. Perham, ed., *The Renewal of Common Prayer: Unity and Diversity in Church of England Worship*, Church House Publishing and SPCK 1993.

1995
34. 'Pushing at the Door: (1) The Church of England', in Ruth A. Meyers, ed., *Children At The Table: The Communion Of All The Baptised in Anglicanism*, Church Hymnal Corporation: New York 1995.

CONTRIBUTORS

Horace Allen is Professor of Worship at Boston University and Co-Chair, English Language Liturgical Consultation.

Paul Bradshaw, formerly Vice-Principal of Ripon College, Cuddesdon, is Professor of Liturgy at the University of Notre Dame, Indiana, Editor-in-Chief of Studia Liturgica, and current President of Societas Liturgica.

Anne Dawtry, Assistant Curate of Corfe Mullen, Dorset, is a member of the Committee of the Alcuin Club.

Martin R. Dudley, Vicar of St George's Church, Owlsmoor, Berkshire, is the Secretary of the Alcuin Club and was until recently Visiting Lecturer in Anglican Studies and Liturgy at the Simon of Cyrene Theological Institute, London.

R. William Franklin is SPRL Professor of History and Mission and Professor of Modern Anglican Studies at the General Theologian Seminary in New York City.

Sehon Goodridge, formerly Principal of the Simon of Cyrene Theological Institute in London, is Bishop of the Windward Islands.

Anthony Harvey, Canon and Sub-Dean of Westminster, was formerly Lecturer in Theology, Fellow of Wolfson College and Chaplain of The Queen's College, Oxford; he was Bampton Lecturer in 1980.

Ruth A. Meyers is Diocesan Liturgist in the Diocese of Western Michigan (U.S.A.)

Michael Perham is a Canon of Norwich Catehdral and a member of the Church of England Liturgical Commission.

Bryan Spinks is Chaplain at Churchill College, Cambridge, and Affiliated Lecturer in Liturgy in the Divinity Faculty of the University.

Kenneth W. Stevenson is Rector of Holy Trinity and St Mary's, Guildford, and a member of the Church of England Liturgical Commission and the Faith and Order Advisory Group.

Gordon Wakefield was formerly Principal of Queen's College, Birmingham.

1

A Word from the New Testament?

A. E. Harvey

I HAVE a distant recollection of a lecture given in Cambridge nearly forty years ago by one of the greatest New Testament scholars of his generation, C. F. D. Moule. In his characteristically deferential way he was suggesting certain respects in which recent scholarship in his own field of study might make a contribution to the life of the church. One of these was liturgical. It was a period when, in Moule's words, 'it was fashionable to find liturgy everywhere'.[1] It was as if, through the application of modern critical methods to the text, we were beginning to feel that we could overhear the early Christian communities at their worship and reconstruct their liturgical ceremonies. In which case, might this not have consequences for ecumenical understanding? If it could be shown that the primitive church had developed certain common forms of worship, and that these were available to us with the authority of their transmission in Holy Scripture, might this not open the way for new agreements between the churches on what should properly be done in any act of worship that deserved the name of Christian?

This promise has not been fulfilled. After surveying the work of New Testament scholars over the last fifty years, Paul Bradshaw is forced to conclude that 'There is relatively little about which we can be sure with regard to this subject, and so the New Testament generally cannot provide the firm foundation from which to project later liturgical developments that it has frequently been thought to give'.[2] Oscar Cullmann's study of the Fourth Gospel,[3] which was entitled *Early Christian Worship* and argued for a sacramental interpretation of no less than thirteen passages of the text, was standard reading for a whole generation of theological students but has now come to be regarded as an 'extreme' of Johannine interpretation.[4] Even Moule, though he continued to place his chapter on 'The Church at Worship' at the very beginning of each successive edition of his *Birth of the New Testament*, and to claim that 'The Christian community at worship ... must always stand in the very front of our search for the settings in which the component parts of the New Testament came into existence', was ready to concede that 'liturgical conclusions should be drawn with care and caution'.[5] Certainly a search through recent commentaries on texts once regarded as liturgically significant reveals little of the enthusiasm once felt for this kind of liturgical archaeology, and scholars have revealed that their real interest is not so much to reconstruct primitive liturgical practices from New Testament texts as to use those texts as evidence for the early formulation of certain doctrines.[6] Many of the previous attempts at liturgical reconstruction have been found to depend on a problematical reading-back of later liturgical forms,[7] and more recent 'lectionary theories' of the origin of the gospels have run into similar criticism.[8] So far as students of liturgy are concerned, it would seem that there is very little enlightment to be expected from modern study of the New Testament; and in any case any optimism that the divided churches might find a new source of unity in New Testament texts should surely have been extinguished from the outset by the simple observation that no established eucharistic liturgy seems ever to have consisted of the direct quotation of any of the relevant New Testament texts.

Yet if the New Testament, even when studied under the powerful lens of modern critical procedures, has failed to offer normative examples of early liturgical language and practice, it does not follow that it has nothing to say to the liturgist. If the details remain obscure and the actual forms of worship are too diverse and elusive to provide any secure guidance for modern Christian assemblies, there are nevertheless certain questions of principle on which the New Testament may still be found to have a significant bearing. It is not, after all, on matters of precise wording and procedure that the historic churches have differed from one another so much as in the characteristic structure and emphasis of their acts of worship. The relative importance of word and sacrament, the place of words and actions inspired by the Spirit, the degree of formality and the extent of personal repentance and preparation required for worship – these are the issues which have divided denominations, and sometimes even congregations within denominations, from each other. Has the New Testament nothing to say on such matters? At one time it would have been taken for granted that the Letter to the Hebrews, for example, had a powerful message for the worshipper. Today, such concerns hardly surface at all in commentaries and monographs.[9] Yet if a New Testament scholar is to pay tribute in his own coinage to a distinguished liturgist, it is surely in this broader area of interpretation that he must locate his treasury.

I

I propose to begin with a selection of the sayings of Jesus. In doing so, I may appear to be deliberately setting myself against established principles of contemporary scholarship. Certain texts in Paul's letters are undoubtedly far earlier, and therefore more appropriate as a historical starting point, than anything in the gospels; moreover so much critical doubt has now accumulated over the authenticity of virtually any of the sayings recorded in the gospels that none of them is likely to offer a secure point of departure for an exploration of the beginnings of a distinctively Christian approach to worship. But in fact the particular sayings with which I am concerned have generally scored an unusually high mark for authenticity by reason of their apparent originality, and my reason for attending to them at the outset is precisely that these sayings, though intensely challenging, have failed to make any significant impact on the worship or the order of the church. A prime example, though it need not concern worship as such, is Jesus' startling admonition to his disciples – reinforced by his unprecedented gesture of placing a child in front of them as an example – 'if anyone wishes to be first, he shall be the last of all and the servant of all' (Mark 9.35). In its Lukan form (22.26), this seems already to have been applied to some form of organization in the church:

'The greater among you should become as the younger, and the leader as the servant'; but it is fair to say that, even if some recollection of this uncomfortable principle has been kept alive in the title of the 'deacon', none of the historic churches has taken the risk of systematically entrusting leadership to its youngest or most humble members,[10] let alone given liturgical expression to the principle by encouraging its most unpretentious and least qualified member to preside over the eucharistic assembly – had it done so, 'Faith and Order' discussions between the churches might well have run a very different course!

Closer to our theme of the principles that should underlie our worship is the saying of Jesus,

> In your prayers, do not go babbling on like the heathen, who imagine that the more they say the more likely they are to be heard.   *(Matthew 6.7 REB)*

The exact meaning of the word translated 'babbling on' (βαττο-λογεῖν) is not known,[11] but its general sense is clear from the following clause; it involves 'much speaking'. Commentators note that this is one of a number of sayings in Matthew's gospel which are distinctly derogatory about non-Jews, and are therefore inclined to attribute it to the evangelist rather than to Jesus.[12] Certainly, a preference for short prayer appears frequently in the Jewish tradition,[13] and there are some instances (particularly in the magical papyri) of a propensity to repetition among pagans. But the opposite is also true,[14] and it is difficult to see why a Christian writer should have attributed such a saying to Jesus if he was not the author of it: the early Christian prayers which have come down to us are seldom notable for their brevity,[15] and the evangelist is hardly likely to have found support in the practice of his own church for attacking the alleged prolixity of 'heathen' prayers. Rather we should take the verse as evidence that Jesus did in fact intend his followers to pray with an economy of words, and offered the Lord's Prayer as an example.[16] If so, we have to record again that the churches have taken singularly little notice. Whether it be in the prolonged repetitions of Orthodox worship, the prolixity of spontaneous prayer in Reformed churches or the periphrastic phrases of Cranmer's collects ('Create and make ...

remission and forgiveness'), liturgical practice has gone its way in direct opposition to Jesus' injunction.

A more serious departure from principles laid down by Jesus may be seen in the traditional response of the churches to another saying of Jesus:

> So if you are presenting your gift at the altar and suddenly remember that your brother has a grievance against you, leave your gift where it is before the altar. First go and make your peace with your brother; then come back and offer your gift. (*Matthew 5.23–24 REB*)

This has a good claim to be an authentic saying: not only does it score high marks on the technical grounds of multiple attestation[17] (Mark 11.25–26; Matthew 6.12, 14–15), but it conveys a point that is a theme of one of the parables (the unforgiving servant, Matthew 18.23–35) and is expressed here with a hint of exaggeration characteristic[18] of Jesus: the somewhat grotesque idea of leaving, say, a brace of live pigeons in the temple precincts while one goes to search for an unreconciled 'brother' in the back streets of Jerusalem – or even further afield – is typical of the way Jesus sharpens the impact of his ethical teaching. It is possible, of course, to make the pedantic objection that the injunction could have been observed only when the Temple was actually standing: after 70 C.E. it had no relevance. But the fact that it was nevertheless preserved in Matthew's gospel (almost certainly composed some years later), and that 'offering sacrifice' had been used as a metaphor for the worship of the heart for at least five hundred years, makes it certain that its application to any form of worship was immediately perceived. Any religious devotions were to be preceded by an act of forgiveness towards anyone by whom one had been offended. Without this, God could not be expected to forgive the offences one had caused oneself.

The practical application of this group of sayings tends to be seen most clearly by Jewish commentators.[19] In Matthew's version of the Lord's Prayer the point is made with great precision: 'Release us from our debts, as we have released our debtors from theirs' (6.12). The Law of Moses gave great prominence to the question of loans. Charging interest was forbidden, and prospects of repayment might be uncertain. Prudence would therefore suggest refusing to make a loan without guaranteed security. But given the social necessity of providing the poor with a modest capital to tide them over times of bad harvest or other vicissitudes, responding to a request for a loan was regarded as a mark of righteousness.

> If there be among you a poor man ... you shall not harden your heart ... but you shall open your hand wide to him and lend him as much as he needs.   (Deut. 15.7–8 RSV)[20]

Jesus evidently endorsed and extended this: 'Give to *anyone* who asks; and do not turn your back on *anyone* who wants to borrow' (Matthew 5.42). But the relationship between creditor and debtor is always an uneasy one. When a whole class is in debt, the cohesion of society is threatened – hence the biblical Law of Release in the seventh year, by which outstanding debts were to be regularly cancelled. Similarly, when one individual is in debt to another, the sense of obligation is a constraint on friendship and trust; hence the creditor may actually have an interest in writing off the debt. The released debtor will have replaced his debt by a personal sense of obligation and will be likely to seek ways of returning the favour in the future.

The point, of course, can be generalized. Monetary indebtedness is not the only way in which human beings place themselves under restrictive obligations to others: damaging the interests or reputation of another creates a similar, if not more serious, constraint on their relationship. These also can be 'released' by an act of forgiveness, and both Matthew and Mark have taken the saying on 'debts' as applying equally to other kinds of 'offences' or 'sins' committed against another (παραπτώματα, Matthew 6.14: Mark 11.25). The necessity of exercising such forgiveness towards others was well understood in Jewish piety. 'Forgive your neighbour any wrong he has done you; then, when you pray, your sins will be forgiven' (Sirach 28.2). And the converse is true also: whether in public worship or in private prayer the offender must seek forgiveness from the one who has been offended before God's forgiveness for the offence can be expected. But however widely the principle is spread over human wrong-doing, one feature of the original example of debts and indebtedness remains constant: before there can be genuine prayer or acceptable worship there must have been some act of forgiveness and reconciliation *between the parties themselves*. God may release me from my sins; but no one can release my debtor from his debt except me. Similarly, even the Day of Atonement 'does not expiate transgressions between human and human, unless the guilty one has first appeased the neighbour'.[21] The implication of Jesus' sayings is absolutely clear. God's forgiveness is conditional upon us first settling the debts and offences which have arisen among ourselves.

It is instructive to notice the way in which Christian interpreters tend to soften the force of this injunction by reducing the emphasis on settling accounts *between persons* before petitions are made for God's forgiveness. Georg Strecker, for example, speaks of 'human readiness to forgive' (not the actual performance of an act of forgiveness) as a precondition of God's forgiveness.[22] Eduard Schweizer speaks of the act of forgiveness 'that is really performed at the very moment the worshipper pronounces this petition'.[23] These scholars, and indeed the majority of Christian interpreters (under the influence, no doubt, of church practice) evidently think of 'forgiving' as something that takes place simply in the mind and heart of the individual at prayer or in worship, as a consequence of which God can forgive in his turn. But this is to forget that the roots of the idea are expressed in the metaphor, as well as the reality, of lending. You cannot remit someone's debt simply by forming an intention in your mind to do so; you have actually to tell the debtor that the debt is cancelled. Similarly, you cannot forgive a personal injury without informing the offender that the offence is no longer a barrier to friendship. The point is well made by the Jewish scholar, Pinchas Lapide: 'the horizontal re-establishment of peace, which is much more difficult than communal prayer or repentance, is an absolute prerequisite for the right to beseech God for vertical reconciliation ... only the self-transcendence of asking for forgiveness and the personal courage of extending one's hand (with all the danger of being rebuffed) can bring the forgiveness that comes from above'.[24] It is beyond doubt that this is the meaning of Jesus in the Lord's Prayer, in the saying about leaving one's gift at the altar, in the parable of the unforgiving servant and in the

summary commands to 'forgive' in Mark and Luke. Yet liturgical
practice has consistently failed to recognize the practical implications. The command to be reconciled with our sisters and brothers has given place to an invitation to confess *to God* (not to them!)
that we may have offended them, and the idea that there may be
offences on their part from the consequences of which we must
personally release them seems not to have found expression in any
known Christian liturgy, nor indeed in the thinking of the church
on sin, penitence and forgiveness from the apostolic age onwards.

II

Why has the liturgical practice of the churches paid so little attention to the practical implications of these sayings? It can be argued,
of course, that they were originally spoken in relation to customs
and practices characteristic of Jewish worship in Jesus' own time,
and have little relevance to Christian worship today. In any case
there is a prior question to be asked: how far did the church initiate a new style of worship that was distinct from its Jewish prece-
dents? Did Christians after the resurrection, and in the light of their
conviction that Jesus now enjoyed divine status at the right hand
of God, begin to adopt new procedures in their gatherings for
prayer and worship, or did they continue in a style inherited from
the Temple and synagogue apart from certain necessary adapta-
tions? If attention is confined to the details of what they said and
did, the question is susceptible to historical enquiry. Clearly the
institutions of baptism and eucharist became distinguishing features
of Christian worship, apparently right from the start; in other
respects, it is usually assumed that Christians borrowed freely from
Jewish liturgical forms, though any reconstruction based on this
assumption is made precarious by our lack of information about
those Jewish forms in the New Testament period. But the question which concerns us is not so much one of words and outward
forms as of inner motivation and disposition. To put the question
in its most succinct form: did the crucifixion and resurrection of
Jesus and his exaltation to the right hand of God make any fundamental difference to the way in which Christians addressed them-

selves to their heavenly Father when they gathered together for worship?

We may begin with a text which, however difficult to interpret with any certainty, at least raises the question whether Christians went on as before or sensed that a significant change had taken place that would affect their whole approach to worship. At the climax of his passion narrative Mark (followed by Matthew) juxtaposes two sentences which, to us, seem to belong to two quite different styles of discourse. First, 'Jesus gave a loud cry and died'; then, without any pause or explanation, we are told that 'the curtain of the temple was torn in two from top to bottom' (Mark 15.37–38). The run of the sentences suggests that the second should be understood as literally as the first: the evangelist appears to be narrating a series of events, and gives no hint that he may be changing gear and adopting a figurative or symbolical mode of speech. Accordingly, in an age when it no longer seems adequate to put down an inexplicable event quite simply to miracle, valiant attempts have been made at a rational explanation. Among the most notable was that of G. R. Driver,[25] who suggested that in the season of the *hamsin* wind, which often brings with it a cloud of sand from the eastern desert sufficient to obscure the sun completely, a sudden gust of exceptional violence could have rent the curtains inside the Temple, of which the doors would have been open towards the east. A similarly literal approach is attempted by the most recent major commentator on Mark, R. H. Gundry,[26] for which purpose he has to locate Golgotha on the Mount of Olives, the only place from which the centurion could have 'seen' (Mark 15.39) the events, including the miraculous rending of the curtain, which persuaded him that Jesus was the Son of God.[27] But none of these attempts has won general assent. The great majority of commentators, from antiquity[28] to the present day, has assumed that the report is intended to be symbolical.

But symbolical of what? Of judgment on the Temple, its administration and its cult? Of the destruction of Jerusalem and the ending of its role as the centre of Jewish religious faith and practice? Of a new era in the relationship between God and his human worshippers? One writer lists no less than thirty-five different interpretations that have been suggested.[29] The question is still further complicated by the fact that the word used for 'curtain' (καταπετασμα) could mean either the inner one covering the entry to the Holy of Holies or the outer one covering the entry to the outer room of the Temple; moreover the further miraculous events recorded by Matthew – earthquake, rending of rocks, raising of the saints – appear themselves to have symbolic value, indicating the cosmic and eschatological significance of Jesus' death,[30] and inspired perhaps in part by the visual image of the rending of the (outer) curtain which was itself a pictorial representation of the firmament of heaven.[31] This is not the place to argue for one interpretation against all the others; indeed to insist that a symbol has just one meaning is to do violence to the very nature of symbolical language, which is capable of stirring the imagination in several directions at once and is never subject to the control of a single 'correct' interpretation. But given that one obvious symbolic meaning of the curtain was that of a sign of the *separation* which existed between the presence of God in his sanctuary and his worshippers outside, even the priests (with one annual exception) being unable to pass through it, and given a number of other New Testament references to the abolition of any such separation through the death of Christ, it is reasonable to accept the judgment of a large number of commentators that one way at least in which Mark's report would have been understood is as a statement that the crucifixion effected a crucial change in the accessibility of God to human beings, a change that might be expected to be particularly apparent in the way in which the followers of Jesus address themselves to God in prayer and worship.

For about a quarter of a century it has been believed that evidence for such a change lies to hand in the simple but allegedly surprising fact that Jesus himself used, and encouraged his followers to use, the Aramaic word *Abba* when addressing their heavenly Father. In an important study published in Germany in 1966[32] and translated into English in the following year with the title *The Prayers of Jesus*,[33] Joachim Jeremias argued that *Abba* was a word belonging to the vocabulary of small children; that Jesus' use of it when addressing God was unprecedented; and that its appearance in the repertory of early Christian prayer demonstrated a consciousness of 'the new relationship with God given by the Son'.[34]

The somewhat unguarded enthusiasm with which he presented this argument aroused immediate interest, and gave rise to a mass of popular books proclaiming that Jesus addressed God, and authorized his followers to address God, by a name roughly equivalent to 'Daddy'. Five years later Jeremias published a warning against the assumption that 'Jesus adopted the language of a tiny child when he addressed God as "Father"', though he admitted to having believed this himself for a while; rather, 'Jesus regarded *Abba* as a sacred word ... *Abba* should be revered ... *Abba* ... expresses the ultimate mystery of the mission of Jesus'.[35] But the damage was done. A generation of Christians has been led to believe that Christian prayer is to be conducted in an almost infantile intimacy with God. Only now, under the influence of the strictly philological arguments advanced by James Barr[36] and Geza Vermes,[37] is the traditional and sensible view beginning to regain scholarly support, namely, that any form of address to God must be essentially *serious*.

III

This necessary seriousness which attaches to any approach to God is one of the dominant themes of the Letter to Hebrews. 'Everything lies bare and exposed to the eyes of him to whom we must render account' (4.13); 'it is a terrifying thing to fall into the hands of the living God' (10.31); 'worship God ... with reverence and awe; for our God is a devouring fire' (12.28–29). The sheer awesomeness of God is a reality that broods over every page of Hebrews. It demands intensely serious preparation before one may attempt to draw near to the divine presence (12.18ff; 12.14: 'aim at sanctification (ἁγιασμός), for without that no one will see God'); and it provides the rationale for the entire organization of the Temple cult. 'Beyond the second curtain was the tent called the Most Holy Place' (9.3) – and there follows a brief roll-call of the sacred objects which had at one time adorned that dark, mysterious and awesome chamber. But these are not at the centre of the writer's interest here (9.5). His concern is not with the detail, but with the general *arrangement* (9.6). The people stood outside, in the great Temple court; the priests were privileged to enter the outer room ('the first tent') in the performance of their duties. Before them was the curtain concealing the entrance to the dark inner room where the presence of God was at its most intense. But this 'is entered by the high priest alone, and that only once a year ... the way into the sanctuary has not been opened up' (9.8). 'All this', says the writer, 'is symbolic'. The arrangement of outer and inner rooms, of a curtain concealing the entrance, of the purification rites required for the ordinary worshipper even to approach the building, of the limitation even on priests to go no closer than the outer room, of the yearly, once-only and ultimately ineffectual entry to the inner room by the High Priest – all this symbolizes one over-riding reality: the remote and awesome inaccessibility of God.

Yet the writer was a Christian. He, like other Christians, was conscious of a new sense of intimacy with God. How could this have come about? The reality symbolized by the careful arrangement of the Temple – the outer and inner rooms, the second curtain barring entrance to the Holy of Holies where God might be supposed to be most intensely and awesomely present – this reality was still in place.[38] The sheer unapproachability of God was in no way to be compromised. But this symbolism also held the clue to a new reality. Could it be that what Christ had done was to 'go through' the curtain, as the High Priest did, but (unlike the High Priest) with decisive and enduring effect, opening a way for believers that would enable them to draw near with confidence to the dread presence of God? Much of the letter is taken up with a demonstration that Jesus did indeed fulfil the requirements for discharging this high-priestly function in a way that made the old cultic observances obsolete. But, throughout, the author's vocabulary betrays again and again his conviction that a new ease of access to God in his majesty was the direct consequence of Jesus' priestly offering.[39] Jesus was a high priest who had 'gone through' (4.14) as the High Priest, just once a year, 'went through' (9.6–7); he has 'gone through' himself (9.12) as a 'pioneer' (2.10) and a 'fore-runner' (6.20). He is a kind of 'anchor' which has 'gone in behind the curtain' (6.19), creating a 'way in' for believers (9.8; 10.19). The consequence is a new possibility of 'drawing near' to God, with a new-found 'confidence' (παρρησία) even in the presence of the Holy (4.16; 10.19; 10.35).

It is in the context of this elated sense of access to a God who is still a source of awe and dread and yet can be approached with 'confidence' by the believer who has 'passed through' the barriers which had always existed between the divine and the human that we must approach the verses which come closest to our subject:

> So now, my friends, the blood of Jesus makes us free to enter the sanctuary with confidence by the new and living way which he has opened for us through the curtain, the way of his flesh. *(10.19–20)*

As is well known, the construction of the Greek sentence allows for two possibilities: the words 'of his flesh' can be taken with either the 'curtain' or the 'way'. Generations of English-speaking Christians, under the influence of the King James Version ('through the veil, that is to say, his flesh') have assumed the first: Jesus' flesh was a 'veil' which concealed his divinity: by the crucifixion and resurrection he 'passed through' it so as to make a way for others into the direct presence of God. But the line of thought is difficult; and the weight placed by the whole sentence on the newness of the 'way' strongly suggests that it is this which is being daringly connected with Christ's 'flesh', his humanity. So it was taken by Tyndale and the great English versions before the KJV,[40] by Westcott[41] and Nairne,[42] by the NEB and the REB. And so the logic of the passage demands. In this writer's theology there is nothing new about the 'curtain': it is that which always existed in the Temple, assuring the necessary separation of God from sinful humanity. To identify this with the flesh of Christ would be to make Christ's flesh a part of the old order that had been transcended by the new reality. But this (apart from its dubious christological implications) runs against the author's repeated conviction that the separation between God and human kind is an absolutely valid presupposition of all religion, but that, for believers, it has been decisively overcome by Christ's priestly act in 'going through'. There is no room for the suggestion that in 'going through' Christ left his flesh behind as part of the barrier. It is our high priest who 'shared our flesh and blood' (2.14) who has opened for us 'the way'. We can say that it is he, in all his physicality, who *is* 'the way'.

But we cannot read this passage without the crucifixion narrative coming to mind. Did this author know of the tradition that the curtain was rent when Jesus died? Does he, too, use the curtain as a symbol of that separation between human and divine which has been dismantled by Christ's death? It is the force of this association which has led many commentators[43] to prefer the alternative construction: 'the curtain, that is, his flesh'. The dissolution of Jesus' fleshly and physical being on the cross symbolizes, or is symbolized by, the destruction of the barrier between God and human kind. But this is not the author's argument. He never says that the curtain has been abolished. It remains in place as a necessary symbol of the essential inaccessibility of God. What Christ has done is 'gone through' – not by tearing it, but by assuming and transcending the High Priest's privilege of parting it to enter the Holy of Holies on behalf of others. And the 'way' he followed to perform the decisive action was a fleshly, physical one: his own death.

Yet the fact that these two writers used the symbol differently does not mean that it did not have the same basic significance. As we saw at the beginning, symbols are not constrained to yield just one meaning; yet the meanings they have will cluster round a single concept. In this case, though their use of the symbol was different, the authors of Mark and Hebrews both saw 'the curtain of the Temple' (whether the inner or the outer one is immaterial for this purpose) as representing that which denied direct access to God by human beings and of which the power to enforce this separation was decisively broken by Christ. Mortals would not normally dare to 'go through' into the immediate presence of God. The entire sacrifical system ordained in the scriptures, culminating in the annual sacrifice performed by the High Priest, effected only a token and provisional passage of a human being into the sphere of the divine. But the death of Christ not only led this new high priest into the presence of God and enthroned him in the heavenly places, but opened a way for others to follow. As a result, Christian worshippers can now draw near with a *confidence* never before experienced in their religious tradition. The word for this confidence – παρρησία – occurs with some frequency in Hebrews and carries great emphasis. Its secular meaning derives from a situation of social distinction where an inferior, conscious of total innocence and a just case, feels able to speak with frankness, boldness and confidence before his superior. Such confidence, as was observed by Philo,[44] could be maintained before God only if one were totally blameless and without reproach – and who could aspire to such a qualification? But now, in the words of our author, 'the blood of Jesus makes us free to enter the sanctuary *with confidence*' (10.19). And that same confidence is the experience of other New Testament writers: of Paul, who contrasts this παρρησία with the veil which 'lies over the mind of the hearer' when the law of Moses is read (2 Cor. 3.12–15); of the author Ephesians, who speaks of having, in Christ, 'παρρησία and free access'; and of the Johannine writer, who is able to look forward to the moment of judgement with a new confidence, with παρρησία (1 John 4.17).

If we ask whether this παρρησία is, and always has been, characteristic of Christian worship, there is an easy answer: since the time of Gregory of Nyssa[45] it has been sensed that one expression of this confidence is the liturgical use of the Lord's Prayer, and modern liturgies reproduce this with the somewhat stilted phrase, 'we are bold to say'. But if the question is asked of Christian worship in general, the answer is not so obvious. There are, of course, many Christians who, since they are accustomed to acknowledge Jesus as their 'personal Saviour', testify to an intensely personal relationship with him, such that any sense of dread or awe in his presence would be quite out of place: their personal prayer, and consequently their worship, exhibit an intimacy and spontaneity which may certainly be called 'confidence', παρρησία. Yet, though this is doubtless fully justified and validated by their spiritual experience, it must be said that such an easy and informal approach to Jesus receives no support in anything that the New Testament has to say about worship. The παρρησία which has been created by the crucifixion and resurrection is always to be understood in the context of the unapproachable majesty of God, of the distance that must be felt by all his sinful human creatures as they seek to participate in the heavenly worship, and of the necessary fear with which they must look forward to the moment of

judgment. Jesus is our advocate and friend; he is the expression of
God's love towards us, and we have the assurance that no evil
forces can prevail over this love. But this does not mean that our
worship of God, which is now directed also towards Jesus, can
presume on an easy familiarity. According to New Testament texts
which are almost universally acknowledged to contain early
Christian liturgical language, the name of Jesus is now above every
name, 'that at the name of Jesus every knee should bow' (Phil.
2.9–10); Jesus has been 'raised to heavenly glory' (1 Tim. 3.16); he
is 'Lord' in a way that can be acknowledged only 'under the influence of the Spirit'. (1 Cor. 12.3). The παρρησία which should be
a distinctive mark of Christian worship must be exercised in
constant tension with the worshipper's sense of the essential
awesomeness of God in which Jesus now shares. It may reasonably
be asked where this tension can be felt in modern liturgical practice, other than in the stylized use of 'bold' in the introduction to
the Lord's Prayer.

IV

But it is a tension which is by no means only a matter of appropriate attitudes to worship; it points to the very heart of the distinc-
tiveness of all Christian liturgy. From earliest days Christians have
incorporated Jesus in their worship, yet they have remained rigidly
monotheistic, able to continue the centuries-old tale of Jewish
worship of the one God and yet acknowledging in their prayers
and praises the divinity of Christ. The tension involved in recon-
ciling this inherited and instinctive monotheism with christology
and (in due course) trinitarian theology gave rise in subsequent
centuries to subtle intellectual distinctions; but in the New Testament it is felt primarily in the language of worship, and resolved
not by doctrinal formulations but in visionary and mystical experience. This is seen most clearly in the Book of Revelation, where
the seer has direct apprehension of the worship in heaven and of
the place of the Lamb in the midst of it. As Richard Bauckham has
recently observed, the author was totally committed to a traditional monotheism by his sustained polemic against the idolatrous

worship of imperial paganism. He was therefore forced to 'reflect deliberately on the relation of christology to monotheism'.[46] To resolve the conflict, he did not coin new *words* to be addressed to the deity in order to allow for the new situation: the hymns of praise scattered through his work are a cento of scriptural allusions. Instead, he used the resources of visual imagery and even of grammar to emphasise that Jesus, though distinct from God, has this strictly monotheistic worship addressed to him as part of God's identity. In Bauckham's words, 'he is evidently reluctant to speak of God and Christ as a plurality. He never makes them the subjects of a plural verb or uses a plural pronoun to refer to them both. The reason is surely clear: he places Christ on the divine side of the distinction between God and creation, but he wishes to avoid ways of speaking which sound to him polytheistic'.[47] The alternative – that of addressing less exalted or more intimate language to Jesus than to God – is a way that evidently never occurred to the author.

We may perhaps find a clue to this mysterious ability of the first generations of Christians to worship God and Christ as a single entity in what may properly be called a mystical strand in Jewish reflection upon God. In Ezekiel's throne-vision, which lay at the root of the entire tradition of Merkabah mysticism,[48] there was seen 'a likeness as it were of a human form' (1.26). That is to say, despite the dazzling radiance which attended any glimpse of the divine glory, it was possible to discern *something human* in the very nature of God. It has been argued by Alan Segal[49] that Paul's 'conversion' was an experience of this kind, involving a mystical 'transformation' of the beholder into a member of that company which could attend on this divine self-manifestation; and in general we can surely say that the absolute conviction of the church that Jesus, in fulfilment of Psalm 110, was now 'seated at the right hand of God' (the most frequently quoted scriptural text in the New Testament) and was one to whom 'every knee should bow' – i.e. who should be universally worshipped – was one for which their religious heritage had in some way prepared them: where Ezekiel had seen 'something human' in God, Christians could now identify this human-ness as Jesus Christ. As a result, Jesus could now be addressed by any of the names or attributes – including 'Lord' itself – which were traditionally reserved for God. Though there was now a new 'confidence' in drawing near to this majestic and awesome presence, nothing had happened that could allow Christians to claim intimacy or ease of access. The suggestion that Jesus might be prayed to or worshipped apart from God, or addressed in language more personal and informal than that appropriate to God (such as is practised in certain forms of Christian piety) finds no support in the New Testament. For all its boldness, and despite any innovation authorized by the presence of the Spirit in the assembly (another distinctive feature in early Christian worship which has found spasmodic expression in later centuries), Christian worship, if it is to be true to its New Testament origins, must somehow sustain the tension (so clearly expressed in Hebrews and implicit elsewhere) between, on the one hand, a newly-granted freedom of access to God in his holiness and, on the other, the awesome reality of the God with whom we have to do.

V

In this discussion I have suggested that, even if an earlier promise of contributions to liturgical practice from the quarter of New Testament scholarship has not been fulfilled, there are nevertheless certain aspects of worship on which our scriptures have something to say. It was wrong to expect that further study would establish firm historical perspectives from which liturgical disagreements might be assessed or provide liturgical formulae that could serve as a basis for ecumenical reconstruction. But I have given some examples of principles which might have some application to any form of worship that could be called 'Christian', and if these principles are sometimes difficult to detect in modern liturgies this does not necessarily mean that they have lost their relevance. Indeed the closet analogy may be in the relationship between the ethical teaching of Jesus and the traditional moral reasoning of the church.[50] Since Jesus' teaching is too unsystematic, too related to particular instances and too challenging to be incorporated in received rules or standards, it holds little place in treatises of moral theology or the day-to-day practice of Christians in ethical matters; yet it remains a source of inspiration and disturbance such that no Christian can ever be content with routine moral standards. And so it may be with worship: though the study of the New Testament may yield little in the way of rules, standards or formulae of assured early acceptance, it may nevertheless help to identify teachings of Jesus and perceptions of the first generations of Christians which, though barely capable of incorporation into formal liturgical practice, may nevertheless constitute the 'word' which is still spoken to us by our scriptures and is still capable of challenging and inspiring those who (like the liturgist which this volume seeks to honour) carry the heavy responsibility of maintaining the Christian character of our worship amid the rapidly changing circumstances of the church today.

NOTES

1. C. F. D. Moule, *Worship in the New Testament* (London 1961) p. 7.
2. Paul Bradshaw, *The Search for the Origins of Christian Worship* (London 1992) p. 55.
3. Oscar Cullmann, *Urchristentum und Gottesdienst* (Zürich 1950), E. T. *Early Christian Worship* (London 1953).
4. S. S. Smalley, *John Evangelist and Interpreter* (Exeter 1978) p. 205.
5. C. F. D. Moule, *The Birth of the New Testament*, 3rd Edition (London 1981) p. 38.
6. See, for example, E. Schweizer, *A Theological Introduction to the New Testament* (London 1992) pp. 28ff: the relevant section is headed, significantly, TRANSMISSION IN THE LITURGY, and considers the texts, not as evidence for liturgical practice, but as sources for early doctrinal formulae.
7. Bradshaw, *op.cit.* pp. 36–7.
8. Cf. Leon Morris in R. T. France and D. Wenham eds., *Gospel Perspectives 3* (Sheffield 1983) pp. 129–156.
9. Compare A. Nairne, *The Epistle of Priesthood* (Edinburgh 1913), which has had a profound influence on the Anglican understanding of sacramental ministry, with Barnabas Lindars SSF, *The Theology of the Letter to the Hebrews* (Cambridge 1991), in which there is virtually no reference to worship or sacraments at all.
10. Nor is this implication much noticed by commentators. Even Howard C. Kee for all his interest in the social aspects of Mark's gospel, simply dismisses this as one of Jesus' 'enigmatic sayings', *Community of the New Age* (London 1977) p. 42.
11. See the possible derivations listed in W. D. Davies and Dale C. Anderson, *The Gospel according to St Matthew I* (Edinburgh 1988) pp. 587–8.
12. See, for example, Graham N. Stanton, *A Gospel for a New People: Studies in Matthew* (Edinburgh 1992) p. 94: '... evidence for reading Matthew as a sectarian writing'.
13. Eccles 5.2; Sirach 7.14; B. Ber. 61a. Many other passages are noted in S. T. Lachs, *A Rabbinic Commentary on the New Testament* (Hoboken. N. J. 1987) p. 117.
14. Davies and Anderson (see n. 12) p. 588.
15. The whole of the first three chapters of Ephesians are in the form of a prayer!
16. Presumably for use in corporate prayer. Fixed forms for private or silent prayer are a later development.

17. This is, of course, a precarious principle. It is overturned in this case by G. Strecker, *The Sermon on the Mount* (Edinburgh 1988) p. 125, who assumes that all other instances derive from this text.
18. A. E. Harvey, *Strenuous Commands: The Ethic of Jesus* (London; Philadelphia 1990) p. 64.
19. Cf Pinchas Lapide, *The Sermon on the Mount* (New York 1986) pp. 52–4; S. T. Lachs, *A Rabbinic Commentary* (see note 13) pp. 121–2, who sees Matthew 6.12 as a deliberate challenge to Hillel's *prosbul*.
20. See also Ps 37.21,26; Sirach 29.1–9.
21. M. Yoma 8.9.
22. *The Sermon on the Mount*, p. 125
23. *Good News according to Matthew* (London 1976) p. 155.
24. *The Sermon on the Mount*, pp. 53–54. The point is trenchantly discussed by J. D. M. Derrett, *New Resolutions of Old Conundrums: a fresh insight into Luke's Gospel* (Shipston-on-Stour 1986) pp. 142–148.
25. J. T. S. 16 (1965) pp. 334–6.
26. Robert H. Gundry, *Mark* (Grand Rapids 1993) p. 950. The commentary is a sustained attempt to show that 'Mark's meaning lies on the surface' (p. 1).
27. Id. ib. pp. 955, 970, 973.
28. Jerome Ep. 120.5 quod … omnia legis sint revelata mysteria.
29. T. J. Geddert, *Watchwords: Mark 13 in Markan Eschatology* (J.S.N.T. Sup 26, Sheffield 1989) pp. 141–43, quoted by Gundry, *Mark*, p.972.
30. Donald P. Senior, *The Passion Narrative according to Matthew* (Leuven 1975) pp. 311–323
31. Josephus, *Bell.* 5.213.
32. *Abba. Studien zur neutestamentlichen Theologie und Zeitgeschichte* (Göttingen 1966).
33. London pp. 11–65.
34. *The Prayers of Jesus*, p. 65
35. *New Testament Theology* (London) pp. 67–8.
36. 'Abba isn't Daddy', J.T.S. 39 (1988) pp. 28–47.
37. *The Religion of Jesus the Jew* (London 1993) pp. 180–83.
38. Whether or not the Temple was still standing when Hebrews was written is immaterial. The argument is that the arrangement was symbolic, and the details are drawn, not from observation, but from scriptural references to 'The Tent'.
39. Cf Barnabas Lindars SSF, *The Theology of the Letter to the Hebrews* (Cambridge 1991) p. 46.
40. Coverdale, the Great Bible, the Geneva Bible.
41. B. F. Westcott, *The Epistle to the Hebrews* (London 1906) p. 322.
42. A. Nairne, *The Epistle to the Hebrews* (Cambridge 1917) p. 101.
43. E.g. C. Spicq, *L'Epître aux Hébreux* (Paris 1953) II p. 316.
44. Q.R.D.H. 7.
45. *Or. dom.* 2 (MPG 44.1137D).
46. Richard Bauckham, *The Theology of the Book of Revelation* (Cambridge 1993) p. 61
47. Pp. 60–61.
48. Cf G. Quispel, 'Ezekiel 1.26 in Jewish Mysticism and Gnosis', *Vigiliae Christianae* 34 (1980) pp. 1–13.
49. Alan Segal, *Paul the Convert* (Yale 1990) pp. 9–10, 39ff.
50. I have developed this point at length in my *Strenuous Commands: The Ethic of Jesus* (London; Philadelphia 1990).

2

From Word to Action:
The Changing Role of Psalmody
in Early Christianity

 *Paul Bradshaw*

ALTHOUGH PSALMS have played a major part in traditional Christian worship, many twentieth-century worshippers appear to be very uncertain what it is they are supposed to be doing when they say or sing them in church services. As in so many other liturgical matters, one naturally turns to the traditions of the early Church for some illumination of this question. However, we do not find there a single consistent apology for the Christian use of psalms, nor an unchanging practice. Instead, a number of quite different ways of using the psalms can be seen, together with their individual explanations for the particular custom. While some of these appear to have emerged in parallel with one another, others seem to have developed out of earlier forms of psalmody. This evolution in practice and interpretation over the centuries brought about a significant shift in the role that psalms played in Christian liturgy and spirituality, which we shall now attempt to trace.

1. *Psalms as prophecy*
The Book of Psalms is cited more frequently in the New Testament than any other Old Testament scripture, and it is here chiefly viewed as being a book of prophecy – or one might say as *the* prophetic work *par excellence* of the Old Testament – written by King David under the inspiration of the Holy Spirit. Thus, for example, Jesus himself is said to have cited Ps. 110.1 as a messianic prophecy:

How can the scribes say that the Christ is the son of David?
David himself, inspired by the Holy Spirit, declared:
'The Lord said to my Lord,
Sit at my right hand,
till I put thy enemies under they feet.'
David himself calls him Lord; so how is he his son?[1]

Similarly, in the Acts of the Apostles, Peter refers in his speech on the day of Pentecost (Acts 2.14–36) both to that same psalm text and also to Ps 16.8–11 as messianic prophecies fulfilled in Jesus Christ.

This same prophetic/christological method of interpreting psalms was continued by Christian theologians and preachers in the succeeding centuries. Among early examples is Justin Martyr's *Dialogue with Trypho*, which features an extensive treatment of Ps. 22.[2] But it was from the third century onwards, apparently under the influence of the exegetical method adopted by Origen from classical literature,[3] that christological interpretation was gradually extended to encompass virtually all the psalms. The words of the psalms were understood either as addressed by the Church to Christ, or as speaking about Christ, or as the voice of the Christ himself. Indeed, even those texts that referred explicitly to God were commonly interpreted as really meaning the divine Christ.[4]

In the light of the above, we might well expect that at least certain psalms – or parts of psalms – that were easily susceptible of a messianic interpretation would have been used in early Christian assemblies as prophetic readings, like the other books of the Old Testament. Traces of such a custom can perhaps be seen in Luke 24.44 (where Jesus says that 'everything written about me in the law of Moses and the prophets and the psalms must be fulfilled') and in the third-century Syrian *Didascalia Apostolorum*, where the paschal vigil is said to have taken place 'with readings from the prophets, and with the gospels and with psalms' (5.19.1). However, the meaning of both of these passages has been challenged. Some scholars have argued that the Lukan text is using the term 'psalms' in a broader sense to refer to the 'Writings', the third of the traditional Jewish divisions of the Old Testament along with the Law and the Prophets.[5] It has also been noted that the description of the paschal vigil does not say explicitly that the psalms were being used there as readings, still less as prophetic readings.[6] On the other hand, somewhat more sure is the statement in the diary of the fourth-century pilgrim Egeria that at Jerusalem on Good Friday the readings were 'all about the things that Jesus suffered: first the psalms on this subject, then the Apostles which concern it, then passages from the Gospels. Thus they read the prophecies about what the Lord would suffer, and the Gospels about what he did suffer.'[7]

Since this evidence is so limited, we have no way of knowing whether the psalms might have had a place in every formal ministry of the word alongside other prophetic readings from the Old Testament in the first three centuries, or whether they were only used occasionally in place of such readings, or whether indeed they only featured once a year in connection with the paschal celebration. Our only other explicit reference to psalms in a formal ministry of the word during this period occurs in a description by Tertullian of a Montanist service led by a woman.[8] While the same same practice may also have existed in the Catholic tradition of the day, we cannot automatically conclude that this was so, nor even that by the word 'psalms' Tertullian here necessarily means biblical psalms, since the term tended to be used quite loosely by patristic writers.

2. Psalms as the summary of scripture

It was among the ascetics and early monastic communities of the fourth century, and especially those in the Egyptian desert, that the psalms came to assume a position of pre-eminence within the books of the Old Testament and to be used extensively within regular worship. While it appears that the early Pachomian communities of Upper Egypt read passages from a variety of biblical books in their daily worship and did not give any special place to the psalms (although this conclusion has recently been challenged[9]), other groups singled out the psalter from the rest of the scriptures, and encouraged their members to commit its contents to memory and recite it constantly, both during formal times of daily prayer and also throughout the rest of their waking hours.[10] Several sayings of the desert fathers tell of individuals completing the whole psalter in the course of a single night.[11] While such stories certainly go far beyond normal practice, they clearly illustrate the ideal towards which the the serious Christian ascetic was expected to strive.

It has sometimes been thought that the psalms were here functioning as a form of prayer. But that is not the case. The sources frequently speak of prayer *and* psalmody, and reveal that the characteristic way of using the psalms in this tradition was to alternate the saying or chanting of a psalm with a period of silent prayer. When two or more people prayed together, only one of them said the psalm and the other(s) listened to it. Then all prayed in silence, and after that another psalm was said, and so on. Thus the psalm was functioning not as prayer itself, but as a reading, as the source of inspiration for the meditative prayer that was to follow it.[12] This was true not only of the Egyptian tradition but also of ascetic practice in Syria. For example, Theodoret of Cyrus describes how Julian of Abiadene (c. 350) instructed his disciples 'to go out into the desert in pairs at dawn, and while one knelt to offer to the Master the worship due to him, the other was to stand and chant fifteen psalms of David; and then they were to change roles, the one standing to chant, the other kneeling on the ground to worship. And they continued doing this from morning until evening.'[13]

Why those who took to the deserts should have shown such an overwhelming preference for psalms above all other scripture for this purpose has been a source of puzzlement for scholars. But perhaps the answer lies in the prophetic/christological interpretation described earlier. As is well known, Origen's ideas exercised a strong influence over the spirituality of the desert fathers, and hence it is likely that his christological exegesis of the psalms would have commended itself to the early ascetics, whose fundamental aim was to conform their lives to the pattern of Christ. What better way could there be to do that, therefore, than by meditating upon the mind of Christ as revealed in the psalms?

Yet, whatever the original cause for their adoption, the psalms soon came to be regarded in this tradition as much more than christological prophecy. The psalter was thought to 'embrace all Scripture',[14] to encapsulate all that the rest of the Old Testament had to offer. And this idea soon spread far outside monastic circles, since in the second half of the fourth century there occurred what James McKinnon has described as a 'psalmodic movement' in Christianity. Because virtually every outstanding Christian personality of the period had lived as a monk at one time or another during their career, the form of spiritual life that they advocated to ordinary lay people was essentially monastic in character, and this was one of the major factors that gave rise to what McKinnon calls 'an unprecedented wave of enthusiasm' for the psalms.[15] While these figures certainly continued to acknowledge the prophetic dimension of the psalter,[16] they made much greater claims for it, asserting it to be a summary of all Christian teaching and the remedy for all spiritual ills. St Basil typifies the attitudes of his contemporaries:

> Now the Prophets teach some things, the Historians other things, the Law still other things, and the form of advice of the Proverbs something else, but the Book of Psalms encompasses what is valuable from them all. It prophesies what is to come; it recalls history; it legislates for life; it gives practical advice; and it is in general a common treasury of good teachings, carefully finding what is suitable for each person. For it heals the old wounds of souls; it brings swift recovery to the recently wounded; it treats what is diseased; it preserves what is pure; and as far as possible it takes away the passions that in many ways dominate souls in the life of human beings. And it does this with a certain diligent persuasion and sweetness that engender a moderate disposition.[17]

Those who viewed the psalter from this perspective did not lose sight of the fact that the psalms were hymnic in form. Indeed, they could hardly do so, since (as we shall see below) psalms were being sung as hymns in the church services that they themselves attended. But they still argued that the teaching function was primary, and that God had deliberately arranged matters in this way in order to make learning more pleasurable for human beings:

> When the Holy Spirit saw that the human race was with difficulty led toward virtue, and that because of our inclination

toward pleasure we neglected an upright life, what did he do?
He mixed sweetness of melody with the teachings so that by
the pleasantness and softness of the sound heard we might
receive without realizing it the benefit of the words, just like
wise physicians, who often smear the cup with honey when
giving the fastidious rather bitter medicines to drink.
Therefore he devised these harmonious melodies of the
psalms for us, so that those who are children in age or even
those who are young in their ways might appear to be singing
but in reality be training their souls.[18]

Of the fourth-century advocates of psalmody, only Athansius,
who in any case belonged to a slightly older generation than the
others, dissented from this latter explanation: 'Some of the simple
ones among us, even while believing the texts to be divinely
inspired, still think that the psalms are sung melodiously for the
sake of good sound and the pleasure of the ear. This is not so.'
Instead, in typical Alexandrian fashion, he adopted an allegorical
explanation for the use of chant: 'to recite the psalms with melody
is not done from a desire for pleasing sound, but is a manifestation
of harmony among the thoughts of the soul. And melodious reading is a sign of the well-ordered and tranquil condition of the
mind.'[19]

3. Psalms as hymns

At the same time as psalms were in the ascendancy in desert
monasticism, a small number of them were also finding a place
within the so-called 'cathedral' office that was emerging after the
Peace of Constantine.[20] However, their inclusion here was not
derived from the monastic custom, since they had an entirely
different function. They were explicitly described as 'hymns', and
performed in a quite distinct manner: after each verse chanted by
the cantor, the assembly repeated a refrain, and there was apparently no period of silence following the psalm. Nor was this usage
a complete innovation of the fourth century. Tertullian at the
beginning of the third century informs us that 'those who are more
diligent in praying are accustomed to include in their prayers
Alleluia and this type of psalms, with the ending of which those

who are present may respond',[21] by which he seems to mean that it was the psalms that already included an Alleluia response in their text (e.g., 148–150) which were being selected for this purpose.

Biblical psalms were also included along with non-canonical compositions that were sung by individuals to others at mealtimes: Tertullian again states that at the end of a Christian community supper 'after the washing of hands and the lighting of lamps, each is invited to stand in the middle and sing a hymn to God, from the holy scriptures or of his own composition as he is able'.[22] This usage may very well be the source of the later adoption of psalms in other occasions of corporate prayer, in the same way that the ritual lighting of the lamp was taken over into the evening office of the 'cathedral' tradition from earlier Christian communal meals.

Singing psalms and hymns in connection with meals was certainly very ancient. The Jewish writer Philo of Alexandria, in recounting the customs of a sectarian community known as the Therapeutae, describes their practice in similar terms to Tertullian. At their festival meals 'the president rises and sings a hymn addressed to God, either a new one which he has composed or an ancient one by poets of old ... After him the others take their turn in the order in which they are arranged, while all the rest listen in complete silence, except when they have to chant the closing lines and refrains, for then they all, men and women, sing ...'[23] In the New Testament 1 Cor. 14.26 includes a 'psalm' among the verbal contributions that individual participants might bring to a Christian ministry of the word, and Eph. 5.19 speaks of believers 'addressing one another in psalms and hymns and spiritual songs ...'. Both of these occasions may well have been in connection with a meal.[24] We cannot of course be sure that canonical psalms were included here as well as psalms and hymns composed by Christians themselves, but it seems likely that they were, given the high regard for the psalter displayed by the New Testament writers.

It appears probable, therefore, that the use of psalms as hymns has its roots in the use of psalms as prophecy. Individual first-century Christians would have sung selected Old Testament psalms to demonstrate that Christ was the expected Messiah, having fulfilled what had been prophesied in the scriptures, and the assembled community would have responded to each verse with an acclamation of praise. Yet by the time that we are in a position to identify the particular psalms being sung as hymns in the fourth-century 'cathedral' office, any former connection with the prophetic usage must have been lost along the way. It is not the obviously christological ones that constitute the regular core here, but instead psalms inviting praise which include within them the Alleluia response (Pss. 148–150), and also those appropriate to the particular hour of the day (e.g., 63 in the morning, 141 in the evening).

Nevertheless, the use of the responsorial method of psalmody clearly implies an affiliation to the two preceding uses that we have examined. Although they were called 'hymns', it was actually the refrain, and not the psalm itself, that constituted the song of praise to God. The psalm verses were still apparently viewed as the word of God, since they are proclaimed by one voice alone to the listening assembly. And Augustine can on occasion refer to the responsorial psalm in the eucharistic ministry of the word as a 'reading'.[25] Of course, one might want to argue that, in the absence of printed texts and in any case in a culture in which there was a large measure of illiteracy, the responsorial method was the only practical way to use unfamiliar liturgical texts. But, while this may be true, we need to remember that the psalms employed in the 'cathedral' office were very few in number and were generally repeated every single day throughout the year. The problem of unfamiliarity therefore cannot have lasted for long, and does not really explain the universal adherence to this method of psalm-singing.

Moreover, John Chrysostom offers an explanation of the significance of the refrain that supports this conclusion:

> Do not then think that you have come here simply to say the words, but when you make the response, consider that response to be a covenant. For when you say, 'Like the hart desire the watersprings, my soul desires you, O God', you make a covenant with God. You have signed a contract without paper or ink; you have confessed with your voice that you love him more than all, that you prefer nothing to him, and that you burn with love for him ...[26]

4. *Psalmody as praise*

We have suggested above that a distinction should be drawn between the use of psalms in Egyptian desert spirituality, where the whole psalter was recited in its biblical order as the basis for individual meditation, and the use in the fourth-century 'cathedral' office, where selected psalms were sung by a cantor as a proclamation of God's word, to which the community responded with a refrain expressing their praise of God. This distinction, however, rapidly became blurred, and in later centuries disappeared altogether, with the result that in both monastic and secular circles in the West the chanting of psalms came to be thought of as itself an act of praise to God.

Two factors seem to have been chiefly responsible for this development. First, there was the practice of fourth-century Cappadocian and Syrian monastic communities, often called by scholars 'urban monastic' because, in contrast to the desert monastic traditions of Egypt, they lived in towns and cities in close association with the Church around them. Although the basis of their prayer life actually lay in the common practices of ante-Nicene Christianity,[27] these communities eventually came to include in their daily worship both the selective psalmody of the 'cathedral' office with which they were familiar and the consecutive psalmody of the desert tradition.[28] And it was their hybrid practice that became the foundation for the worship patterns of virtually all later forms of the daily office.

This mingling of the two traditions effectively obscured the previous contrast between the psalms as scripture and selected psalms as hymns, and caused leading church figures of the fourth century both to advocate the use of much more extensive psalmody by ordinary Christians and to offer explanations for its dual function, as we noted earlier. It also, in turn, encouraged monastic communities to take greater cognizance of the hymnic character of the psalms and to introduce more elaborate forms of their performance. 'Monasticism made a quantitive contribution to the song of the fourth-century church, and received in exchange the gift of musicality.'[29] However, the defence mounted by certain patristic writers with regard to these innovations suggests that at first not everyone welcomed them.[30]

The second principal factor was that from the early fifth century onwards communities of monks were given responsibility for maintaining the prayer and sacramental life of basilicas in the city of Rome. Even though the external *form* of their daily offices of psalmody may have remained unchanged, yet in this new context their *function* was effectively transformed from the spiritual advancement of the individual members of the community to the celebration of the praise of the Church. Moreover, this Roman institution provided a model that was imitated by others, including the establishment by the Franks of similar foundations in connection with sanctuaries dedicated to specially venerated saints.[31]

In this way Christians came to accept that the whole psalter and not just selected psalms could be used for the praise of God. But what of the difficulty that not all of the psalms actually expressed words of praise to God – indeed that some of them were prayers of desperation and others called down fire upon the psalmist's enemies? This did not present a serious obstacle to this new understanding, because it was thought that it was the *act* of psalm-singing rather than what the *text* of the psalms themselves said that was pleasing to God: we chant the psalms because God likes to hear them. One can see this attitude emerging in the *Rule of the Master*, a forerunner of the *Rule of Benedict* that was written in the late fifth or early sixth century:

> So great must be the reverential seriousness and the manner of chanting the psalms that the Lord listens more lovingly than we say them; as Scripture declares: 'You take delight in the coming of the morning, and in the evening', and again: 'Sing the psalms to him joyfully and skilfully, for direct is the word of the Lord', and again: 'Exult in him with fear', and again: 'Sing to the Lord wisely'. Therefore if it commands the singing of psalms to be done wisely and with fear, the person singing them should stand with body motionless and head bowed, and should sing praises to the Lord with composure, since he is indeed performing his service before the Godhead, as the prophet teaches when he says: 'In the presence of the angels I will sing your praise'.
>
> So the singer of psalms must always be careful not to let his

attention wander elsewhere, lest God say to us when our mind has strayed to some other thought: 'This people honours me only with lip-service, while their hearts are far from me', and lest it likewise be said of us: 'With their mouth they blessed and in their heart they cursed', and lest when we praise God with the tongue alone, we admit God only to the doorway of our mouth while we bring in and lodge the devil in the dwelling of our heart.[32]

It is true that this chapter of the rule, like other sources of the period,[33] later goes on offer a second and more traditionally monastic reason why the singer should pay attention to every single verse of the psalm, 'because if each verse is noted the soul derives profit for salvation and therein finds all it seeks, for "the psalm says everything for edification"; as the prophet declares: "I shall sing and understand in the way of integrity, when you come to me".' Yet it is clear from the rest of the chapter that praise has succeeded edification as the primary purpose for the use of psalms, and that what makes the psalm acceptable to God as praise is not the words that are spoken but the attitude and intention of the singler.

As a result of this change of function, it was inevitable that less importance would be accorded to the silent prayer that came between the psalms. The *Rule of the Master* directed that these periods of silence should always be kept short, to avoid the risk of any of the community falling asleep or being tempted to evil thoughts.[34] The *Rule of Benedict* echoed all the above exhortations, although expressing them more succinctly and giving as the reason for brevity in prayer that 'we are not to imagine that our prayers will be heard because we use many words'.[35]

In the light of all this, it is not surprising to find that the period of silence between psalms eventually disappeared altogether in later western usage, and that the usual method of psalm-singing itself changed. Already by the late fourth century, in an effort to relieve the monotony of the responsorial method, especially during the long night vigils, a variation had emerged – antiphonal psalmody – in which the assembly was divided into two choirs that took it in turns to sing the response to the verses sung by the soloist, or sometimes by two soloists alternating the verses.[36] By the ninth century, however, the two choirs themselves, instead of a soloist, began to sing the verses alternately, and the response (or antiphon, as it came to be called) was relegated merely to the beginning and end of the psalm. Joseph Dyer has argued that this change came about as a result of an increasing emphasis on the efficacy of individual effort towards growth in grace. 'Prayers and good works which were frequently repeated added to the soul's store of grace and helped overcome uncertainty about personal salvation. From this perspective active participation in chanting the sacred words of the psalms would have seemed more meritorious than merely listening to them.'[37] While they may certainly be some truth to his claim, such an attitude required as its prerequisite that the act of psalm-singing already be thought of as directed towards God rather than towards the edification of others.

5. *Psalmody as penance*
The use of certain psalms in order to express contrition for one's sins is clearly attested in sources from the late fourth century. For example, several writers refer to the presence of Ps. 51 ('Have mercy on me, O God ...') at or near the beginning of each day's worship.[38] Since the use of this psalm in this position is a universal feature of later forms of the daily office, this suggests that the practice may have been widely observed in this earlier period. Other psalms, too, were to be used by individuals in order to ask for the forgiveness of their sins.[39]

In addition to this use of particular psalms, however, we find that at this period the whole of a daily office could be thought of as an occasion to express one's penitence. The anonymous ascetic rule *De virginitate*, for instance, instructs its readers to recite as many psalms as they can during their nightly vigil from midnight until dawn, 'and after each psalm let there be a prayer and genuflection, confessing your sins with tears to the Lord and asking him to forgive you'.[40] While this interpretation of the function of daily prayer may well have had its origin in the strongly penitential atmosphere of early monasticism, by the late fourth century its influence was already spreading outside ascetic and monastic circles. Thus John Chrysostom counsels new converts to Christianity.

> to show great zeal by gathering here in the church at dawn to make your prayers *and confessions* to the God of all things, and to thank him for the gifts he has already given ... Let each one ... spend his working hours in the knowledge that at evening he should return here to the church, render an account to the Master of his whole day, *and beg forgiveness for his faults.*[41]

It is to be noted that there is no evidence to suggest that at this time the rites themselves included any explicitly penitential prayers or litanies, apart from Ps. 51 in the morning. It was only much later that publicly recited prayers of confession emerged among the preparatory elements in Western daily offices, and that the offering of incense in Eastern rites gave rise to a strongly penitential liturgical unit around it, since incense was seen in the Old Testament as having expiatory power for the sins of the people.[42]

Although, therefore, our fourth-century sources see the office as an opportunity for individuals to acknowledge their faults privately and ask for forgiveness, rather than thinking of the psalms of the office themselves functioning as an expression of penitence, yet it is not really surprising to find this latter idea developing in later centuries. Thus Caesarius of Arles in the sixth century lists psalmody among the pious exercises in which a penitent person might engage: 'I believe that in the mercy of God he will deign to inspire you in such a way that you do not pursue sinfulness through neglect, bur rather through repentance are able to reach the remedy of forgiveness by fasting, prayer, singing the psalms, and almsgiving.'[43] Similarly, he includes it along with fasting, prayer, and the keeping of vigils as an appropriate Lenten practice.[44]

From this use, psalms then found their way into more formal penitential discipline. The Celtic penitential system, which often assigned the performance of extremely demanding penances for many sins, also permitted commutation – the substitution of an easier or shorter penance for a more arduous or lengthier one. Hence the recitation of a certain number of psalms frequently became the permitted – and much preferred – alternative to other forms of penitential practice. A very early example of this development appears in the so-called *Canones hibernenses*, where as a substitute for a *superpositio* (a double fast-day) one hundred psalms may be recited instead.[45] Other Celtic sources regularly speak of multiples of fifty psalms functioning in this manner.

6. *Psalmody as intercession*

The roots of the use of psalms for intercessory purposes seem to lie in the funeral customs of the early Church. A notable characteristic of early Christian practice was the singing of psalms and hymns that proclaimed the hope of the resurrection, as death approached, as the body was prepared for burial, and in procession to the grave. One of the most common texts used for this purpose was Ps. 116. This custom stood in sharp contrast to the usual pagan practice of the period, which was to accompany death and burial by wailing and lamentation.[46] As the centuries went by, however, Christianity was increasingly influenced by the surrounding culture, and the fear of judgement and condemnation began to displace confident hope of the resurrection in the liturgies surrounding death. As a result, funeral psalmody took on a more penitential tone, as those present began to recite on behalf of the dying and deceased the sort of psalms that they believed that those persons themselves would have said as prayers for the forgiveness of their sins, had they been able to do so.

Our earliest testimony to this development appears to be a document dating from the second half of the eighth century, which describes the monastic observances of Monte Cassino. This states that on the day of the burial of a monk, the community were to chant the seven penitential psalms after vespers.[47] Later sources reveal further developments from this practice: the psalms used were no longer restricted to those that were penitential in character, and the act of intercession could now be for the living as well as the departed. Thus various documents prescribe 50, 100, or the whole 150 psalms to be said on the occasion of a death, and monthly or annually thereafter.[48] Similarly, the biography of Benedict of Aniane (*d.* 821) recounts that he directed that the monks of his monastery, on going to their places in the choir each morning, should recite privately fifteen psalms before the office began. These were arranged in three sets of five, the first set being for the living, the second for all the faithful departed, and the third for all the recently deceased. Each set was concluded with a short collect related to the intention for which the preceding psalms had been said. Although the biographer does not specify which particular psalms were used for this purpose, scholars are generally agreed, because of the evidence from later sources, that they were the fifteen gradual psalms (Pss. 120–134).[49]

Conclusions

What emerges from this survey is that an important distinction has to be drawn between the first three ways of using the psalms described above and the second three. In the first group, it is the *content* of the psalms that is all-important. It is because of what the psalms say, that they can be used as prophecy, as teaching, or as hymns. While the roots of the second group may lie in this same area, in their later development content recedes into the background, and it is the *action* of singing the psalm and the particular *intention* of the singer that renders it a vehicle for praise, for penitence, or for intercession. One might go so far as to say that in this second group of uses, psalms have simply become the accepted currency for divine-human interchange: their value lay not in their intrinsic merit but solely in the fact that God was thought to favour them. God could just as easily have preferred the performance of some other form of religious activity, but because he apparently liked to hear psalms, he could in that way be paid what was due to him in praise, be repaid what was owed to him in penitence, or be induced to grant the desires or the supplicants.

The use of content-related psalmody did not of course thereafter vanish from the Christian liturgical tradition. Appropriate psalms and sections of psalms went on being appointed for a wide variety of occasions in the ecclesiastical calendar, and certain psalms continued to be regarded as especially suitable to express particular sentiments. Yet there was now an underlying sense that one psalm was really just as good as another, and that what the words of a text said mattered less than the intentions of those using it. These attitudes have lingered on down to the present day, and often contribute to a lack of sensitivity on the part of those responsible for deciding what psalms shall be used in worship and how they are to be performed, as well as to the confusion of those who are expected to participate in that psalmody.

NOTES

1. Mark 12.35–37; parallels in Matt. 22.42–45 & Luke 20.41–44.
2. Chs. 97–106 (PG 6:704–724). For other examples, see Graham W. Woolfenden, 'The Use of the Psalter by Early Monastic Communities', *Studia Patristica* 26 (1993), p. 89.
3. See Marie-Josèphe Rondeau, *Les Commentaires patristiques du Psautier (IIIe-Ve siècles)* II (Orientalia Christiana Analecta 220, Rome, 1985), pp. 39ff.
4. The classic study of this phenomenon in early Christianity is Balthasar Fischer, 'Christ in the Psalms', *Theology Digest* 1 (1951), pp. 53–57.
5. See, for example, Roger Beckwith, *The Old Testament Canon of the New Testament Church* (London, 1985), pp. 110–118.
6. See J. D. Crichton, *Christian Celebration: The Prayer of the Church* (London, 1976), p. 60.
7. John Wilkinson, *Egeria's Travels* (London, 1971), p. 137.
8. *De anima* 9.4 (PL 2:660).
9. Frans Kok, 'L'office pachômien: *psallere, orare, legere*', *Ecclesia Orans* 9 (1992), pp. 69–95, has argued that their daily services included psalmody in addition to other biblical readings and prayer.
10. See Robert Taft, *The Liturgy of the Hours in East and West* (Collegeville, 1986), pp. 57–73.
11. See, for example, *Apophthegmata patrum*, Serapion 1 (PG 65:413–416).
12. See further Adalbert de Vogüé, 'Psalmodier n'est pas prier', *Ecclesia Orans* 6 (1989), pp. 7–32.
13. *Historia religiosa* 2.5 (PG 82:1309).
14. A saying of Abba Philimon, in G. E. H. Palmer, P. Sherard, K. Ware (eds.), *The Philokalia* (London, 1979), II, p. 347.
15. James W. McKinnon, 'Desert Monasticism and the Later Fourth-Century Psalmodic Movement', *Music and Letters* 75 (1994), pp. 505–521.
16. See, for example, Pierre Salmon, *The Breviary through the Centuries* (Collegeville, 1962), pp. 42–61.
17. *Homilia in psalmum* 1.1 (PG 29:212). See also Ambrose, *Explanatio psalmi* 1.7 9 (PL 14:923–925); Athanasius, *Epistola ad Marcellinum in interpretationem psalmorum* (PG 27:12–45); John Chrysostom, *Expositio in Psalmos* 41.1 (PG 55:156); Niceta of Remesiana, *De psalmodiae bono* 5.
18. Basil, *Homilia in psalmum* 1.1 (PG 29:212). See also John Chrysostom, *Expositio in psalmos* 41.1 (PG 55:156); *Homilia in Colossenses* 9.2 (PG 62:362); Niceta of Remesiana, *De psalmodiae bono* 5.
19. *Ep. ad Marcellinum* 27, 29 (PG 27:37, 41); English translation from James W. McKinnon, *Music in Early Christian Literature* (Cambridge 1987), pp. 52–53.
20. See Taft, *The Liturgy of the Hours in East and West*, pp. 31–56.
21. *De oratione* 27 (PL 1:1194).
22. Tertullian, *Apologeticum* 39.18 (PL 1:477). This custom also continued in later centuries: see, for example, John Chrysostom, *Expositio in psalmos* 41.2 (PG 55:157–158).
23. *De vita contemplativa* 80.
24. See Paul F. Bradshaw, *Daily Prayer in the Early Church* (London, 1981), pp. 44–45.
25. *Serm.* 165; 176 (PL 38:902, 950). On the origin of this psalm in the eucharist, see the

suggestion by James W. McKinnon, 'The Fourth-Century Origin of the Gradual', *Early Music History* 7 (1987), pp. 91–106.

26. *Expositio in Psalmos* 41.5 (PG 55:164).

27. See Paul F. Bradshaw, 'Cathedral vs. Monastery: the only alternatives for the Liturgy of the Hours?', in J. Neil Alexander (ed.), *Time and Community* (Washington DC, 1990), pp. 131–132.

28. See Taft, *The Liturgy of the Hours in East and West*, pp. 75–91.

29. McKinnon, 'Desert Monasticism and the Later Fourth-Century Psalmodic Movement', p. 519.

30. See especially Basil, *Ep.* 207.3 (PG 32:764); and Niceta of Remesiana, *De psalmodiae bono* 2.

31. See Angelus Häussling, *Mönchskonvent und Eucharistiefeier* (Liturgiewissenschaft Quellen und Forschungen 58, Münster, 1973), pp. 123–142.

32. *The Rule of the Master*, ch. 47; English translation by Luke Eberle (Kalamazoo, Michigan, 1977), pp. 205–206.

33. See, for example, Caesarius of Arles, *Sermones* 75.

34. Ch. 48.

35. *Rule of Benedict*, chs. 19–20. See also Adalbert de Vogüé, *The Rule of St. Benedict: A Doctrinal and Spiritual Commentary* (Kalamazoo, Michigan, 1983), pp. 139–149.

36. See Taft, *The Liturgy of the Hours in East and West*, p. 139.

37. Joseph Dyer, 'Monastic Psalmody of the Middle Ages', *Revue bénédictine* 99 (1989), pp. 41–74; quotation from pp. 70–71.

38. Pseudo-Athanasius, *De virginitate* 20 (PG 28:276); Basil, *Epistola* 207.3 (PG 32:764); John Cassian, *De institutis coenobiorum* 3.6 (PL 49:136). See Bradshaw, *Daily Prayer in the Early Church*, pp. 101–103, 108.

39. See, for example, Athansius, *Ep. ad Marcellinum* 21 (PG 27:33).

40. *De virginitate* 20 (PG 28:276).

41. *Baptismal Instruction* 8.17–18; English translation from P. W. Harkins, *St. John Chrysostom: Baptismal Instructions* (Westminster, Maryland, 1963), pp. 126–127 (emphasis added).

42. Num. 16.46–47. See further Gabriele Winkler, 'L'aspect pénitential dans les offices du soir en Orient et en Occident', in *Liturgie et rémission des péchés* (Bibliotheca "Ephemerides Liturgicae" Subsidia 3, Rome, 1975), pp. 273–293.

43. *Sermones* 208; English translation from M. M. Mueller, *Saint Caesarius of Arles – Sermons* 3 (Fathers of the Church 66, Washington DC, 1973), p. 89.

44. *Sermones* 202, 238; ibid., pp. 68, 224.

45. Text in F. W. H. Wasserschleben, *Die Bussordnungen der abendländischen Kirche* (Halle 1851), p. 139. Cyrille Vogel, 'Composition légale et commutations dans le systèm de la pénitence tarifée', *Revue de droit canonique* 9 (1959), p. 3, dates this section of the document to the sixth century.

46. See Geoffrey Rowell, *The Liturgy of Christian Burial* (Alcius Club Collection 59 London, 1977), pp. 19–30.

47. See Edmund Bishop, 'The Prymer', in *Liturgica Historica* (Oxford, 1918), p. 216.

48. For examples, see ibid., p. 216, and esp. n. 4.

49. Ibid., p. 214; Joseph Jungmann, *Christian Prayer through the Centuries* (New York, 1978), p. 82.

3

The Wisdom of God and the Word of God: Alcuin's Mass 'of Wisdom'

 *Ruth A. Meyers*

AMONG THE many votive masses appearing in sacramentaries of the eighth and ninth centuries, a series of masses attributed to Alcuin of York are particularly well-known. (Anglicans may be most familiar with the Collect for Trinity Sunday and the Collect for Purity, both found in this 'little missal'.) While many of these masses remained in the missal up to the Reformation and subsequently found a place in the 1570 *Missale Romanum*, one mass from this collection, the mass of wisdom, disappeared after 1570.[1] Yet its continuing presence in liturgical books throughout the Middle Ages suggests that it was of some significance (although certainly the frequency of its use cannot be determined). The title 'Of Holy Wisdom Who Is Christ'[2] offers the intriguing possibility that this mass honours not just the quality of wisdom but the Wisdom from on high whom some patristic writers identify as the Word.

Alcuin's Votive Masses
The existence of a collection of votive masses known to Alcuin is attested by two frequently cited letters of Alcuin, both written during his tenure as abbot of the monastery of St Martin, Tours. At some point during his abbacy (which lasted from 796 until his death in 804), the monks of St Vaast near Arras requested from Alcuin inscriptions for their churches and their altars. In his response, Alcuin included a series of masses taken from the missal in use at St Martin's: 'And I have also taken some masses from our

39

missal, for your use in the customary daily offices of the church'.[3]
Alcuin sent a similar series of masses in a letter to the monks of
Fulda dated to 801 or 802: 'I have sent you, holy priests, a little
missal, that you may have, for every day of the week, prayer forms
that one may wish to direct to God.'[4]

The two lists, although not identical, each include five masses
listed in similar order and with nearly identical description. Each
begins with a mass in honour of the Holy Trinity, and each
contains masses for the intercession of the angels, for all the saints,
in honour of Mary, and for sins. The letter to Fulda enumerates
several masses not found in the letter to St Vaast, including one 'for
the love of wisdom'.[5]

Although in his letters Alcuin suggests that these masses are
offered for daily use, he does not specify any for use on particular
days. Such a day-by-day assignment can be found in the *Liber
Sacramentorum* ('Book of the Sacraments'), included in the
collected works of Alcuin edited by Froben in 1777 and reprinted
in the Patrology of J. P. Migne.[6] Here three masses are assigned to
each day of the week, followed by additional votive masses.
Virtually all the masses identified in Alcuin's letters to St Vaast and
St Fulda appear at some point in this collection.

Froben based his work on an edition of the Gregorian
Sacramentary edited in 1571 by the liturgist J. Pamélius. However,
the latter relied only upon two manuscripts from Cologne dating
to the end of the ninth century, nearly a century after Alcuin
completed his work. As Jean Deshusses has pointed out, this lapse
of several decades opens the possibility of alterations or interpola-
tions in Alcuin's original work.[7]

Collaborating in the early stages of his work with Henri Barré,
Deshusses reviewed ninth-century manuscripts of sacramentaries
in order to assess Alcuin's authorship of these votive masses and to
produce a critical edition. Although these sacramentaries include
large numbers of votive masses and masses for the dead, Barré and
Deshusses eliminated from consideration masses clearly borrowed
from eighth-century sacramentaries and thus antedating Alcuin,
and those appearing in only a few manuscripts. The sacramentary
of St Martin of Tours, that is, Alcuin's church, was considered a
primary witness, although the earliest manuscript dates only to the

last quarter of the ninth century. Deshusses and Barré were able to identify a small number of votive masses which appear in this sacramentary of St Martin of Tours and were also identified by title in one or both of Alcuin's letters and had a wide diffusion as indicated by their presence in a significant number of ninth-century manuscripts. These masses are listed in nearly identical order in Alcuin's letters and in the various manuscripts.[8]

Examining the style and structure of these votive masses, Barré and Deshusses identified distinctive characteristics marking these as a strikingly homogeneous grouping. Each mass comprises four prayers: a first prayer given without title; prayer over the gifts (*Super oblata*); postcommunion prayer (*Ad complendum* or *Post communionem*); and prayer over the people (*Super populum* or *alia*). Several of the masses also include a preface. Most of these prayers have no known antecedents in earlier manuscripts. The appearance of the same terms and identical expressions suggests a single author. Furthermore, the Latin is written with strict grammatical accuracy and elegant constructions. The vocabulary, style, and rhythms reproduce those of ancient prayers and thus suggest an author quite familiar with these liturgical texts consciously mimicking them.[9]

Barré and Deshusses found support for Alcuinian authorship in later medieval manuscripts. In his *Micrologus* (eleventh century), Bernhold of Constance describes a list of daily masses as the work of Alcuin. Beginning at the end of the ninth century, some medieval manuscripts preface a list of daily votive masses with a title attributing them to Alcuin, while others ascribe to Alcuin individual masses in the series. Morever, Alcuin's biographer, writing no later than 823–829, states that Alcuin celebrated mass daily with masses assigned to each day of the week. These various witnesses lend support to the claim of Alcuin's authorship of this series of votive masses.[10]

Several masses can thus be identified with near certainty as the work of Alcuin. Deshusses lists the following criteria:

> indication of the title in at least one of the letters of Alcuin;
> inclusion in the sacramentary of St Martin of Tours;
> widespread diffusion in the manuscript tradition;

the characteristic structure of four prayers;
the distinctive style.[11]

While these criteria allow the authorship of the masses to be
assigned to Alcuin, the designation of masses for particular days of
the week does not seem to go back to Alcuin, the comments of his
biographer notwithstanding.

Based upon the manuscript evidence, Barré and Deshusses identified two distinct schemes designating specific masses for each day
of the week. These emerged by the middle of the ninth century
and spread rapidly. One scheme, which seems to have appeared
first at Reichenau, assigns one mass to each day of the week, beginning with the Holy Trinity on Sunday. Barré and Deshusses cate-
gorized these as masses *in honore*, in honour of God and the saints,
to wit, the Trinity, the divine attributes of wisdom and charity, the
cross, Mary, the angels, and the saints. In contrast, the sacramentaries of Cologne are distinguished by the provision of three masses
for each day. Those 'in honour' appear first in each daily group
(except on Monday, where a mass for sins is placed first), and a
series of masses 'for need' comprises the second daily mass (except
on Saturday, where the second mass is a commemoration of
Mary). The third mass each day is a 'mass of St Augustine', a series
whose author is most certainly not Alcuin.[12]

The Mass of Wisdom
The title 'for the love of wisdom' appears as the second item in the
list of masses given in Alcuin's letter to the monks of Fulda.
Moreover, a mass 'of wisdom' is found in the sacramentary of St
Martin of Tours and in virtually all of the ninth-century manuscripts used by Deshusses to establish a critical edition of Alcuin's
votive masses. In the first stage of the manuscript tradition, prior to
the assignment of masses for specific weekdays, the mass of wisdom
is usually the second mass provided. It follows the mass of the Holy
Trinity, the same order given in Alcuin's letter to the monks of
Fulda. This order remains in the daily scheme originating at
Reichenau, with the mass of the Holy Trinity placed on Sunday
and that of wisdom assigned to Monday (although in a tenth-
century manuscript from Tours the mass of wisdom has shifted to

Wednesday). In the pattern represented by the sacramentaries of Cologne, the mass of wisdom is the first of the three masses assigned to Wednesday.[13]

The text of the mass includes the four characteristic prayers as well as a preface, although the latter is missing from several manuscripts. The distinctive style of the Alcuinian series of votive masses is evident. Thus the text translated below meets all criteria established by Deshusses and can be attributed to Alcuin with virtual certainty.

MASS OF WISDOM[14]

O God, who through your coeternal wisdom fashioned human beings when they did not yet exist and mercifully restored them when they were lost: grant, we pray, that, by that same [wisdom] inspiring our breaths, we may love you with our whole minds, and run to you with our whole hearts. Through.

Over the gifts. Lord God, we pray that the gift of this our offering may be made holy in cooperation with your wisdom, so that it may please you to your praise and profit us to our salvation. Through.

Preface.[15] ... whose will it was to reveal to us in your coeternal wisdom the knowledge of your name and the glory of your power, that confessing your majesty and holding fast to your commands we might have eternal life with you. Through Christ.

Postcommunion. Pour into our hearts, we pray, Lord God, through these holy things we have taken, the light of your wisdom, that we may know you truly and love you faithfully. Through.

Over the people. O God who sent your Son and manifested the Creator of creatures: look favourably upon us your servants and prepare in our hearts a dwelling-place worthy of *hagia sophia.*[16] Through.

In addition to these prayers, a few manuscripts include readings for the mass of wisdom. These readings are not, however, widely attested, nor are they the same in all manuscripts where they do appear, suggesting that they were not appointed by Alcuin. Alternatives for the first reading include Wisdom 9.1–5, James 1.5–6, James 1.3–6, and Ephesians 1.16–20. The Gospel assigned is Matthew 11.25–30 in some manuscripts and John 17.1–3 in others.[17]

The Gift of Wisdom

In his survey of Alcuin's votive masses, Josef Jungmann asserts that this mass of wisdom describes the divine gift of wisdom sought by people and only in passing calls to mind 'the uncreated Wisdom.'[18] But Jungmann based this observation primarily upon the appointed lessons, which, as noted above, are not widely attested. His assessment was further limited by his reliance on the *Liber Sacramentorum*, supplemented by Odilo Heiming's study of the Milanese manuscript tradition,[19] with the result that he did not know the alternative readings in Ephesians and Wisdom of Solomon.

Certainly portions of the prayers reflect the human desire for the divine gift of wisdom. This is most evident in the postcommunion prayer, in which 'the light of [God's] wisdom' is sought in order to attain true knowledge of God and to love God faithfully. A similar end is the intent of the opening prayer, which asks that through divine wisdom inspiring us (literally 'breathing into our breasts') we might love God fully and wholeheartedly seek God. The purpose of this gift is thus to enhance the human relation to the divine, rather than any increase of wisdom in wordly affairs. This is the gift of wisdom described in Ephesians, that is, a 'spirit of wisdom' bestowed by God 'so that, with the eyes of your heart enlightened, you may know what is the hope to which [God] has called you' (Eph. 1.17–18).[20]

The only hint that wisdom might be understood as 'common sense' or 'practical wisdom' comes in the letter to James. The passage selected suggests that anyone 'lacking in wisdom' should 'ask God … and it will be given you' (James 1.5), although the purpose of this wisdom is not specified here. However, it can be inferred from the overall content of the book, which provides practical guidance for Christian living. Given that this passage is a later addition appearing in only a few manuscripts, we can conclude that the notion of wisdom as knowledge or skill for daily living was at most a minor dimension of this mass of wisdom.

A very different view of wisdom is evident in other elements of the prayers. The phrase 'your coeternal wisdom' appears in the opening prayer and again in the preface. The dative of reference is employed: 'wisdom coeternal to you', i.e., to God. This is not a gift of divine wisdom to human beings, but a divine attribute which is part of God's work of creation, redemption and revelation. The petition of the opening prayer, calling upon 'that same [wisdom]', is referring to the wisdom coeternal to God and not solely to the divine gift of wisdom desired by people. The prayer over the gifts, while not specifying God's coeternal wisdom, speaks of wisdom 'cooperating', in this case in the sanctification of the bread and wine. Here again is a divine action involving wisdom rather than a gift of wisdom bestowed upon humankind.

That the 'uncreated Wisdom' (to use Jungmann's term) is a significant dimension of this mass is underscored by a few manuscripts. Although the title most frequently used is 'mass of wisdom', or simply 'of wisdom', in several manuscripts it is entitled 'mass of *holy* wisdom'.[21] This could still be understood as reference to a divine gift to humanity, but the addition of 'holy' emphasizes the sacred or divine nature of this wisdom. A much more explicit title supplied in one manuscript is 'mass of wisdom, who is Christ'.[22] Here the focus on uncreated Wisdom, the wisdom coeternal to God, is unmistakable.

Also striking is a manuscript which uses the title 'mass of holy *sophia*',[23] echoing Alcuin's use of the transliterated Greek phrase *hagia sophia* ('holy wisdom') in the postcommunion prayer. The choice of the Greek term is curious. It suggests that the Latin translation was in some way inadequate to convey the full meaning inherent in the Greek. If this is so, then it must have a meaning beyond or other than that of 'practical wisdom', 'rules for upright conduct', or even 'intimate knowing which draws one closer to God'. Perhaps *sophia* refers to 'uncreated Wisdom', or even the personification of wisdom, who first appears in post-exilic Jewish wisdom tradition and is subsequently identified with Christ in New Testament and patristic texts.

The Wisdom of God

The personification of wisdom emerges first in the Book of Proverbs. She (the grammatical gender of the Hebrew *chokmah* and the Greek σοφια as well as the Latin *sapientia*, is feminine) speaks in three sections of the introduction to Proverbs (ch. 1–9), material understood by contemporary scholars as most probably the work of a post-exilic editor. In these discourses (1.20–33; 8.1–36; 9.1–6), Wisdom appears as a noisy street preacher, proclaiming her goodness and her worth; challenging those who refuse to listen to her and threatening punishment to them; inviting 'the simple' to eat her bread and drink her wine; exhorting her listeners to heed her words and keep her ways.

In addition to offering her gifts and confronting those who spurn her, Wisdom speaks of her origins (8.22–31). While Job 28 hints at the pre-existence of Wisdom, in Proverbs it is obvious. The first of God's created works, Wisdom was at God's side as 'master worker' or 'little child' (the translation is disputed) at the creation of the world, when God established the heavens, set the bounds of the seas, and carved the foundations of the earth. She rejoiced in the world and took delight in the human race.

Although in existence at the creation of the world, in Proverbs Wisdom is not identified with God. In the Book of Sirach, usually dated to about 180 B.C.E., she is identified with *Torah* (Law). In a song of self-praise (24.1–22), Wisdom proclaims that she 'came forth from the mouth of the Most High' and at the command of the Creator pitched her tent in Israel. At the conclusion of her speech, the author of Sirach steps in to make an identification: 'All this is the book of the covenant of the Most High God,/ the law that Moses commanded us/as an inheritance for the congregations of Jacob' (24.23).

The personification of Wisdom is further developed in the Wisdom of Solomon, dating to the first century B.C.E. Here Wisdom is clearly divine, a manifestation of God to humanity.[24] Pseudo-Solomon describes her as 'a breath of the power of God', 'a pure emanation of the glory of the Almighty', 'a reflection of eternal light,/a spotless mirror of the working of God,/ and an image of his goodness' (7.25–26). In the act of creation, wisdom and word are synonymous: 'O God of my ancestors and Lord of mercy,/ who have made all things by your word,/ and by your wisdom have formed humankind' (9.1–2a). Wisdom has the power to arrange the world (8.1) and is involved in bringing people to God (7.27). An agent of salvation, Wisdom was the saving power in the history of Israel, from Adam to the Exodus (9.18–10.21).

This personification of Wisdom in the Hebrew scriptures forms the background to a 'Wisdom christology' that developed during the first century C.E. The language and imagery of the Wisdom tradition appear repeatedly in the New Testament. In places, Jesus is the messenger or child of Wisdom, particularly in the Q tradition. For example, in Luke 7.31–35, Jesus compares his ministry to that of John the Baptist and concludes, 'wisdom is vindicated by all her children', suggesting that both he and John are children of Wisdom. While Jesus is not identified with Wisdom in Q, a shift occurs in Matthew's redaction of Q. 'Wisdom is vindicated by her children' becomes 'wisdom is vindicated by her deeds' (Matt 11.19), implying that Jesus himself is Wisdom. This Matthean identification of Jesus with Wisdom may be seen as analogous to the Jewish concept of Wisdom as abiding in the *Torah* (Sir. 24), and is in keeping with the Matthean theology of Jesus as the fulfillment of the Law.[25]

The identification of Jesus with Wisdom also appears in Matthew 11.25–30, one of the passages appointed for the wisdom mass in a few manuscripts. Some scholars argue that the description of the exclusive mutual knowledge of the Father and the Son (11.25–27) is elsewhere applied only to Wisdom, that is, only Wisdom knows God (Wis. 7.25–26, 8.4) and only God knows Wisdom (Job 28; Sir. 1.6–10), and thus Jesus is presented as Wisdom.[26] An even clearer parallel with Wisdom is evident in Jesus' invitation to those who are weary: 'take my yoke upon you, and learn from me … For my yoke is easy, and my burden is light' (11.28–30), echoing the words of Sirach: 'Put your neck under [Wisdom's] yoke/and let your souls receive instruction;/ … See with your own eyes that I have laboured but little/and found for myself much serenity' (Sir. 51.26–27; cf. Sir. 6:24–30).

Elsewhere in the New Testament, Jesus is also understood in

light of the Wisdom tradition. In 1 Corinthians, Paul identifies Jesus with Wisdom: 'Christ the power of God and the wisdom of God' (1.24); 'Christ Jesus, who became for us wisdom from God' (1.30). James Dunn argues that Paul drew upon the language and ideas of Wisdom, familiar to his audience, to explain the significance of Jesus. 'Jesus is the exhaustive embodiment of divine wisdom', Wisdom who makes known God's activity in creation, revelation, and salvation.[27] The language and ideas of Wisdom are also evident in some early Christian hymns extolling Christ. In the hymn found in Colossians 1.15–20, Jesus is lauded as 'the image of the invisible God, the firstborn of all creation', in whom 'all things in heaven and on earth were created', language which recalls descriptions of Wisdom (e.g., Prov. 8.22; Wis. 7.26, 9.2; Sir. 24.9). Likewise, Hebrews 1.3, '[the Son] is the reflection of God's glory and the exact imprint of God's very being', echoes pseudo-Solomon's praise of Wisdom (Wis. 7.26).[28]

The use of wisdom language to describe Jesus is especially evident in the Gospel of John. As Wisdom is a pure emanation of the glory of God (Wis. 7.25), Jesus manifests the Father's glory (John 8.50; 17.4–5). Wisdom teaches people what is of God (Wis. 9.17), utters truth (Prov. 8.6–7), and leads people to life with God (Prov. 8.35, 9.6), as Jesus is the revealer and source of truth (John 3.11–12, 14.6, 18.37). The symbols of bread, wine and water and the invitation to eat and drink also relate Jesus to Wisdom (Prov. 9.2–5; Sir. 24.19–21; John 4.13–15, 6.35, 51ff.). Noting the extensive parallels to Wisdom literature found in the Gospel of John, Raymond Brown concludes, 'in John, Jesus is personified Wisdom'.[29]

The identification of Jesus with Wisdom extends to the identification of Wisdom and Word in the prologue to John. Wisdom and the Word existed 'at the beginning' before the creation of the world (Prov. 8.22–23; Sir. 24.9; John 1.1). Like Wisdom, the Word is an agent of creation (Wis. 9.2; John 1.3). Both Wisdom and the Word are reflections of the light of God (Wis. 7.26; John 1.4). Just as Wisdom pitched her tent in Israel (Sir. 24.8), the Word pitched his tent among humanity (John 1.14). Brown comments, 'in the Old Testament presentation of Wisdom, there are good parallels for almost every detail of the prologue's description of the

Word ... Jesus is divine Wisdom, pre-existent, but now come among [people] to teach them and give them life'.[30]

Thus the Jewish concept of Wisdom played a significant theological role for the early Christians. Dunn asserts that the use of Wisdom categories allowed Christians to understand Jesus as the embodiment of the creative and saving activity of God, reaching out to humanity. He concludes, 'Herein we see the origin of the doctrine of the incarnation'.[31]

Christians in the ante-Nicene period continued to draw upon the category of Wisdom. Although the figure of Wisdom was an essential element of Gnosticism,[32] orthodox Christian writers used the concept of Wisdom to assert the pre-existence of Christ and the role of Christ in creation. Countering Gnostic claims, Irenaeus asserts, 'there is one only God, the Creator ... who made those things by Himself, that is, through His Word and His Wisdom'.[33] Elsewhere Irenaeus relates Wisdom to the Spirit, but maintains the pre-existence of Wisdom and Word and their role in creation:

> ... the Word, namely the Son, was always with the Father; and that Wisdom also, which is the Spirit, was present with Him, anterior to all creation ...
>
> There is therefore one God, who by the Word and Wisdom created and arranged all things.[34]

While Wisdom and Word were thus distinguished by Irenaeus, for other writers Wisdom was one christological title among others. Origen reflects at length on Wisdom as a name for Christ:

> And therefore we have first to ascertain what the only-begotten Son of God is, seeing He is called by many different names ... For He is termed Wisdom...
>
> Whatever, therefore, we have predicated of the wisdom of God, will be appropriately applied and understood of the Son of God ...
>
> For through Wisdom, which is Christ, God has power over all things.[35]

Throughout this chapter, Origen returns repeatedly to pseudo-Solomon's description of Wisdom (especially Wis. 7.25–26), as

well as the letters of Paul and the prologue to John's Gospel. Later,
Origen employs the category of Wisdom to comment on the
incarnation:

> But of all the marvellous and mighty acts related of [God], this
> altogether surpasses human admiration ... how that mighty
> power of divine majesty, that very Word of the Father, and
> that very wisdom of God, in which were all created things,
> visible and invisible, can be believed to have existed within
> the limits of that man who appeared in Judea; nay, that the
> Wisdom of God can have entered the womb of a woman, and
> have been born an infant, and have uttered wailings like the
> cries of little children! [36]

The equivalence of Wisdom and Word is also noted by Tertullian,
who writes, '[it is] evident that it is one and the same power which
is in one place described under the name of Wisdom, and in
another passage under the appellation of the Word'.[37]

The identity of Wisdom and Word had some significance in the
Arian controversy. Both sides cited Wisdom texts to defend their
respective positions, arguments made possible because some
passages of the Hebrew scriptures describe Wisdom as subordinate
to God, while elsewhere Wisdom is equated with divine presence
and activity.[38] In deciding in favor of the equality of the Son with
the Father, the equivalence of Wisdom and Word was not dis-
carded. Augustine later asserted in his treatise on the Trinity: '[the
Son] was not sent in respect to any inequality of power, or substance, or anything that in Him was not equal to the Father ... for
the Son is the Word of the Father, which is also called His
wisdom'.[39]

Wisdom did not disappear altogether in the Middle Ages, but
was manifest in various forms. She was honoured in the great
cathedral of Hagia Sophia in Constantinople, where she was associated with Christ and eventually also with Mary. Some medieval
writers continued to identify Wisdom with Christ. But elements
of personified Wisdom appear as well in devotion to Mary, in
writings about Holy Mother Church, and in the figures of Lady
Philosophy and Charity.[40] Thus it is not surprising that Wisdom
appears as well in Alcuin's writings.

Wisdom in the Writing of Alcuin

Alcuin had great respect for the wisdom that is the source of knowledge, and at times he describes wisdom in the narrower sense of skill in writing and speech or as inspiration for learning. But he also speaks of divine Wisdom. In some texts he uses the translitered *sophia* or *hagia sophia*, while elsewhere *sapientia* or *sancta sapientia* appear.[41]

In his handbooks on the seven liberal arts, Alcuin describes them as steps leading to the temple of Philosophy, who is supreme wisdom. The steps were established by divine Wisdom herself, who built a house with seven pillars (Prov. 9.1). One is led to perfect knowledge by ascending these columns or steps.[42] Wisdom also teaches the four cardinal virtues (cf. Wis. 8.7).[43] Newman comments, 'the figure of Wisdom was thus a central link between devotion and pedagogy, prayerful adoration and liberal education'.[44]

Alcuin did not limit his writings on wisdom to the topics of knowledge and learning. In his treatise *De fide sanctae et individuae Trinitatis*, he draws upon the identification of Christ as Wisdom (1 Cor. 1.24) and extends it to all the persons of the Trinity: 'behold the Father, who is power and wisdom, and the Son, power and wisdom, and the Holy Spirit, power and wisdom; yet not three powers nor three wisdoms, but one power and one wisdom, Father, Son and Holy Spirit'.[45] Alcuin returns to the Pauline description of Christ as the wisdom of God at several points in the treatise.

The same biblical citation is alluded to in the first line of Alcuin's 'Poem on the Bishops, Kings, and Saints of the Church of York'.[46] More intriguing in this poem is Alcuin's description of a church built by his friend and patron Ælberht, archbishop of York (773–778), and dedicated to holy Wisdom, *alma Sophia*.[47] Although there is no other extant record of a church with this name in York, Richard Morris proposes that the site was subsequently inherited by the religious community in York known alternatively as Christ Church and as Holy Trinity. Morris notes that the dedication of the church to Wisdom could have been suggested by pilgrims returning from Constantinople. But he turns instead to a church dedicated to Sancta Sophia, built in the dukedom of Benevento in southern Italy during the middle of the eighth century, and suggests that, during a journey overseas with Ælberht, Alcuin may have heard conversation about the approaching completion of this church. However, Morris also acknowledges that the dedication of the church in Benevento is a direct imitation of Hagia Sophia in Constantinople.[48] Thus even if Morris' speculation is accurate, the York church was at least indirectly influenced by the Constantinopolitan prototype.

The designation 'alma' sophia is curious. The translator of Alcuin's poem offers no explanation of the use of this adjective, literally translated 'dear' or 'cherished', but refers in his commentary to 'Sancta [Holy] Sophia'. Perhaps alma was not the actual title of the church, but rather was employed here by Alcuin to describe his love of wisdom. Certainly Alcuin cherished wisdom throughout his life, a fact he emphasizes in the penultimate line of his epitaph (which he himself composed): 'My name was Alcuin; wisdom [sophia] was always dear to me'.[49]

While it is tempting to suggest that Alcuin's use of sophia always refers to divine Wisdom, this may not be entirely accurate. In Alcuin's poem, just a few lines after his description of alma Sophia, he describes Ælberht's division of his estate. One son received 'government of the church, treasure, lands, and money', the other 'his choice learning [sophia], his study and collection of books'.[50] Sophia in this instance cannot refer to divine Wisdom; it seems most unlikely that Alcuin would view this divine gift as being under human control. At most, the term may suggest that the learning acquired by Ælberht in his life was inspired by the heavenly wisdom.

Perhaps all that can be said about Alcuin's use of sophia and sapientia is that the terms are used interchangeably both in a narrower sense as relating to learning and the liberal arts and in a much broader sense as the divine Wisdom who is Christ. These understandings are not mutually exclusive for Alcuin, but form a continuum.[51] Hence the context of each use of these terms is of particular importance in interpreting Alcuin's intent.

One final work is of interest as background to Alcuin's mass of wisdom. A compilation of private prayers is attributed to Alcuin and said to have been offered to his friends and his patron Charlemagne.[52] Included is a 'prayer for wisdom':

God of my ancestors and Lord of mercy, you have made all
things by your word, and by your wisdom you have fashioned human beings, so that they might rule the creatures
whom you have made, might govern the world with justice
and righteousness, and might judge with upright hearts: Give
me the wisdom that sits by your throne, and do not reject me
from among your children, for I am your servant and the
child of your handmaid. Deal with your servant according to
your mercy, and teach me your precepts. I am your servant.
Give me understanding, that I may know your command-
ments.[53]

The majority of this prayer is simply a citation of pseudo-
Solomon's prayer in Wisdom 9.1–5a, while the conclusion, beginning 'Deal with your servant', is a quotation from Psalm 119 (vss.
124–5).[54] However, in the manuscript this private prayer is
followed by a collect which is identical to the opening prayer of
Alcuin's mass of wisdom, leading Barré and Deshusses to suggest
that this collection may represent an early draft of the masses of
Alcuin.[55]

The Mass of Wisdom: A Closer Look

Despite Alcuin's love of wisdom as the source and summit of
learning, this concept is not in evidence in the mass of wisdom. As
noted above, the gift of wisdom is sought in order to enhance the
human relation to the divine, that is, to turn our hearts to God and
to increase our knowledge, love, obedience, and praise of God.
This is the gift not only of the abstract concept of wisdom, but
most especially of personified Wisdom, who stands in the streets
and calls people to eat her fruits and walk in her ways, that they
might have life (Prov. 9.3–6).

The work of divine Wisdom is referred to repeatedly in the
mass. She is agent of creation. Through this coeternal wisdom God
is said to have formed human beings, calling to mind Wisdom's
discourse on her origins (Prov. 8.22–31) and the prayer of pseudo-
Solomon, who identifies both divine Wisdom and divine Word as
agents of creation (Wis. 9.1–2). She is agent of salvation, one
through whom God 'restored human beings when they were lost',

as the address of the opening collect states. This is Wisdom who seeks out human beings (Prov. 1.20ff.), challenges and forms them (Prov. 9.6, Sir. 6.20–26), and makes them friends of God (Wis. 7.27). She is agent of revelation, through whom, in the language of the preface, God reveals 'the knowledge of [God's] name and the glory of [God's] power'. Her instructions teach people what pleases God and how to obey the divine will (Prov. 8.35; Wis. 8.4–8, 9.13–18). The postcommunion prayer asks that the light of divine wisdom be poured into our hearts, an allusion to Wisdom, 'a reflection of eternal light' (Wis. 7.26; see also Eccles. 2.13; Prov. 4.18–19), who brings light to the world.

The parallels with the Word, as extolled in the Johannine prologue, are obvious. Again and again this mass speaks of Wisdom in ways which suggest that this is a christological title parallel to 'Word', as used by some patristic writers. But von Lilienfeld, cautioning that 'wisdom' cannot be associated exclusively with Christ, points out that *infunde*, the verb used in the petition of the postcommunion prayer for God to 'pour into our hearts the light of your wisdom', is a verb associated in particular with the work of the Holy Spirit.[56] For example, the prayer over the people in a mass for the gift of tears asks God to 'pour (*infunde*) the grace of the Holy Spirit into our hearts'.[57] Likewise, the noun *infusio*, a cognate of the verb *infundo*, is employed in the prayer for the Holy Spirit included among Alcuin's masses and familiar to Anglicans as the Collect for Purity.[58]

In addition to the verb *infundo*, the phrase 'in cooperation with your wisdom', used in the prayer over the gifts in the mass of wisdom, suggests the Holy Spirit as Wisdom.[59] To this can be added the petition, in the opening prayer, that Wisdom might 'inspire our breaths'. The language calls to mind God breathing the breath of life into the nostrils of the first human being (Gen. 2.7), the same verb, *inspiro*, 'breathe into', being used both in the Vulgate and in Alcuin's mass. This too implies the work of the Holy Spirit more than that of the Word.

As further evidence that Alcuin may be equating Wisdom with the Holy Spirit, von Lilienfeld cites the petition, in the concluding prayer over the people, asking God to 'prepare in our hearts a dwelling-place worthy of *hagia sophia*', but substantiates this claim on the basis of the concluding formula. Since the indwelling is to take place through Christ, Christ cannot be the immediate or exclusive intent of the term *hagia sophia*.[60] Perhaps this argument has merit, but it must be remembered that the concluding formula is just that, a formula included in the prayer as only one word, *per* ('through').[61] The content of this formula would thus be one step removed from conscious consideration in the composition of the prayer.

More compelling in the identification of *hagia sophia* with the Holy Spirit are the parallels in other prayers of the masses of Alcuin. In the mass for the grace of the Holy Spirit, the opening prayer asks God to 'free our hearts from the temptations of evil thoughts, that we may be made worthy dwelling-places for the Holy Spirit'.[62] The prayer over the gifts in the mass 'for the cleansing of our hearts by the Holy Spirit' asks God to 'cleanse our hearts of [every] stain, that we may be made worthy dwelling-places for the Holy Spirit'.[63] In both these prayers, as in the mass of wisdom, the intent is that our hearts may become dwelling-places worthy of the divine, identified variously as the Holy Spirit or as Wisdom. Thus one can conclude that *hagia sophia* refers to the Spirit, a parallel also drawn in the Wisdom of Solomon: 'Who has learned your counsel,/unless you have given wisdom/ and sent your holy spirit from on high?' (Wis. 9.18).

But 'Holy Spirit' may not be the sole meaning of *hagia sophia*. The prayer over the people asks that our hearts become fit 'dwelling-places' for *hagia sophia*. This brings to mind Wisdom's statement that she established her dwelling in Israel (Sir. 24.8) and the parallel statement of the Johannine prologue that 'the Word became flesh and dwelt amoung us' (John 1.14). Taken independently of Alcuin's other masses, this is the primary allusion made in this prayer, that is, that *hagia sophia* who is to indwell our hearts is the very Word of God.

Perhaps Alcuin associates Wisdom with both the Holy Spirit and with the Word who is Christ. That dual parallel is evident not only in the petition for the indwelling of *hagia sophia*, but also in the allusions to creation. The agency of both Wisdom and Word in creation (Wis. 9.1–2) is implied by the address of the opening prayer. But that same prayer also speaks of Wisdom breathing into us, activity more commonly associated with the Spirit.

Furthermore, 'the light of your wisdom' may also imply both the Holy Spirit and the Word. In the mass for the grace of the Holy Spirit, the prayer over the gifts asks God to 'enlighten our souls by the grace of the Holy Spirit'.[64] Yet in that same mass the prayer over the people associates enlightenment with the Word: 'O God, who comes into this world to enlighten all people, enlighten our hearts with the splendor of your grace, that we might worthily contemplate your majesty and love you'.[65] The wording in the address is almost verbatim that of the prologue to John (1.9), suggesting that enlightenment is a function of the Word as well as a function of the Holy Spirit.

There are thus three divine activities, creation, enlightenment, and indwelling, attributed to Wisdom and associated with both the Holy Spirit and with the Word. The multiple allusions of this Wisdom mass do not permit more careful distinctions. Furthermore, it should be remembered that Alcuin, who referred in his writings to the identification of Christ as the wisdom of God (1 Cor. 1.24), extended that description to all three persons of the Trinity and to the one God. And if Alcuin is imprecise in his identification of Wisdom, patristic writers who preceded him differed in their identification, some understanding Wisdom as the Holy Spirit and others using this name as a christological title equivalent to 'Word'.[66]

Who, then, is Wisdom who is honoured in this mass of Alcuin? She is a personification of God, a manifestation of God's gracious activity toward humankind. She is both Word and Spirit, an agent of creation, revelation and salvation. She is the light who enlightens human hearts and the fullness of God dwelling amongst humanity. Through her outreach, human beings are drawn ever more deeply into the knowledge and love of God.

NOTES

1. Gerald Ellard, 'Alcuin and Some Favored Votive Masses', *Theological Studies* 1 (1940):37–61.

2. Ellard, pp. 39, 61, uses this title, which is a variant reading. See below, p. 45.

3. 'Missas quoque aliquas de nostro tuli missali ad cotidiana et ecclesiasticae consuetudinis officia', Letter 296, in *Monumenta Germaniae historica* (hereafter *MGH*), *Epistolae* IV, p. 455; trans. Gerald Ellard, *Master Alcuin, Liturgist: A Partner of Our Piety* (Chicago 1956), p. 147.

4. 'Misi chartulam missalem vobis, o sanctissimi presbyteri, ut habeatis singulis diebus, quibus preces Deo dirigere cuilibet placeat', Letter 250, *MGH, Epist.* IV, pp. 404–5; translated by Ellard, *Master Alcuin*, p. 147.

5. Letters 250 and 296, *MGH, Epist.* IV, p. 404–6, 454–5.

6. *Liber Sacramentorum*, in *PL* 101:445–66.

7. Jean Deshusses, 'Les messes d'Alcuin', *Archiv für Liturgiewissenschaft* 14 (1972):7.

8. Henri Barré and Jean Deshusses, 'A la recherche du Missel d'Alcuin', *Ephemerides liturgicae* 82 (1968): 17–27; Deshusses, 'Les messes', pp. 8–14; Deshusses, *Le sacramentaire Grégorien: ses principales formes d'après les plus anciens manuscrits*, vol. II: *Textes complémentaires pour la messe*, 2nd ed. (Fribourg 1988), pp. 25–6. Barré and Deshusses identified 18 votive masses meeting these criteria; in his subsequent work Deshusses identified 21 such masses. The mass 'of wisdom' is included in both lists.

9. Barré and Deshusses, 'A la recherche', pp. 36–37; Deshusses, 'Les messes', pp. 10–11; Deshusses, *Le sacramentaire Grégorien*, II:25–6.

10. Barré and Deshusses, 'A la recherche', pp. 33–8; cf. Ellard, 'Alcuin and Some Favored Votive Masses', p. 61.

11. Deshusses, 'Les messes', p. 10.

12. Barré and Deshusses, 'A la recherche', pp. 24, 27–32. The series of three masses assigned to each day is reproduced in the *Liber Sacramentorum* (*PL* 101:445–66).

13. Barré and Deshusses, 'A la recherche', pp. 24–32.

14. '*Missa de Sapientia*

'Deus qui per coaeternam tibi sapientiam hominem cum non esset condidisti, perditumque misericorditer reformasti, praesta quaesumus ut eadem pectora nostra inspirante, te tota mente amemus, et ad te toto corde curramus. Per.

'*Super oblata.* Sanctificetur quaesumus domine deus huius nostrae oblationis munus, tua cooperante sapientia, ut tibi placere possit ad laudem, et nobis proficere ad salutem. Per.

'*Praefatio.* VD [Vere dignum ...] Qui tui nominis agnitionem et tuae potentiae gloriam nobis in coaeterna tibi sapientia reuelare uoluisti, ut tuam confitentes maiestatem, et tuis inherentes mandatis, tecum uitam habeamus aeternam. Per christum.

'*Ad complendum.* Infunde quaesumus domine deus, per haec sancta quae sumpsimus, tuae cordibus nostris lumen sapientiae, ut te ueraciter agnoscamus et fideliter diliamus. Per.

'*Super populum.* Deus qui misisti filium tuum et ostendisti creaturae creatorem, respice propitius super nos famulos tuos, et praepara agiae sophiae dignam in cordibus nostris habitationem. Per' (Deshusses, *Le sacramentaire Grégorian*, II:41; cf. Deshusses, 'Les messes', pp. 16–7).

15. Because the preface does not appear in the Cologne manuscripts, it is not included in the text of the *Liber Sacramentorum* (*PL* 101:451).

16. Because the Latin text uses the transliterated Greek phrase 'agiae sophiae' ('holy wisdom') rather than its Latin equivalent 'sanctae sapientiae', the Greek phrase is retained in this English translation.

17. Deshusses, *Le sacramentaire Grégorien*, Vol. III: *Textes complémentaires divers* (Fribourg 1982), pp. 301–2. One of the Cologne manuscripts appoints James 1.3–6 and Matthew 11.25–30, and hence these readings are included in the *Liber Sacramentorum* (*PL* 101:451).

18. Jungmann, *Pastoral Liturgy* (ET, New York 1962), p. 257.

19. Heiming, 'Die mailändischen sieben Votivmessen für die einzelnen Tage der Woche und der Liber Sacramentorum des sel. Alkuin', in *Miscellanea liturgica in honorem L. Cuniberti Mohlberg*, Vol. II (Rome 1949), pp. 317–39; text of 'Missa de Sapientia', including lections, on pp. 326–7.
20. All citations of scripture are from the New Revised Standard Version.
21. Deshusses, *Le sacramentaire Grégorien*, II:41; emphasis added.
22. *Ibid.*
23. 'Missa de sancta sophia' (*ibid.*).
24. See, for example, James L. Crenshaw, *Old Testament Wisdom: An Introduction* (Atlanta 1981), pp. 176–8.
25. James M. Robinson, 'Jesus as *Sophos* and *Sophia*: Wisdom Tradition and the Gospels', in *Aspects of Wisdom in Judaism and Early Christianity*, ed. Robert L. Wilken (Notre Dame 1975), pp. 1–8; James D. G. Dunn, *Christology in the Making* (Philadelphia 1980), pp. 197–8. For another example of Matthew's use of Q, compare Luke 11.49 ('the Wisdom of God said, "I will send them prophets and apostles ..." ') with Matt. 23.34 ('I send you prophets, sages and scribes ...').
26. Robinson, pp. 8–10. For a different conclusion, that in Matt. 11.25–27 Jesus is presented not as Wisdom but as the righteous person charged with bringing God's wisdom to humanity, see Dunn, pp. 198–200.
27. Dunn, pp. 194–6.
28. Dunn, pp. 165–6, 187–96; see further in Elisabeth Schüssler Fiorenza, 'Wisdom Mythology and the Christological Hymns of the New Testament', in *Aspects of Wisdom*, pp. 17–41.
29. Raymond Brown, *The Gospel According to John (i–xii)*, The Anchor Bible, vol. 29 (Garden City, NY 1966), p. cxxv.
30. *Ibid.*, pp. 5234. Brown, pp. 520–4, notes other concepts that underlie the Prologue, namely, 'the word of the Lord' (*debar yhwh*), 'Jewish speculation on the Law (*Torah*)', and 'the Targumic use of *Memra* ["word" in Aramaic]'.
31. Dunn, pp. 209–12, quotation on p. 212.
32. Ulrich Wilkens, σοφια, in *Theological Dictionary of the New Testament*, ed. Gerhard Friedrich, trans. and ed. Geoffrey W. Bromiley (Grand Rapids, MI 1971), VII:509–14.
33. Irenaeus, *Adversus haereses* 2.30.9, in *The Ante-Nicene Fathers*, ed. Alexander Roberts and James Donaldson (10 vols, Buffalo 1885–1896), I:406 (hereafter cited as *ANF*).
34. *Adv. haer.* 4.20.3, 4, in *ANF* I:488.
35. Origen, *De principiis* 1.2.1, 4, 10, in *ANF*, IV:246, 247, 250.
36. *De prin.* 2.6.2, in *ANF*, IV:281–2.
37. Tertullian, *Adversus Praxean* 7, in *ANF* III:602.
38. Jaroslav Pelikan, *The Emergence of the Catholic Tradition (100–600)* (Chicago and London 1971), pp. 186–93.
39. Augustine, *De Trinitate* 4.20.27, in *A Select Library of the Nicene and Post-Nicene Fathers of the Christian Church*, ed. Philip Schaff (Buffalo 1886–1889), 1st ser., III:83.
40. Barbara Newman, 'The Pilgrimage of Christ-Sophia', *Vox Benedictina* 9 (1992):8–37.
41. Fairy von Lilienfeld, 'Frau Weisheit in byzantinischen und karolingischen Quellen des 9. Jahrhunderts', in *Typus, Symbol, Allegorie bei den östlichen Vätern und ihren Parallelen im Mittelalter*, ed. Margot Schmidt and Carl Friedrich Geyer (Regensburg, 1982), p. 152.
42. Alcuin, *De grammatica* and *De dialectica*, PL 101:849, 853, 966.
43. Alcuin, *De animae ratione liber ad Eulaliam virginem*, cited by von Lilienfeld, p. 152.
44. Newman, pp. 25–6; see further in Wolfgang Edelstein, *Eruditio und sapientia: Weltbild und Erziehung in der Karolingerzeit* (Freiburg 1965).
45. 'ideo Pater, virtus et sapientia, et Filius virtus et sapientia; et Spiritus sanctus virtus et sapientia; non tamen tres virtutes, nec tres sapientiae, sed una virtus, et una sapientia Pater et Filius, et Spiritus sanctus' (Alcuin, *De fide sanctae et individuae Trinitatis* 2.7.11).

46. 'Christe deus, summi virtus sapientia patris', 'Christ divine, strength and wisdom of the Father Almighty' (Alcuin, *The Bishops, Kings, and Saints of York*, trans. and ed. Peter Godman [Oxford 1982], line 1, pp. 2–3).

47. *Ibid.*, lines 1515–20, pp. 120–1.

48. Richard Morris, 'Alcuin, York, and the *Alma Sophia*', in *The Anglo-Saxon Church: Papers on History, Architecture, and Archaeology in Honour of Dr H. M. Taylor*, ed. L. A. S. Butler and R. K. Morris (London 1986), pp. 80–9; see pp. 83–4 for discussion of the church of Sancta Sophia in Benevento.

49. 'Alcuine nomen erat, sophiam mihi semper amanti' (in Barré and Deshusses, 'A la recherche', p. 39, n. 56.)

50. Alcuin, *The Bishops, Kings, and Saints of York*, line 1533, pp. 120–1.

51. See von Lilienfeld, pp. 152–3.

52. Ellard, *Master Alcuin, Liturgist*, p. 171.

53. 'Oratio pro sapientia. Deus patrum meorum et domine misericordiae meae. Qui fecisti omnia verbo tuo. Et sapientia tua constituisti hominem, ut dominaretur creaturae quae a te facta est, ut disponat orbem terrarum in aequitate et iustitia, et in directione cordis iudicium iudicet. Da mihi sedium tuarum adsistricem sapientiam. Et noli me reprobare a pueris tuis quoniam ego servus tuus sum et filius ancillae tuae. Fac cum servo tuo secundum misericordiam tuam et iustificationes tuas doce me. Servus tuus sum eo. Da mihi intellectum, ut sciam testimonia tua' (*Libellus Turonensis* 13, in *Precum libelli quattuor aevi Karolini*, ed. André Wilmart [Rome 1939] pp. 101–2).

54. The citations are practically verbatim from the Vulgate, using for the Psalter the translation of the Septuagint.

55. Barré and Deshusses, 'A la recherche', p. 38; see *Libellus Turonensis* 13, in *Precum libelli*, p. 102.

56. von Lilienfeld, pp. 154–5.

57. 'gratiam sancti spiritus domine deus cordibus nostris clementer infunde' (Deshusses, *Le sacramentaire Grégorien*, II:130). See also the preface in the mass for the grace of the Holy Spirit: 'gratiam sancti spiritus animae meae clementer infundere digneris' (*ibid.*, II:127).

58. 'purifica per infusionem sancti spiritus cogitation e cordis nostri' (*ibid.*, II:125) see also the preface in the mass for the gift of tears: 'per infusionem sancti spiritus' (*ibid.*, II:130).

59. von Lilienfeld, p. 155.

60. *Ibid.*, p. 154.

61. This is the reading in the critical edition of Deshusses (*Le sacramentaire Grégorien* II:41), although some manuscripts, including those from Cologne, add *eundem* ("the same"). Von Lilienfeld used the text in *PL* (101:454) and thus would have known the latter reading.

62. 'liber cor nostrum de malarum temptatione cogitationum, ut sancti spiritus dignum fieri habitaculum mereamur' (Deshusses, *Le sacramentaire Grégorien*, II:126.)

63. 'Haec oblatio domine deus cordis nostri maculas emundet, ut sancti spiritus digna efficiatur habitatio' (*ibid.*, II:125).

64. 'quatenus animam nostram sancti spiritus gratia inluminare digneris' (Deshusses, *Le sacramentaire Grégorien*, p. 127).

65. 'Deus qui inluminas omnem hominem uenientem in hunc mundum, inlumina quaesumus cor nostrum gratiae tuae splendore, ut digne maiestati tuae cogitare et diligere uaeleamus' (*ibid.*).

66. See above, pp. 11–14.

4

The Decline of the Cult of the Old English Saints in Post-Conquest England: A Case of Norman Prejudice or of Liturgical Reform?

 *Anne Dawtry*

The abbey of Thorney possesses the bodies of many saints but I must decline to give their names for they strike us as barbarous. Not that I would deny that they were saints. What authority have I to dispute what holy antiquity has consecrated? But because, as I have said, their names have an uncouth ring and rough flavour I have no wish to expose these saints to the derision of foolish men who are produced in such plenty in our age. Also since not even the community reads their lives it seems silly to preach the merits of men whose miracles cannot be found.[1]

In these words the early twelfth century historian, William of Malmesbury, ridiculed the cult of some of the Anglo-Saxon saints whose popularity had not entirely vanished after the Norman Conquest. And William was not alone in his prejudice. Almost half a century before William wrote these words Warin, the first Norman abbot of Malmesbury, found such a surfeit of relics at the abbey that he is said to have turned many of them out with a jest.[2] Paul, abbot of Saint Albans and nephew of Archbishop Lanfranc, was equally ruthless. He not only slighted the tombs of his predecessors, whom he regarded as a group of simpletons, but also destroyed the tomb of King Offa in the abbey church and caused his bones to be scattered.[3] Meanwhile at Evesham Walter de

Cerisy[4] carefully examined, on the advice of Archbishop Lanfranc, all the relics which he found in his monastery and put to a trial by fire all those which he considered to be dubious.[5]

Not all the purging was carried out so violently, however. At Abingdon, the feasts of St Aethelwold and St Edmund the Martyr were merely discontinued by Abbot Athelelm on the grounds that the English were boors,[6] whilst at St Augustine's, Canterbury, the feasts of eight Anglo-Saxon saints simply disappear from the abbey's calendar after the Conquest.[7]

At Westminster no cult, as such, was destroyed but it is significant that all attempts to establish a new cult devoted to Edward the Confessor failed there before the middle of the twelfth century. Sulcard, the historian of the house in the 1070s, records virtually nothing of Edward's life except that he died very soon after rebuilding the abbey church.[8] The site of Edward's tomb, before the high altar, had almost been forgotten thirty years after his death, and its opening in 1102 may well have been to establish its site rather than to prove any incorruptibility surrounding the body of the saint. Certainly the event was rather low key. Significantly, Archbishop Anselm was not present. The ecclesiastical authorities were instead represented by Gundulf of Rochester.[9] It was not until the 1130s that the cult of Edward began to take off in any meaningful way, because of the enthusiasm of the prior, Osbert of Clare, for the cause. Yet even Osbert found it difficult to relate more than circumstantial evidence concerning the supposed miracles of the king[10] and it was probably only political expediency which finally ensured Edward's canonisation in 1161.

There was then in the first half century after the Norman Conquest a noticeable decline in the popularity of many Anglo-Saxon saints. But why was this so? Was it simply a case of Norman distaste for anything English as unsophisticated and outmoded? Certainly Athelelm's comment about 'English boors'[11] and William of Malmesbury's complaint that the names of many of the Anglo-Saxon saints have a rough and uncouth flavour[12] would seem to support this interpretation. Yet, if this attitude was generally held then we would expect to find a wholesale rejection of the cult of every Anglo-Saxon saint by the Normans. And this is certainly not the case. At Malmesbury, although Abbot Warin turned out many of the relics which he found in his church, he nevertheless retained and even encouraged veneration towards St Aldhelm. Meanwhile, at Canterbury, Archbishop Lanfranc by no mean swept the church as clean as has often been supposed.[13] Although the feasts of Ermenhilda and Edward the Martyr were removed from the calendar,[14] Lanfranc treated with respect the bones of the saints which had to be removed from the old church when rebuilding began in 1070. He first rehoused them decently in the monk's refectory during the rebuilding, and then reburied them before the high altar in the new church. Two of the most important Canterbury saints, Dunstan and Aelfheah were even given new shrines either side of the choir altar.[15]

Moreover the feasts of both saints appear amongst the principal feast days commemorated in the *Monastic Constitutions*.[16] It was not then the case that the Normans wished to reject the cult of the Anglo-Saxon saints simply because they were English. Many of the more important saints, although perhaps initially regarded with suspicion[17], were venerated long after the Conquest and their cults received a renewed boost in the twelfth century when things English became once again fashionable under King Henry I. The Normans were, however, worried by the huge number of saints who had been venerated in England before the Norman Conquest. Many of these had no written life and there was little proof of their sanctity beyond the popular veneration which they enjoyed. William of Malmesbury's comment that it was silly to preach the merits of men whose miracles cannot be found was a very real concern – and not only at Thorney.[18]

The chief reason for the decline of veneration towards the Anglo-Saxon saints in the late eleventh century, however, was probably the doctrinal change which was sweeping Europe at this time in the wake of the papal reform movement. Local cults everywhere paled into insignificance in the face of a new emphasis upon the Incarnation of Christ, itself rooted in a new devotion towards the Eucharist. One of the chief proponents of this new devotion was Lanfranc, who, during the 1050s and 1060s had vigorously defended the doctrine of the physical presence of the body and blood of Christ in the elements at the Eucharist against Berengar of Tours. Berengar, whilst not denying the doctrine of the real presence in the Eucharist, nevertheless tried to draw a distinction between the elements themselves and what they symbolised.[19]

Lanfranc won and a new devotion to the Eucharist began in which miracles concerning the presence of real flesh and blood on the altar abounded.[20] Following his appointment as Archbishop of Canterbury, Lanfranc continued to preach and teach devotion to the Eucharist above all else. In a letter which he wrote to Domnall, Bishop of Munster in 1086, for example, he stressed the necessity for people of all ages to take the opportunity of fortifying themselves with the Eucharist.[21] His desire to mark out the Eucharist as something special was further revealed in a letter to John, Archbishop of Rouen, in which he condemned the archbishop's practice of wearing a chasuble for the whole of the service of consecration for a church. He claimed that the chasuble should, instead, be reserved as a special vestment to be used only during the celebration of the Eucharist.[22]

Lanfranc's eucharistic devotion was also visible in his dealings with Christchurch, Canterbury and with the community of monks there. His whole plan for the new church, which he began to build soon after his arrival in 1070, was focused on this devotion. Whereas in the old Saxon cathedral the whole focus of attention had been the shrines of the old English saints, several of which had crowded in on and dwarfed the high altar,[23] now, in Lanfranc's church, the whole focus was upon an uncluttered high altar with a large space around it and with the archbishop's throne behind it from which he presided at the Eucharist.[24] A secondary focus was the choir altar situated somewhat to the west of, and presumably at a lower level than, the high altar.[25] Above, at the entrance to the choir was a huge crucifix supported on either side by two cherubims. These cherubims, watching over the crucifix and the church itself, were a reminder of those cherubims who had guarded the Ark of the Covenant. As such they were themselves a powerful reminder of all that the Eucharist stood for. For just as in the Old Testament the peoples' sins had been forgiven by the sprinkling of the Ark with blood on the Feast of the Atonement so now, through the Eucharist, God's people found new and perfect reconciliation in Christ.[26]

Lanfranc's eucharistic devotion was also visible in the gifts which he made to Christchurch. He provided for use during the Mass gold embroidered copes and chasubles, stoles and a number of dalmatics and tunicles[27] in order that each minister from president to subdeacon might wear the garment appropriate to his office. This was in direct contrast to the practice of the *Regularis Concordia* in which priest, deacon and subdeacon were all vested in chasubles.[28] Detailed provision was also made for preparing the vessels and elements for the Eucharist. Those monks who made the wafers for Communion were instructed to dress in alb and amice for the task and were also to recite special prayers during the baking process.[29] In addition very special care was to be taken in the washing of the chalices which was to be carried out twice a week. The chalices could only be cleaned by a monk in priests' orders who must first vest himself in an alb and place an amice over his head.[30]

In Lanfranc's spirituality then, and in that which he imposed upon Christ Church, Canterbury, the Eucharist was paramount. It was not that he was hostile to the cult of the Anglo-Saxon saints *per se*; it was just that there was very little room for them beside his all devouring veneration for the Eucharist. The same is true at Winchester where the new church was begun by Walkelin in the 1080s. Whereas the focus of the Saxon church had been on the westwork, where the shrine of Swithun was to be found, so in the Norman church the focus was now the high altar with the translated shrine now almost hidden behind it.[31] At Westminster, too, the importance of eucharistic devotion might well explain why the cult of Edward the Confessor failed to be of any real significance before the middle of the twelfth century. Edward had not designed the church as a shrine to focus on his own tomb. It had been designed, according to contemporary continental custom, with the altar as its focus.[32] Moreover, we know that by the time of the abbacy of Gilbert Crispin, the *Monastic Constitutions of Lanfranc* were being used at Westminster and were indeed still influential when Abbot Ware drew up a new customary for the house in the thirteenth century.[33] Could it not then have been that the very cult of Edward seemed unimportant alongside the re-enactment of the central mysteries of the faith in the celebration of the Eucharist?

Popular devotion, however, was hard to kill. By the early

twelfth century some of the more respectable of the Anglo-Saxon saints had re-established their cults. Moreover as the century progressed the cult of these saints was supplemented by the growth of other new saints' cults. Devotion to Edward the Confessor, for example, really became popular after his canonisation in 1161 and reached its climax in the devotion to the saint of King Henry III. At Canterbury, popular piety found a new focus, after 1170, in devotion to Thomas Becket, whose shrine remained a popular place of pilgrimage for the rest of the Middle Ages. Yet these new cults were never to be as all consuming and dominant as those of the Anglo-Saxon saints had been in the tenth and early eleventh centuries. Edward the Confessor and Thomas Becket now shared the glory and the devotion of the people with Christ himself, present to his people each time the Eucharist was enacted.

NOTES

1. William of Malmesbury, *Gesta Pontificum* ed. N. E. S. A. Hamilton (Rolls Series, 1870), p. 327–8.
2. *ibid.* p. 421.
3. *Gesta Abbatum Monasterii Sancti Albani* ed. H. T. Riley, 3 vols, (Rolls Series, 1867), 1 p. 62. '*Tumbas venerabilium antecessorum suorum abbatum nobilium – quos rudes et idiotas consuevit appellare – delevit.*'; D. Knowles, *The Monastic Order in England* (Cambridge, 1962), p. 119 n. 1.
4. Walter was appointed on the death of Abbot Aethelwig in 1077.
5. *Chronicon Monasterii de Evesham* ed. W. D. Macray (RS, 1863), pp. 323–4, 335–6.
6. *Chronicon Monasterii de Abingdon* ed. J. Stevenson, 2 vols., (RS, 1858), 2 p. 284.
7. These were the Feasts of Werburga, Ermenhilda, Aldhelm, Aelgifu, Swithun, Eadburga, Withburga and Ceolfrith. A. F. Dawtry, 'The Benedictine Revival in the North: The last Bulwark of Anglo-Saxon Monasticism' *SCH* 18 (1982) pp. 87–98, p. 89.
8. Sulcard, writing in the 1080s, used the text of the earlier *Vita Aedwardi Regis* in his description of the abbey church built by Edward, but completely ignores the hagiographical elements in the work; B. Scholz, 'Sulcard of Westminster's *Prologus de Construccione Westmonasterii*', *Traditio* 20 (1964) pp. 59–91.
9. F. Barlow ed, *Vita Aedwardi Regis* (London, 1962) p. 114.
10. Osbert refers to 'numerous miracles which he has left untold so as not to weary the reader' Osbert of Clare, *Letters* ed. E. W. Williamson (Oxford, 1929), p. 84 but this seems rather lame. Of the five supposed miracles earlier related by the writer of the *Vita Aedwardi Regis* only one was performed directly by Edward himself, the rest being enacted by courtiers using water in which Edward had washed his hands; *Vita Aedwardi Regis* p. 72 n. 3.
11. *Chronicon de Abingdon* 2 p. 284.
12. *Gesta Pontificum* p. 327–8.

13. Williamson p. 13 says that Lanfranc purged the calendar at Canterbury with 'the ferocity of a sixteenth century reformer'.

14. Dawtry, 'Benedictine Revival', p. 89.

15. In the thirteenth century *Instructions for Novices* from Canterbury which is nevertheless based upon the *Monastic Constitutions* the novices are instructed on entering the choir to bow first to right and left to the altars of Dunstan and Aelfheah before bowing to the choir altar itself. See D. Knowles, *The Monastic Constitutions of Lanfranc* (London, 1951) p. 137.

16. *Monastic Constitutions* p. 59; Barlow, *The English Church 1066–1154* (London, 1979) p. 191.

17. According to tradition Lanfranc was initially worried by the cult of Aelfheah who had been murdered by the Danes in 1012. He was, however, persuaded to change his mind by Anselm some time between 1079 and 1081. Eadmer, *The Life of St Anselm* ed. R. W. Southern (London, 1962) pp. 50–54; Barlow, *English Church 1066–1154* p. 191.

18. *Gesta Pontificum* pp. 327–8. William was mistaken about one of the Thorney saints, however, namely St Botulf, for whom there was a written life. See F. Barlow, *The English Church 1000–1066* (London, 1979) p. 26.

19. This distinction is quite a modern one and was not understood by Berengar's adversaries who believed that he was denying the real presence of Christ in the Eucharist. For the dispute with Berengar see Gibson, *Lanfranc of Bec* pp. 63–97.

20. Lanfranc himself reported a miracle concerning a priest who had actually found flesh and blood on the altar which had later been preserved as a relic. *Patrologia Latina* vol CXLIX 1449d–50a; Gibson p. 84.

21. H. Clover M. Gibson eds, *Letters of Lanfranc, Archbishop of Canterbury* (Oxford, 1979) no. 49 p. 156.

22. *ibid.* no. 14 p. 85.

23. For the Anglo-Saxon cathedral and its shrines see the article by H. M. Taylor in *Archaeological Journal* 126 (1969) pp. 101–30.

24. C. Brooke, 'Religious sentiment and church design in the later Middle Ages' in *Medieval Church and Society* (London, 1972) p. 173.

25. This altar is referred to in the *Monastic Constitutions* p. 55.

26. Gibson p. 165.

27. Eadmer, *Historia Novorum* ed. G. Bosanquet (London, 1964) pp. 13–14.

28. T. Symons ed, *The Regularis Concordia* p. 33. This represents the practice of the English monasteries before 1066. In the *Monastic Constitutions* on the other hand Lanfranc stipulate that the deacon and subdeacon are to be arrayed in dalmatic and tunicle respectively. (*Monastic Constitutions* p. 55).

29. *Lanfranc Constitutions* p. 83.

30. *ibid.*

31. R. B. and C. Brooke, *Popular Religion in the Middle Ages* (London, 1984) pp. 38–40; F. Barlow, M. Biddle eds., *Winchester Studies* 1 (Oxford, 1976) pp. 306–13.

32. R. D. H. Gem, 'The Romanesque rebuilding of Westminster Abbey' *Anglo-Norman Studies* 3 (1980) pp. 33–60, p. 34.

33. A. W. Klukas, 'The Architectural Importance of the *Decreta Lanfranci*' *Anglo-Norman Studies* 6 (1983) pp. 135–71, p. 143.

5

Vox clara: The Liturgical Voice in Advent and Christmas

 *Martin Dudley*

LITURGY IS a performed text. Sacred space, an assembly and its ministers, ornaments and vestments, together with gestures, tones of voice, and styles of music belong to the essential nature of the liturgy. Without them there is no liturgy, only words written on a page.[1] The text is performed within and interacts with an environment specifically intended for its performance. It involves a repertory of symbols, both in the shape, structure and decoration of the liturgical space and in the movement, posture and gestures of the assembly and its ministers. Liturgical ritual delivers up its secrets only when celebrated in community.[2] Sung or spoken, the performed text takes its place in a context defined by its position within a cycle of liturgical celebrations, by the literary genre employed, and by its relation to other texts and the mode of their performance. The liturgy is capable of indicating and explicating a complex variety of levels of meaning and it is not limited in this by the original placing of the written text in Scripture. An apocalyptic or eschatological text can be given a quite different meaning defined by its liturgical context.[3]

By performance we do not mean, however, something extroverted and self-conscious. Medieval Latin has no exact equivalent of the English verb 'to perform'[4] and the liturgy, even though it can be interpreted using principles drawn from the semiotics of drama, is not a performance in the same way that plays are. They primarily operate horizontally, using dramatic methods to communicate with and to involve and engage an audience. The liturgy operates both horizontally and vertically, addressing both the human assembly and the divine presence. Liturgy involves an inner appropriation of the outward expression. In singing the psalms St Benedict called for behaviour appropriate to the presence of the Divinity and his angels so that 'our mind may be in harmony with our voice.'[5]

The intention of this essay is, first of all, to set down an understanding of the voice in liturgy, and then to explore the resonances of the liturgical voice in Advent and, more briefly, in some aspects of the Christmas season. After a discussion of the meaning of 'voice', it goes on to consider the origin and perceived meaning of Advent. It then examines the text and context of the medieval liturgy of Advent and the many voices to be heard therein. Next it examines the ways in which liturgical reformers have rethought Advent.

Voice and Word

What is meant here by 'voice'? The liturgy is dialogic in its nature. The human voice, praising God and making intercession, is replying to the call of the divine voice.[6] The divine word is addressed to humankind. The voice that enunciates the word is as varied in divine as in human utterance. The voice of the Lord – qol Yahweh, φωνη κυριου, vox Domini – is powerful, full of splendour, shakes the wilderness and resounds over the waters. It crushes the cedar trees, makes the oak trees writhe and splits the flame of fire.[7] But the Lord may also eschew the wind and the earthquake and the fire and be found instead in a still small voice,[8] a faint murmuring sound,[9] in a sound of sheer silence[10] that caused the prophet to wrap his face in his mantle.

The progression of languages has tended to refine the distinction between word, voice, discourse and sound. The Hebrew dabar means a spoken utterance of any kind, but it also means a matter, event, act and thing.[11] There is, in consequence, little clear differentiation between word and event, and the word brings the event into being because it is not separate from it. All words had special power, particularly curses and blessings, but the divine word is of a different order. 'The words of the Lord always had power appropriate to their particular character, and were effective for their particular purpose.'[12] A good example of this is found in Isaiah 55 in a text used in the American Book of Common Prayer 1979 as a canticle at morning prayer:

> For as rain and snow fall from the heavens
> and return not again, but water the earth,
> Bringing forth life and giving growth,
> seed for sowing and bread for eating,
> So is my word that goes forth from my mouth;
> it will not return empty;
> But it will accomplish that which I have purposed,
> and prosper in that for which I sent it.[13]

The Greek φωνη means a sound, a cry, a voice, as well as speech, discourse, and language. The Latin *vox* means not only the voice but also authority and even vote. Though the *vox Dei* is the voice of God, *vox sola* is the mere word and *vocalis* means nominal or so-called. The English *voice* has a similar range of meaning but there is a clear movement away from the performative Hebrew word. Voice is sound but the sound is that of opinion, a report, a statement, and no longer that which brings into being. The universal acclamation of biblical readings as 'the Word of the Lord' has carried this devaluation into the liturgy. Not every reading gives full expression to the divine word and this uncritical announcement fails to distinguish the levels at which the word operates. Yet we can truly say that the Word of God is heard in the liturgy.

The liturgical voice takes many forms and has many tones. For the medieval liturgy celebrated with full participation the voice was always one that sang or chanted. The dialogic nature is most clear when a single voice or a schola enunciates the word and the assembly replies; it is less clear or absent in antiphonal singing. The hymn, sung by the whole assembly, does not have a dialogic character at all.

For an utterance to make sense, sound must be punctuated; the punctuation is provided by silence. The word must issue into silence if there is not to be an incomprehensible babbling. Silence is followed by speech; speech by silence; and in dialogue, discourse and conversation, silence is further followed by response. This pattern exists in the divine discourse more perfectly than in human discourse. It also provides a fundamental structure for the liturgy.

This is a deep underlying structure essential to liturgical performance.[14]

Advent and its relation to Christmas

We turn now to our specific purpose: the investigation of the liturgical voice in Advent and Christmas. A word of caution is necessary. The period of liturgical time which we call Advent is a source of some perplexity for liturgical scholars. The historical evidence concerning its origin and original purpose is conflicting and inconclusive.[15] Before the liturgical reforms of the period 1960–80 the liturgy of the Roman Church was a modified version of medieval liturgy. Pius Parsch contrasted therein the older and newer feasts in the liturgy. The former, he said, were like virgin forests; the latter, like artistically kept flower gardens.[16] Something rather similar can be said of the Advent liturgy but I would want to draw my analogy from architecture and specifically from Romanesque architecture. Hans Erich Kubach says of Romanesque that 'it proves to be a new creation which utilised and transformed whatever stimuli were received from elsewhere' and when we compare it with what went before – in Egypt, Palestine, Syria, Asia Minor, Armenia and Byzantium – or with parallel developments in Armenia and Russia 'we find that there is often a disconcerting similarity but very rarely anything we can define as a truly tangible relationship'.[17] The Advent and Christmas liturgies of the Western Church are built on a site which already had both pagan and Christian buildings standing on it. There are Eastern influences. There are creative interchanges between the Roman and Franco-Germanic worlds. There are influences – such as those of the Roman stational churches – which are slight and yet which contribute something distinctive to the whole. The Advent liturgy taken as a whole is indeed a new creation which utilises and transforms whatever is available for the project. The existing buildings, notably the Epiphany, the Ember Days and some older saints' days, are incorporated into the new structure, modified, extended and enabled to serve a new function.

The traditional liturgical year pivots on two points, Christmas and Easter. The former has a fixed date and therefore a variable day. The latter is always on a Sunday and has a variable date. The early Capitularies begin with the Masses of Christmas Day rather than with Advent. The length of the pre-Christmas period is variable, being as short as one Sunday or as long as six or seven. In Spain, it was, like Lent, of forty days duration and so began on November 16th. In Gaul, the opening day was the feast of St Martin, November 11th, and it was known as *Quadragesima sancti Martini*. Within the Carolingian empire there are also traces of a three month preparation, beginning on the *Conceptio sancti Johannis*, September 24th.[18] In Rome, it seems to have been first six weeks in duration, then five, and finally settled to four.[19] The 'Earlier Gospel Series' and 'Standard Series' of Roman Gospels, dating from early and late in the eighth century, number the weeks *ante natale domini*; the former has five and the latter four.[20] The four-Sunday scheme was normal throughout most of the Latin Church by the 10th century and it passed by way of the Sarum Use into the Book of Common Prayer. Advent therefore has a variable length in terms of number of days, ranging from twenty-one to twenty-eight. It is possible for the Fourth Sunday to be Christmas Eve, as shown in this table:

	Advent 1	Advent 2	Advent 3	Advent 4
Earliest	November 27	December 4	December 11	December 18
Latest	December 3	December 10	December 7	December 24

In non-religious observance in the West today the period of preparation for Christmas has been pushed back to the end of October but Advent has become co-terminous with the twenty-four days of December prior to Christmas to enable secular 'Advent calendars' to begin on December 1st every year.

As its very title – *Adventu Domini* – makes clear, the season celebrates the coming of the Lord. The Dominican Jacobus de Voragine (*c*. 1230–*c*. 1298) tells us that the four weeks of Advent signify the fourfold nature of the Lord's coming.[21] Guerric of Igny (d. 1157) speaks of the first and second comings of Christ but also considers his spiritual coming to his disciples, in the Eucharist and in mystical experiences.[22] St Bernard of Clairvaux's sermons on Advent speak of three comings[23] but another Cistercian preacher,

Helinand of Froidmont (*d.* 1229) also has four.[24] This progression suggests a development of the understanding of Advent during the twelfth century, enabling it to include personal experience of the coming of Jesus to the soul, in life and in death, alongside his Incarnation and coming again in glory.[25] Jacobus gives the four comings: he came to us in the flesh, he comes into our hearts, he comes to us at death, and he will come to judge us and, he continues, the fourth week is seldom completed 'because the glory of the saints, which will be bestowed at the last coming, will never end'. Nevertheless, the two comings, the one in the flesh and the one at the Last Judgement, shape the season and provide its tonality and, as Jacobus says, the season is partly one of rejoicing, by reason of Christ's coming in flesh, and partly one of anxiety at the thought of judgement. The major Advent themes are eschatology, penitence, annunciation, and expectation.

The medieval liturgy was rich in antiphons, versicles, responsories, graduals, sequences, tracts, alleluias and tropes. The liturgical voice could be heard in many and diverse ways. It was not the lections alone that carried, with the collect, as they now do the tonality of the season. The readings set in the Roman and Sarum lectionaries were not identical throughout the Middle Ages. Seven out of eight readings are the same, but they were not used on the same Sundays or in the same combinations. The Sarum readings, following what W. H. Frere calls the 'Standard Series', represent the models promulgated by Charlemagne at the end of the eighth century.[26] The Roman series involves the repetition of the Gospel from *xii lectiones* of Ember Saturday on the Sunday and the consequent movement backwards of the whole sequence of Gospels.[27] Sarum also maintains the series of Epistles found in the *Liber Comitis*, whereas the Roman sequences transposes the third and fourth Sundays.[28]

	Roman 1570	**Sarum**
Advent 1	Romans 13:11–14 Luke 21:25–33	Romans 13:11–14 Matthew 21:1–9
Advent 2	Romans 15:4–13 Matthew 11:2–10	Romans 15:4–14 Luke 21:25–33
Advent 3	Philippians 4:4–7 John 1:19–28	1 Corinthians 4:1–5 Matthew 11:2–10
Advent 4	1 Corinthians 4:1–5 Luke 3:1–6	Philippians 4:4–7 John 1:19–28

The first three masses – *Ad te levavi*, *Populus Sion*, and *Gaudete in Domino* are the same. The Sarum Mass of the fourth Sunday continues the theme from the introit of the third Sunday by using Philippians 4, the introit's source, as its epistle. The same sequence of collects is used throughout, with three beginning *Excita* used on the first, second and fourth Sundays.

The Prayer Book of 1549 and the Book of Common Prayer after it followed the Sarum readings with very slight modification, but the Holy Communion was stripped of the introits, graduals, alleluias and prayers, other than the collect, that had provided the setting for the lections. 1549 had introits but they were whole psalms unrelated to the Sarum texts. There was no provision for a Christmas Vigil. The Advent voice was effectively silenced.

In illa die: the eschatological voice in Advent

The first seasonal words of any Advent liturgy said or sung in the pre-conciliar Roman Church were those of the first antiphon at first Vespers of the first Sunday of Advent, words drawn from Joel (3:18). 'On that day the mountains shall drop down sweetness, and the hills shall flow with milk and honey, alleluia.' The day to which it refers is the eschatological day, the last great day, the day on which the Lord will come. It could as easily have been a verse from Isaiah, the Advent prophet *par excellence*, who spoke constantly of the coming day and of the coming Messiah. The day had three main features: it was the day of judgement, the day of plenty, and the day of fulfilment. Fear has tended to dominate thoughts of Christ's coming and displace the other two aspects. It was not by chance that Austin Farrer began his book on the Church's year, *Said or Sung*, with his own rendering of *the* hymn of judgement: *Dies irae, dies illa*.[29] It represents one aspect of the theme of judgement: the aspect of fear. A little less fearful is the view expressed in the venerable hymn *Condtor alme siderum* which appears in the Advent office in the ninth century at Bern, in the tenth at Munich and at the Abbey of Rheinau; it is also among the Latin hymns of the Anglo-Saxon Church and finds a place in the Sarum Breviary.[30] It holds together the hope of salvation, the expectation of judgement and the need for protection here and now:

> O thou whose coming is with dread
> To judge and doom the quick and dead,
> Preserve us while we dwell below,
> From every insult of the foe.[31]

But the idea of fulfilment is also strong and must not be ignored. It is found in the texts of both the Mass and the Office. The introit of *Gaudete* Sunday does not stand alone, rather the older idea that eschatological fulfilment should bring joy rings out Sunday by Sunday and the late medieval fear of death does not displace it.

Vox clamantis: the penitential voice

The fear of judgement draws sinners to repentance and it is hardly surprising that the eschatological voice should also be a call to penitence. The voice of the herald, John the Baptist, called to repentance and Jesus' own proclamation of the coming of the Kingdom takes up the theme: Repent and believe! Guerric applied John's call to his own community: 'He prepares the way who amends his life; he makes straight the path who directs his footsteps along the narrow way.'[32]

In the Gallican church, Advent had an ascetic and penitential character In the Roman Church it had a purely liturgical nature.[33]

In the liturgical interchange that created the medieval liturgy, the Romano-Frankish Advent became a season of four Sundays with a penitential character, though never as deeply penitential as Lent. Fasting was limited to the Ember Days and there were few other ascetical practices. In general, the joyful chants, the *Gloria in excelsis* and the *Te Deum* were omitted; alleluias remained. Purple vestments were worn in Rome, with rose-coloured vestments, including dalmatic and tunicle, on the third Sunday (when the introit began *Gaudete*). In England it was rather different: white was worn at Westminster Abbey, blue at Wells, and violet at Exeter (under the Roman influence of Bishop Grandison, perhaps, who was Chaplain to John XXII in Avignon).[34] The Sarum *Ordinale* orders the wearing of chasubles, rather than dalmatic and tunicle, by the deacon and subdeacon, but says nothing of the colour.[35] It here means folded chasubles. The chasuble was the common vestment of all ministers and it was folded to facilitate the deacon's functions, freeing his hands and arms, but when the dalmatic became the normal diaconal vestment the folded chasuble was associated with penitential seasons.[36]

O Adonai: the expectant voice

Joyful expectation of the coming of Christ complements and, to an extent, counters the penitential aspect of Advent. Penitence gives way to expectation in the last week. It finds particular expression in the great 'O' antiphons – beginning with '*O Sapientia*' – sung at Vespers from December 17 to 23 since at least the ninth century. Fixed to particular dates the antiphons could begin as early as the third Sunday of Advent itself or as late as the Saturday after that Sunday. The antiphons were sung with special solemnity. Each of them is a fervent appeal for the coming of the Messiah.

Ave gratia plena: the angelic voice

The Stational Mass on the first Sunday of Advent was at St Mary Major, where the relics of Christ's crib are venerated. Since the fourth century it has had this particular association with the Nativity and was often called *S. Maria in praesepe* (= in the stable).[37] The stational Mass of Christmas Eve, and the first and third Masses of Christmas Day were celebrated here. The stational church can

itself give a flavour to the liturgy; here it may be sufficient that
Advent begins in this church. The Roman Mass for Advent
Sunday has no specific mention of the Nativity but the Magnificat
antiphon at Vespers – *Ne timeas, Maria* – has:

> Fear not, Mary, for thou hast found grace
> with the Lord: behold, thou shalt conceive,
> and shalt bring forth a son, alleluia.

Vespers on the third Sunday also has a Magnificat antiphon
concerned with Mary – *Beata es, Maria*.

The major statement of this theme comes not in the Sunday liturgy
but in that of the Ember Days, the Wednesday, Friday and
Saturday after the Third Sunday of Advent. These are one of the
Quattor Tempora, the fasts occurring in each of the four seasons,
which originated in the city of Rome and gradually spread from
there across the Latin Church.[38] Their origin is obscure and
traditionally attributed to Pope Callixtus. Parsch describes them
as occasions of thanksgiving for the three great harvests of
wheat, grapes and olives.[39] The Ember Week ended with ordinations on the Saturday. *The Golden Legend* deals with them entirely
in terms of reasons for fasting: e.g. we fast in winter 'to overcome
the coldness of malice and lack of faith'[40] but their more ancient
form of liturgy provided an opportunity for some significant
preaching, notably by Leo the Great[41] and by Bernard of
Clairvaux. The December days have a pronounced Advent character, though Wednesday and Friday are concerned with Mary and
Saturday with the fullest possible expression of the Advent themes.
This is not their original character and represents the combining of
the existing Ember Day observance with the introduction of
Advent.[42]

The station on the Wednesday is again at St Mary Major. The
introit is *Rorate, caeli*: Drop down dew, ye heavens, from above ...
let the earth be opened and bud forth a Saviour.[43] The Mass retains
the deacon's call *Flectamus genua*, has two proper collects and has
both an Old Testament lesson, from Isaiah 2, and a passage from
Isaiah 7, with the prophecy '*Ecce Virgo concipiet*', in place of the
Epistle. The Gospel is of the Annunciation. The *Ecce Virgo* is

repeated at Communion. The Mass – known as the *Missa Aurea* – was apparently 'particularly esteemed by the faithful as a means of honouring our Lady in this mystery [the Annunciation] which is a preparation for the birth of our Saviour'.[44] It was a Mass that caught the popular imagination. Though generally treated as a solemn votive Mass, using the collect of the Annunciation, and celebrated in white vestments the official ruling was that it was a popular devotion.[45] It clearly caused liturgical legislators some trouble and they grudgingly allowed that by custom and because of the devotion of the people it could be sung daily during the Novena before Christmas and the custom of singing it every day of Advent could be tolerated where it already existed. The geographical focus of this devotion was the *Alpenland* and Bavaria.[46] It was also known there as *Engelamt*, the angels' office.[47] Clearly, in places where the *Missa Aurea* was celebrated daily for the longer or shorter period it changed the whole tone of Advent and oriented it much more directly towards Christmas. On the Ember Friday there is no separate Old Testament reading but Isaiah 11:1–5 is substituted for the Epistle. The Gospel is of the Visitation.

Veni, Domine: the imploring voice

The Ember Saturday liturgy is more complex. It was marked by very great solemnity. It was a night celebration and, as Aemiliana Löhr observed, it retained 'the air of an age which was glad to watch a whole night through in God's praise'.[48] The Mass was a rich one: Löhr wrote of the depth and power presented in the rhythm of texts. All the texts, building on those already used on Ember Wednesday and Friday, speak of the coming of God, ritually expressing 'the primæval advent, the new birth, and the coming of Christ at the last day, advent in all the fullness of its developing meaning'.[49] Certainly the key advent words and themes appear: *adventus* in the Epistle, *veni* as the first word of the introit and in the third gradual and the tract, the coming of the bridegroom from his chamber and of the King to Sion. There is but one hint of the nativity – the mention in a collect of 'the approaching solemnity of your Son' – but the whole liturgy, permeated with Advent expectation, implores God to come and show his face.

This is its structure up to the Gospel:

> Introit: *Veni, et ostende nobis faciem tuam, Domine*
> *Flectamus genua* before the first Collect
> First Lesson: Isaiah 19:20–22
> Gradual
> *Flectamus genua* before the second Collect
> Second Lesson: Isaiah 35:1–7
> Gradual
> *Flectamus genua* before the third Collect
> Third Lesson: Isaiah 40:9–11
> Gradual
> *Flectamus genua* before the fourth Collect
> Fourth Lesson: Isaiah 45:1–8
> *Flectamus genua* before the fifth Collect
> Fifth Lesson: Daniel 3:47–51
> Hymn: *Benedictus es, Domine* (Daniel 3:52–56)
> Collect
> Epistle: 2 Thessalonians 2:1–8
> Tract
> Gospel: Luke 3:1–6

The liturgy went on until Sunday morning and there was originally no separate provision for the Fourth Sunday of Advent. The Mass set was put together from pieces of other Masses, shared a Gospel with the Saturday, and is a relatively late creation; it was given up entirely if the Sunday was Christmas Eve. The Ember Saturday Vigil said all there was to say about Advent. In Löhr's view, Advent could end there; the fourth Sunday adds nothing to it and merely binds together what has gone before.[50] Pius Parsch is of the same view:

> No new avenues remain to be explored in our preparation for Christmas during this fourth week of Advent, for the Church has unfolded her entire Advent message. She has led us to the threshold of Christmas with the joyous cry, 'Rejoice, for the Lord is near!', and more especially by the Ember Day observance. The liturgy has defined the picture of Christ the Saviour as clearly as it can for the time.[51]

Magnum Mysterium: Incarnation

> While all things were in quiet silence[52]
> and the night was in the midst of her course,
> your almighty Word, O Lord,
> came down from your royal throne.

This is the Magnificat antiphon of first Vespers of the Sunday within the Octave of Christmas[53] 'Word' is here *sermo* not *verbum: omnipotens Sermo tuus, Domine.* This may seem a curious choice given that John 1's *In principio erat Verbum* is a central Christmas text. In general use in medieval thought, in Aquinas, for example, *verbum* means the second person of the Trinity and the *verbum essentiale, notiale* or *personale* signifies the essence of God. *Sermo* is rather different; it means not merely a word but a discourse, a conversation, and it is the word used in the text, in the book of Wisdom, from which this antiphon is drawn. The incarnation initiates a new and definitive phase in the discourse between the creation and the Creator. The echoing voices of Advent, culminating in the call for Christ to come here find their reply.

The structure we have already set out – speech, silence and response – is an essential part of Christmas. 'Silence' is a word applied to the night of the Nativity in many texts. It is the *Stille Nacht* and the *heilige Nacht* long before Joseph Mohr used these words or Bishop Phillips Brooks told how silently the wondrous gift is given and Edmond Sears spoke of the world lying in solemn stillness.[54] The Cistercian preacher Guerric, Abbot of Igny, makes much of this in his fifth sermon for Christmas. He contrasts hearing the Word with seeing the Word, pointing out that God, knowing that human minds are incapable of perceiving invisible things, unwilling to be taught about the things of heaven, and slow to yield to faith without visible testimony, made his Word both visible and tangible.[55]

> Truly it is a trustworthy word and deserving of every welcome, your almighty Word, Lord, which in such deep silence made its way down from the Father's royal throne into the mangers of animals and meanwhile speaks to us better by its silence. Let him who has ears to hear, hear what this loving and mysterious silence of the eternal Word speaks to us.[56]

The human response is 'with joyous voice' to loudly sing 'the glory of their new-born King'.[57]

Rethinking Advent

Liturgical renewal and reform has had its effect on Advent. The building site has been effectively cleared of earlier structures and general principles belonging to the whole year have been applied to this season as well. It is a less interesting place to explore! The 1969 General Norms on the Liturgical Year and Roman Calendar issued by the Sacred Congregation of Rites affirmed the twofold character of Advent – preparation for Christmas and the turning of our minds to Christ's second coming – retained the duration and pointed to the special orientation to Christ's birth of the weekdays, December 17 to 24.[58] The season is described as a period of devout and joyful expectation.[59] A moderation reflecting this character is looked for in music and in floral decoration.[60] The only other really significant change to the season itself was the removal of the Advent Ember Days and the remodelling of the calendar, including the removal of the Apostle St Thomas, so that in the General Roman Calendar there is no feast other than the Immaculate Conception above the rank of memorial during December.[61]

There has been a general reluctance to extend Advent as such, not least because to do so would take it even further away from the length of the secular Advent (which, starting on December 1st, can vary between four days shorter or two days longer than the liturgical Advent). The Church of South India, in *The Book of Common Worship* (1962), demonstrated that it was possible to have a pre-Easter season of nine Sundays which changed gear on the sixth Sunday before Easter, the first in Lent. In 1967 the British Joint Liturgical Group (JLG) extended this approach to Christmas by having nine Sundays before Christmas, with the fourth Sunday before designated as Advent 1.[62] In November 1968 the Church of England Liturgical Commission submitted a report to the Archbishops of Canterbury and York that followed the JLG approach to the calendar. It proposed a longer Advent, of nine Sundays before Christmas, 'in order to make room for a fuller treatment of the preparation for Christ's coming'.[63] In 1970, the Standing Liturgical Commission of the American Episcopal

Church rejected this restructuring and followed instead the calendar and lectionary revision undertaken by the Roman Catholic Church after Vatican II. The JLG proposals were rejected as pedagogical rather than kerygmatic, but the psychological value of the British scheme was also questioned and the value of a short, intensive period of preparation was affirmed against a longer more diffuse one.[64] The real failure of *The Alternative Service Book 1980* was not the nine Sunday pre-Christmas period but the way in which the pre-Advent themes were totally unrelated to the tradition. They were drawn from themes appropriate to Easter not Christmas, i.e. the creation, the fall, the election of God's people, the promise of redemption and the remnant of Israel.[65]

In fact the Roman scheme also involved an extension of the pre-Christmas period but it approached it from a different direction. The old system had Sundays after Trinity (Pentecost). The number was variable and spare sets of lections from after the Epiphany were used to fill spaces if necessary. The post-Trinity/Pentecost period always ended, however, with the same set of Sunday propers.[66] In both the Roman and Anglican traditions this 'Sunday next before Advent' had an eschatological flavour and used an *Excita* collect, a remnant of the longer Roman Advent. There were, therefore, five pre-Christmas Sundays with set liturgies. As we will see, the liturgical year as expressed in the Office often differs from the way it is expressed in the Mass. There was an eschatological theme in the breviary readings from the beginning of November as Ezechiel, Daniel, the minor prophets, and Isaiah were read. A strong anticipation of the Second Coming was introduced into the liturgy. Jungmann goes so far as to call it a 'Pre-Advent'.[67] He also finds Advent themes in the introit and epistle of the 18th Sunday after Pentecost and in the processional chants of the 23rd Sunday onwards when the Epiphany Sundays were used, though with an Advent introit.

The revised scheme has eschatological texts assigned to the last two weeks of the year,[68] followed by the feast of Christ the King (moved from the place given it by Pius XI on the last Sunday of October) on the Sunday before Advent begins. The number of Sundays needed after Pentecost, called Sundays in Ordinary Time, is worked out by counting backwards from the end of the series.

The American propers, and those derived from them, use a similar approach. The Sundays are designated by date; thus, American Proper 29 always fall on the Sunday closest to November 23. There are three Sundays before Advent begins that have an esachatological theme, giving a pre-Christmas period of seven Sundays. The English supplementary text *The Promise of His Glory* takes up the logic of this development and designates these three additional Sundays as the first, second and third Sundays of the Kingdom.

These patterns of reading and the calendars underlying them are concerned mainly with the Eucharist. The conformity of the Daily Office to the Church Year was a gradual development and was never completely carried through.[69] The primary focus was the recitation of the psalter and this was only partially complemented by seasonal antiphons, responsories and collects. A difference between eucharistic lections and the office remains in the revised liturgies. The Roman Divine Office, for example, has a set of propers for the period 18–24 December which has no special provision for the Sunday; the set issued without regard for the varying day on which Advent 4 might fall. *Celebrating Common Prayer*, a version of the daily office of the Anglican Society of St Francis, makes provision for the eight days before Christmas but readings set for Advent 4 supersede those of a given weekday.[70] It also extends the so-called Kingdom period prior to Advent to four Sundays, beginning on the first Sunday of November.[71]

The eschatological voice is, therefore, heard more obviously in the Sundays before Advent than in the season itself. In the Roman lectionary the 32nd Sunday in Ordinary Time has Paul's teaching about the general resurrection and the parable of the bridesmaids (Year A – the most obviously eschatological set), a reading about judgement from the Letter to the Hebrews and the story of the widow's mite (Year B) and an admonition from Paul on maintaining the faith and Jesus' answer to a question about marriage and resurrection (Year C). The Old Testament lections are barely eschatological. The 33rd Sunday has Paul's teaching on times and seasons and the parable of the talents (Year A), Daniel on the time of great distress, Hebrews on the single sacrifice of Christ, and part of the 'Little Apocalypse' of Mark 13 (Year B), and Malachi's prophecy of the coming day and the Lucan prophecy of wars and rumours of wars, framing a little piece of Paul on idleness and eating other people's food (Year C). There is near agreement on the NT and Gospel readings in the pre-Advent Sundays but wide variation on the OT reading. The lectionary in *The Promise of His Glory* is out of sequence with the other lectionaries. Its Year 1 (everyone else's Year C) began on Advent Sunday 1989, when the others began Year A. The Canadian OT reading for Year C was that given in Common Lectionary.

In the Roman Catholic Church, the last Sunday before Advent was designated as Christ the King and the Common Lectionary took up this designation. Pius XI instituted this feast, on the last Sunday of October, by his encyclical *Quas primas* of December 11, 1925. In doing so he desired to make solemn proclamation of the social dominion of Christ over the world and to show that organising social life as if God did not exist leads to apostasy and the ruin of society.[72] The introit – *Dignus est Agnus* – begins with the Lamb upon the throne, and the whole Mass set out a kingship both of this world and of the world to come. The collect spoke of all the families of the nations, torn apart by the wound of sin, being made subject to Christ's gentle rule. In the current Roman Missal this strong link to the state of the world is broken.

So, the pre-Advent season – also called the Sundays of the Kingdom – has a strong eschatological flavour. This is continued on the First Sunday of Advent. The following Sunday provide Gospel readings on the themes of John the Baptist (two Sundays) and the events that prepared immediately for the Lord's birth (i.e. Year C – the Visitation) The Old Testament readings are prophecies about the Messiah and the messianic age, especially from Isaiah, and the apostolic readings (Epistle) are exhortations and proclamations.

The pre-Vatican II provisions did not include daily Mass lections and the ferial Mass in Advent was that of the preceding Sunday, except on the Ember days. There is now a weekday lectionary which, as also for the Christmas and Easter seasons, provides a single annual sequence though with two series of readings – one runs from Advent Sunday until 16 December, the other runs from 17–24 December. The Office of Readings provides a reading from Isaiah and another non-biblical reading for each day. It has no provision for Advent 4 as it has specific readings set for each day from December 17.

Ember Days are now gone from Advent. Their significance – apart from the *Missa Aurea* – was anyway much reduced. However, there is still a solemnity in Advent, that of the Immaculate Conception, which will fall between Advent 2 and Advent 3. If it falls on a Sunday, it is observed on the Saturday and it has the Annunciation (Luke 1:26–38) as its Gospel. This involves a change over the pre-conciliar provision in which it displaced the Sunday propers and had a shortened Annunciation (1:26–28) because the focus was on Mary *gratia plena* rather than on the child she was to bear.

There is now a very full, comprehensive and tidy pattern of lections. Those set in the *Revised Common Lectionary* agree for the most part with those of the Roman lectionary and common Advent themes are explored: a general eschatological theme on the first Sunday, John the Baptist on the second and third Sundays, and Joseph (Year 1) or Mary (Annunciation, Year 2 & Visitation, Year 3) on the fourth Sunday. The weekday cycle, especially in the period December 17–24, is a real enrichment.

In Conclusion

I am not entirely clear why the Advent voice or perhaps the voices of Advent resounded so effectively through the older, less systematic structure, and sound so unclear now.[73] It is possible that the strident voice of the commercially-driven Christmas is drowning the other voices. But I think that it is also possible that Advent now looks just too much like every other season, as far as the round of Sunday liturgy is concerned, and lacks its own identity, leaving a space which is filled by the encroaching Christmas. The compilers of *The Promise of His Glory* saw these difficulties.[74] They noted how many Advent Services had the feel of a first Christmas Carol Service and how many relied too much on the darkness/light theme. They provided an abundance of additional material for Advent which can hardly be too highly praised. These included Vigils, with the Service of Light and patterns of readings that explore Advent themes, a penitential rite based on the four Last

Things and another based on the 'O' antiphons, and sentences and prayers for use at Sunday worship. Yet what is really needed is a different tonality, a blending of voices that changes the whole feel of the main Sunday worship, eucharistic or not, during Advent. And that must return us to the way in which the voice sounds within the liturgical context. Old Advent, if I may call it that, had its idiosyncrasies – folded chasubles, rose-coloured vestments, solemn antiphons, and remnants of ancient worship. It lacked the clean lines that liturgical renewal has given it. Yet the liturgical voice sounded clearly in its many tones, repenting, announcing, imploring. It had a passion strangely absent today. I do not think that I am indulging in nostalgia for something which never existed anyway, though there is always a risk. I think that the compilers of *The Promise of His Glory* also saw what I see but are also uncertain how to achieve this tonality.[75] It must, however, be our aim, utilising all the resources of the liturgy.

NOTES

1. Martin Dudley, 'The Ambience of Liturgy', in Michael Perham, ed., *Towards Liturgy 2000: Preparing for the revision of the Alternative Service Book* (London 1989) pp. 59–65.
2. François Kabasele Lumbala, 'Africans celebrate Jesus Christ', in Rosino Gibellini, ed., *Paths of African Theology* (London 1994) p. 78.
3. See Kevin W. Irwin, *Context and Text: Method in Liturgical Theology* (Collegeville 1994) esp. Chapter 3.
4. This point is made by Christopher Page in his notes to the Gothic Voices recording *A feather on the breath of God*, a collection of sequences and hymns of Hildegard of Bingen, Hyperion Record (London 1982).
5. Rule of St Benedict 19.
6. See the discussion of psalmody in Adalbert de Vogüé, *The Rule of St Benedict: A Doctrinal and Spiritual Commentary* (Kalamazoo 1983) pp. 142–145.
7. Psalm 29.
8. 1 Kings 19:12 AV/KJV.
9. 1 Kings 19:12 REB.
10. 1 Kings 19:12 NRSV.
11. Alan Richardson, ed., *A Theological Word Book of the Bible* (London 1950), p. 283.
12. *A Theological Word Book of the Bible*, p. 284.
13. Isaiah 55:10–11; translation by Charles Mortimer Guilbert from the American Book of Common Prayer.
14. See Kevin W. Irwin, *Context and Text: Method in Liturgical Theology*, chapter 3.
15. *The Promise of His Glory* (London 1991) p. 415. See Thomas J. Talley, *The Origins of the Liturgical Year*, 2nd emended ed. (Collegeville 1986), pp. 147–155.
16. Pius Parsch, *The Church's Year of Grace* (Collegeville 1959) vol. 4, 18. See also Martin

R. Dudley, 'Liturgy and Doctrine: Corpus Christi', *Worship*, vol 66, no 5 (September 1992), pp. 417–426.

17. Hans Erich Kubach, *Romanesque Architecture*, rev. ed. (London 1988), p. 8.
18. J. A. Jungmann, *Public Worship* (London 1957) p. 209.
19. See P. Bruylants, *Les Oraison du Missel Romain* (Louvain 1952) p. 1.
20. W. H. Frere, *Studies in Early Roman Liturgy: II The Roman Gospel Lectionary*, Alcuin Club Collection 30 (London 1934) pp. 24–25 and 56.
21. *The Golden Legend*, trans. by W. G. Ryan (Princeton 1993) vol 1., p. 4.
22. *Liturgical Sermons* I, Cistercian Father Series (Shannon 1971), p. 10.
23. See *Sermons Pour L'Année*, Taizé 1990.
24. PL 212:481ff.
25. I have not, however, had an opportunity to do detailed research on extant Advent sermons from a large variety of medieval sources.
26. W. H. Frere, *Studies in Early Roman Liturgy: II The Roman Gospel Lectionary*, Alcuin Club Collection 30 (London 1934) p. 56.
27. The liturgy of the Ember Saturday is set out below.
28. W. H. Frere, *Studies in Early Roman Liturgy: III The Roman Epistle-Lectionary*, Alcuin Club Collection 32 (London 1935), pp. 25–27.
29. London 1960; it is there headed 'The Great Assize'. It is recommended in *The Promise of His Glory* (London 1991) as an office hymn for the week or weeks before Advent and three versions of it are given.
30. The versions in the Roman and Sarum breviaries are different. This was the result of a misguided attempt to reform the Roman hymns under Urban VIII. The revised (and deformed) version has the opening line *Creator alme siderum*. The two versions are set out in parallel by Pierre Batiffol, *History of the Roman Breviary* (London 1912), p. 222.
31. Translation by J. M. Neale in *The English Hymnal*.
32. Guerric of Igny, Fourth Sermon for Advent, *Liturgical Sermons I*, p. 24.
33. Ludwig Eisenhofer and Joseph Lechner, *The Liturgy of the Roman Rite*, edited by H. E. Winstone (Freiburg & London 1961) p. 221.
34. William St John Hope and E. G. Cuthbert Atchley, *English Liturgical Colours* (London 1918) pp. 37–39.
35. W. H. Frere, *The Use of Sarum* (Cambridge 1901) 2:149.
36. See Adrian Fortescue, *The Ceremonies of the Roman Rite Described*, 8th ed. rev. by J. O'Connell (London 1948) p. 245–6.
37. G. G. Willis, *Further Essays in the Early Roman Liturgy* (Alcuin Club Collection 50) (London 1968) p. 56.
38. See G. G. Willis, 'Ember Days' in *Essays in Early Roman Liturgy* (Alcuin Club Collections 46) (London 1964) p. 51–97.
39. *The Church's Year of Grace*, vol 1., p. 104.
40. *The Golden Legend*, vol 1, p. 139–140.
41. Leo The Great, Sermons XII–XIX, On the Fast of the Tenth Month.
42. See notes on OR XXXVII in C. Vogel, *Medieval Liturgy: An Introduction to the Sources*, rev. and trans. by William G. Story and Niels Rasmussen, Washington D.C. 1986, 178 and 216 n. 161.
43. The current Roman Missal continues to provide a Votive Mass of the Blessed Virgin Mary in Advent with the introit *Rorate, caeli*.
44. Note in *The St Andrew Daily Missal* (Bruges 1962) p. 26.
45. Joseph Wuest, Thomas Mullaney and William Barry, *Matters Liturgical*, 10th ed. (New York, 1959), note 272.
46. See the entry '*Rorate*' in G. Podhradsky, *Lexikon der Liturgie* (Innsbruck 1962), p. 328.
47. LThK 3:875.

48. Aemiliana Löhr, *The Mass Through The Year* (London, 1958) vol. 1, p. 30. Sr Aemiliana, a nun of Herstelle, was a disciple of Dom Odo Casel.
49. *The Mass Through The Year*, vol 1, p. 31.
50. *The Mass Through The Year*, vol 1, p. 37.
51. *The Church's Year of Grace*, vol 1., p. 130.
52. The Latin *quietum silentium* is here rendered tautologically; NRSV has 'gentle silence' and REB 'peace and silence'.
53. Now the Magnificat antiphon for Evening Prayer on St Stephen's Day.
54. See the Christmas hymns 'Silent night, holy night', German words by Joseph Mohr (1792–1848), trans. by John Freeman Young (1820–1885), 'O little town of Bethlehem' by Phillips Brooks (1835–93), and 'It came upon the midnight clear' by Edmund H. Sears (1810–76).
55. Guerric of Igny, *Liturgical Sermons* I, pp. 61–62.
56. *op. cit.* 63.
57. Christmas Office Hymn at Vespers *Christe Redemptor omnium*. The quotation is from the English version, 'Jesus, the Ransomer of man', found in *The Monastic Diurnal* (Collegeville 1963, p. 76*, and *The Roman Breviary: An Approved English Translation* (New York 1964), p. 48. In the current Divine Office the hymn, set for Evening Prayer II on Christmas Day, begins 'Christ, whose blood for all men streamed' and the equivalent verse reads:

> Let not earth alone rejoice,
> Seas and skies unite their voice
> In a new song, to the morn
> When the Lord of life was born.

58. Latin text in *Missale Romanum*, editio typica altera, Vatican City 1975, 105; English text in *Roman Calendar*, United States Catholic Conference: Washington D.C. 1970, pp. 12–13.
59. *Ceremonial of Bishops* (Collegeville, 1989), s. 235.
60. *Ceremonial of Bishops* s. 236. It also allows for the wearing of rose coloured vestments on Gaudete Sunday.
61. See *Missale Romanum*, editio typica altera, '*De Rogationibus et Quattor anni Temporibus*', 106. The Weekdays of Advent, December 17–24, rank above all types of memorials.
62. R. C. D. Jasper, ed., *The Calendar and Lectionary; A reconsideration* (Oxford, 1967).
63. *The Calendar and Lessons for the Church's Year* (London, 1969) p. 6.
64. *The Church Year.* (Prayer Book Studies 19) (New York, 1970) p. 8–11.
65. The themes are listed on p. 1092 in ASB.
66. Numbered 24 after Pentecost in the Roman Missal and 25 after Trinity in the BCP.
67. J. A. Jungmann, 'Advent und Voradvent', *Zetschr. kathol. Theol.* 61 (1937) and *Public Worship* (London, 1957), pp. 209–210.
68. General Introduction to the Lectionary, section 104.
69. *The Church Year.* (Prayer Book Studies 19) (New York, 1970) p. 11.
70. Its lectionary is related to the proposed lectionary of *The Promise of His Glory*, but is not identical with it.
71. As do the current proposals (January 1995) from the Church of England Liturgical Commission to the House of Bishops.
72. *St Andrew Daily Missal*, 1533.
73. For my view of the way another feast has been handled in liturgical reform see '*Natalis Innocentum*: The Holy Innocents in Liturgy and Drama', in Diana Wood, ed., *The Church and Childhood* (Studies in Church History, Volume 31) (Oxford, 1994), pp. 233–242.
74. *The Promise of His Glory;* Advent material on pages 13–14, 22–25, 91–144.

75. The French Benedictines who compiled the commentary on the liturgical year *The Days of the Lord*, English trans., (Collegeville, 1991) also perceived the difficulty in enabling the majority of people to enjoy the 'abundance and multiplicity of spiritual foods' to be found in the liturgical texts for Advent. See vol 1, p. 88.

6

Brief and Perspicuous Text; Plain and Pertinent Doctrine: Behind 'Of the Preaching of the Word' in the Westminster Directory

 *Bryan D. Spinks*

By AN Ordinance read in the House of Commons on 13th May 1643, and agreed to by the Lords on 12th June 1643 an assembly of 121 divines with 10 peers and 20 members of the Commons were required to meet and assemble themselves at Westminster, in the Chapel of King Henry VII, on 1st July 1643, for the purpose of

> '... settling of the government and liturgy of the Church of England, and for vindicating and clearing of the doctrine of the said church from false aspersions and interpretations as should be found most agreeable to the Word of God, and most apt to procure and preserve the peace of the church at home, and nearer agreement with the Church of Scotland and other Reformed churches abroad'.[1]

Ignoring the King's prohibition, sixty nine of the nominated divines duly met on 1st July to hear a sermon by William Twisse who had been named as Prolocutor of this assembly. It adjourned until 6th July when it once more assembled in the Abbey and began its work. It was later to transfer meetings to the Jerusalem Chamber. Thus commenced the work of the Westminster Assembly.

Amongst the original remit of this impressive body — it contained many of the Church of England's most learned theologians – was the requirement to confer on matters of liturgy, discipline and government of the Church of England, though its initial work was in fact a revision of the Thirty Nine Articles of Religion. However, when Parliament accepted the Solemn League and Covenant in September 1643, a new remit was to bring the Church of England into conformity with the Church of Scotland and other Reformed Churches in matters of confession of faith, form of Church government, directory for worship and catechizing, and it was thus that the Assembly produced the Westminster Confession of Faith, the Larger and Shorter Catechism, and *A Directory for the Public Worship of God (Directory)*.

The *Directory*, which was the legal replacement for the Book of Common Prayer from 1645 until 1661, was the work of a subcommittee consisting of four Scottish Commissioners, four English divines of Presbyterian sympathies, and two English Independents.[2] As its title suggests, it was but a guide or directory for what the minister might say in public prayer, and in what order. In comparison with the Book of Common Prayer it is but a summary guide and extremely brief. However, in one area it represents a considerable expansion. In the Book of Common Prayer preaching is mentioned only by rubrics. Although these rubrics were backed up by the Injunctions, Homilies and Canons, there was no specific guide for sermon style and scope. In contrast, in the *Directory* there is a lengthy section entitled 'Of the Preaching of the Word' – almost as long as the entire prayer outlines for Sunday worship. This section was the work of Stephen Marshall, the chairman of the subcommittee.

The section begins by stressing that a good education in Arts, Science and Divinity is assumed to be a pre-requisite for ministry; this together with the gift of the Spirit will be used in private preparation of the sermon. Ordinarily the subject will be a *Text* of scripture, and the introduction will be 'brief and perspicuous'; then *Context*, but if the text is long, a paraphrase may be needed. Next comes the *Analysis*, with divisions according to order of matter rather than words, and the audience must not be troubled with obscure terms of Art. Then the *Doctrines* raised from the text should be concerned with the truths of God that the hearers can understand and which will be edifying. It must be expressed in plain terms. Parallel places of scripture confirming the doctrine must be plain and pertinent. *Arguments* or *Reasons* are to be solid. *Doubts* are to be removed. The doctrines are not to be left as general doctrine but brought home to special use. The *Use* of Instruction follows, and *Confutation* of false doctrine. *Exhortation*, to Duties is followed by *Dehortation, Reprehension and public admonition*. However, *Comfort* should be applied to the hearers. The Uses should be those 'most needful and seasonable' to draw souls to Christ.

In the latter part of this guide it is noted that the method is only recommended and 'not prescribed as necessary for every man, or upon every Text', but it is strong recommendation with certain prohibitions, which include 'entising words of mans wisdom', 'an unprofitable use of unknown tongues, strange phrases, and cadences of sounds and words' and urging only sparing use of citations of divines or other writers however elegant these might be.

Why the need for this guide to preaching? Although in this section Marshall actually acknowledges that there must be a latitude in method of preaching, running through his advice is a call that the sermon should be a serious undertaking, but equally it should be direct, plain and pertinent. It was promoting a particular style and approach, and was, indirectly, actively discouraging some other styles and approaches, and particularly what had been fashionable in some quarters, namely the 'metaphysical sermon'. The style advocated by Marshall, and known as the 'Puritan Plain Style' was in direct contrast to the type of sermon represented by John Donne and Lancelot Andrewes.

In his study of the metaphysical preachers, Horton Davies rightly points out that this style should not really be called 'Anglican style' (as, for example, it is by Perry Miller and William Haller) since this metaphysical style was used by definite Calvinists such as Ralph Brownrig, Bishop of Exeter and John Prideaux, Bishop of Worcester.[3] Bearing in mind the misnomer, Perry Miller summarized the general difference in approach as follows:

'The Anglican sermon is constructed on a symphonic scheme of progressively widening vision; it moves from point to point by verbal analysis, weaving larger and larger embroideries about words of the text. The Puritan sermon quotes the text and 'opens' it as briefly as possible, expounding circumstances and context, explaining its grammatical meanings, reducing its tropes and schemata to prose, and setting forth its logical implications; the sermon then proclaims in a flat, indicative sentence the 'doctrine' contained in the text or logically deduced from it, and proceeds to the first reason or proof. Reason follows reason, with no other transition than a period and a number; after the last proof is stated there follows the uses or application, also in numbered sequence, and the sermon ends when there is nothing more to be said.'[4]

What, then, were the hallmarks of the 'metaphysical' or 'Anglican' sermon? There are distinct stylistic differences between such preachers as Donne, Andrewes and Brownrig. However, Horton Davies draws attention to the following common characteristics of this approach:[5]

1. *Wit.* There is a fondness for puns and paronomasia in English and ancient languages, in abstruse and often paradoxical expressions of thought, drawn from a variety of sources.

2. *Patristic citations and references.* This enabled the preacher to gain respect for his learning, and also showed that the Church of England was the direct descendant of the undivided Church of the first five centuries. Thus Andrewes in his fifteenth Easter Day sermon quotes in Latin the words to Mary Magdalene, 'Touch me not' and gives different interpretations from Chrysostom, Gregory the Great and Augustine.

3. *The use of classical literature and history.* There are frequent references to pagan poets, philosophers and historians of Greece and Rome, reflecting the Renaissance rediscovery of the classical world.

4. *Illustrations from 'unnatural' natural history.* Examples include the phoenix, the unicorn and the salamander.

5. *Quotations in Greek and Latin, and etymology.* This is a favourite of Andrewes and Barten Holyday, the archdeacon of Oxford, giving the root meaning of words.

6. *Principles of biblical exegesis.* According to Davies, the metaphysical preachers chose a via media, choosing neither to use the four-

fold medieval Catholic approach (literal, allegorical, tropological and anagogical) nor the single literal sense advocated by Calvinism. However, as the study of Erwin Gane makes clear, it is quite difficult to divide Anglican and Puritan sermon styles on this issue, for both rejected the Roman approach, but both used typology and allegory when it suited.[6]

7. *Sermon structure and divisions.* There was a preference amongst the metaphysical preachers for sermons with complex divisions, something seeming almost a recovered scholasticism.

8. *The Senecan style (and Ciceronian).* Davies gives examples from Donne, Richard Hooker and Taylor, showing the use of these styles.

9. *Pardoxes, riddles, and emblems.* Thus Resurrection as the death of death, adaptation of Samson's riddles, and use of natural symbols.

10. *Speculative doctrines and arcane knowledge.* Davies here cites Donne's speculation on how to interpret 'the messenger of satan' in the Pauline letters, and Barten Holyday's speculation about eternal life. Henry King can quote from Rabbi Jehudah, and Hacket provides Muslim lore.

11. *Liturgical-devotional preaching.* The metaphysical preachers tended to relate their doctrine to the liturgical calendar.

Not all these eleven characteristics appeared in every sermon of every metaphysical preacher, neither were all used by every metaphysical preacher, and some features were less important than others. Some, however, can be illustrated by reference to Lancelot Andrewes.

Andrewes (1555–1626) was without doubt one of the leading preachers of the latter years of Elizabeth and throughout the reign of James I. He was an able scholar with a knowledge of several languages and a good grasp of the Fathers. In 1607 he was appointed as one of the ten scholars responsible for producing the Pentateuch and the historical books from Joshua to 1 Chronicles of the King James Bible. For a quarter of a century he regularly preached at the Court of James I. Davies comments:

> 'The content of his sermons exhibited a profound and detailed biblical knowledge, an exact knowledge of biblical and ancillary languages, a great reverence for the Fathers of

the primitive Church, a deep concern for relating texts to the calendar of the liturgical year, and an almost scholastic division of the text into what critics called 'crumblings'. He also showed a fondness for wit especially in the beginnings, endings, and transitions of his sermons, which are redolent of unostentatious learning and of holiness.'[7]

Something of Andrewes' style, which Lossky prefers to describe as 'mystical',[8] is illustrated in the following extract from a Christmas sermon:

> The Word, 'by whom all things were made', to come to be made Itself ... what flesh? The flesh of an infant. What, *Verbum infans*, the Word an Infant? The Word, and not able to speak a word? ... How borne, how entertained? In a stately palace, cradle or ivorie, robes of estate? No: but a stable for His palace; a manger for his cradle; poore clouts for His array. This was His beginning : Is His end any better? That maketh up all: what flesh then? *Cujus livore sanati*, black and blue, bloody and swollen, rent and torn; the thorns and nails sticking in His flesh: And such flesh He was made ... love respects it not, cares not what flesh He be made, so the flesh be made by it.[9]

In another Christmas sermon, on Isaiah 7.14, Andrewes can say:

> This *cum* we shall never conceive to purpose, but *carendo*; the value of 'with' no way so well as by without, by stripping of *cum* from *nobis*. and so let *nobis*, 'us', stand by ourselves without Him, to see what our case is but for this Immanuel; what, if this virgin's Child had not this day been born us: *nobiscum* after will be the better esteemed. For if this Child be 'Immanuel, God with us', then without this Child, this Immanuel, we be without God. 'Without Him in this world', saith the Apostle; and if without Him in this, without Him in the next; and if without Him there – if it be not *Immanu-el*, it will be *Immanu-hell*; and that and no other place will fall, I fear me, to our share. Without Him, this we are. What with Him? Why, if we have Him, and God by Him, we need no more; *Immanu-el* and *Immanu-all*.[10]

And an example on the theme of the resurrection:

> '... there goeth from His resurrection an influence, which shall have an operation like that of the dew of the spring; which when He will let fall, 'the earth shall yield her dead', as at the falling of the dew the herbs now rise and shoot forth again. Which term therefore, of regenerating, was well chosen, as fitting well with His rising and the time of it. The time, I say, of the year, of the week, and if ye will, of the day too. For He rose in the dawning – then is the day regenerate; and in *prima Sabbati* – that, the first begetting of the Week; and in the spring, when all that were winter-starved, withered, and dead, are regenerate again, and rise up anew.[11]

Here, in the space of a few lines, we have word play, paradox, and Latin, and chopped sentences which give a staccato effect, that 'personal habit of letting off words like squibs so that they break into a number of dazzling images',[12]

Writing in 1928, T. S. Eliot claimed that Andrewes' sermons ranked with the finest English prose of their time and any time, though he admitted that they are not easy reading and are only for the reader who can elevate himself to the subject of which they treat.[13] This was precisely the basis of the criticism made by many Puritans at the time; they were too pedantic and only for highly educated people. But they also failed to bring out doctrine and use. Richard Baxter wrote: 'When I read such a book as Bishop Andrew's [sic] Sermons, or heard such a kind of preaching, I felt no life in it: me thought they did but play with holy things'.[14] Edward Reynolds, a member of the Westminster Assembly who later became Bishop of Norwich, listed what he regarded as vices in methods of preaching which included 'sordidness, tediousness, obscurity, flatness of conceit, arguteness' and minutiae, gaudiness, wordiness, and empty ostentation', and advised that 'the truth of God is indeed fuller of majesty when it is naked, than when adorned with dress of any human contribution'.[15] William Perkins, commenting on 1 Corinthians 2.4 advised: 'observe an admirable plainess and an admirable powerfulness'.[16] The Puritan preference, which underlies Marshall's guide in the *Directory*, was for the very opposite of Andrewes's styles.

What was the origin of this 'Puritan Plain Style'? In much of the secondary literature relating to the period 1559–1640 the words 'Anglican' and 'Arminian' on the one hand, and 'Puritan' and 'Calvinist' on the other, have been used so loosely as to obscure the complexities of theological interests and leanings which made up the Church of England in that era. As we have noted, some of the metaphysical preachers were 'Calvinist', and very few Puritans consciously espoused a pure school of John Calvin. Indeed, T. H. L. Parker has noted that some of Calvin's divisions in his sermons are not too dissimiliar from Andrewes's love of division and subdivision[17], and Bishop Henry King cited Calvin in opposing the Puritan dislike of Latin citations and patristic references.[18] The Puritan read far more widely than just Calvin's works, and absorbed ideas from many Continental theologians, especially Bullinger and Musculus. In the writings of the latter we find recommendations that the sermon should concern itself with doctrine, reason and uses[19], which is a rather different approach to Nicholas Heminge's *The Preacher, or Method of Preaching*, 1576 and Bartholomaus Keckermann's *Rhetoricae Ecclesiasticae, sive Artis Formandi et Habendi Conciones Sacras*. whose reliance on Aristotelian rehetoric seems to have influenced Donne if not also Andrewes.[20]

The type of sermon advocated by Musculus was developed by William Perkins in his *The Arte of Prophecying*, 1592. Anglicanism has not been kind to Perkins (1558–1602) who was a Cambridge conformist Puritan, and in his day the most widely published, translated and read English theologian, completely eclipsing Richard Hooker.[21] This particular work of Perkins was extremely influential amongst English Puritan preachers.

Perkins begins by defining his subject: 'Preaching of the Word is Prophecying in the name and room of Christ, whereby men are called to the state of Grace, and conserved in it.'[22] Preparation for the sermon requires considerable study and use of the Arts and learning, but these are but the preparation, and should not themselves be the sermon. The sermon will require definitions, divisions and explications, together with grammatical, rhetorical and logical analysis. Interpretation is the opening words and sentences of scripture, that one entire and natural sense may appear. Perkins notes that the Roman method of exegesis entails the literal, allegorical, tropological and anagogical, but this must be exploded and rejected. There is only one sense, and that is the literal. Scripture passages fall into two categories – either analogical and plain, or cryptic and dark. Dark passages need to be explained with reference to other passages. The application is either mental or practical. His advice is summarised at the end of the treatise as follows:

'To read the Text distinctly out of the Canonicall Scriptures.
To give the sense and understanding of it being read, by the Scripture it selfe.
To collect a fewe and profitable points of doctrine out of the naturall sense.
To apply (if he have the gift) the doctrines rightly collected to the life and manners of men in a simple and plaine speech.'[23]

Where it becomes clear that the type of sermon of Andrewes is disqualified is when Perkins deals with human wisdom.

'Human wisdom must be concealed, whether it be in the matter of the sermon, or in the setting forth of the words: because the preaching of the Word is the testimony of God, and the profession of the knowledge of Christ, and not of humane skill: and again, because the hearers ought not to ascribe their faith to the gifts of men, but to the power of God's Word.'[24]

This was not to be an excuse for rude or rough speech:

If any man think that by this means barbarism should be brought into pulpits; he must understand that the Minister may, yea and must privately use at his liberty the arts, Philosophy, and variety of reading, whilest he is in framing the sermon: but he ought in public to conceal all these from the people, and not to make the least ostentation.[25]

Perkins thus rules out of play many of those devices which make up the metaphysical sermon. In particular the love of Greek and Latin found in Andrewes is criticised:

'Wherefore neither the words of arts, nor Greek and Latin phrases and quirks must be intermingled in the sermon.

1. They disturb the mind of the auditors, that they cannot fit those things which went afore with those that follow. 2. A strange word hindreth the understanding of those things that are spoken. 3. It drawes the minde away from the purpose to some other matter.'[26]

Much of the tenor of Perkins is reflected in Marshall's piece in the Westminster *Directory*.

The difference in style was presented in stark terms by Abraham Wright in 1656 when he published *Five Sermons in Five Several Styles or Waies of Preaching*. Miller compares the reference to joys in heaven in Wright's 'Presbyterian' sermon to a genuine passage from Donne. Wright has:

'Our bodies therefore shall be endued with most unspeakable perfections, and most perfectly clarified from all imperfections, but they shall not be disrobed of their nautral properties: briefly they shal be spirituall in a threefold sense.'

Donne in contrast waxes lyrical:

'A new earth, where all their waters are milk, and all their milk, honey; where all their grass is corn, and all their corn manna; where all their glebe, all their clods of earth are gold, and all their gold of innumerable carats; where all their minutes are ages, and all their ages, eternity; where every thing, is every minute, in the highest exaltation, as good as it can be, and yet super-exalted, and infinitely multiplied by every minute's addition; every minute, infinitely better, than ever it was before.'[27]

We have already noted that since divines such as Brownrig and Prideaux were amongst the 'metaphysical' preachers, the root difference is not 'Anglican' versus 'Puritan', or 'Arminian' versus 'Calvinist', even if these loose terms are not wholly irrelevant. Nor can it have been just a preference of style. The possible influence of Heminge and Keckermann on Donne and Andrewes has already been noted. These works taught a preaching style based on Aristotelian principles. Miller notes that in contrast, Perkins and many of those dubbed 'Puritans' appear to have espoused Ramism with its radical critique of Aristotle.[28] Petrus Ramus (1515–72) and his colleague Omer Talon (1510–62) had mounted a successful challenge to Aristotelian method, and their methodology was particularly influential at Cambridge in the 1570s and 1580s, though opposed by divines such as Richard Hooker. For Aristotelian logic, predicables and syllogisms were paramount. Ramus urged the banishment of predicables and the curtailment of syllogisms in the interests of utility. Instead of predicables Ramus substituted 'arguments' or 'reasons'. He placed a great emphasis on laying things out in a series. An anonymous translation of Ramus's *Dialecticae* in 1574 advised in the preface:

> 'If thou be a deuine this method willethe thee that in place of the definition, thou sett forthe shortly the some of the text, which thou hast taken in hand to interprete: next to porte thy text into a fewe heads that the auditor may the better retaine thy sayings: Thirdly to intreate of euery heade in his owne place with the ten places of inuention, shewing them the causes, the effectes, the adiontes and circumstances: to bring in thy comparisons with the rest of artificiall places: and last to make thy matter playne and manifest with familiar examples & aucthorities out of the worde of God: to sett before the auditors (as euery heade shall geue the occasion) the horrible and sharpe punyshing of disobedience, and the ioyfull promises appartayning to the obedient and godlie.'[29]

Although with regard to *The Act of Prophecying* Howell concluded that Perkins derived his sources from Ciceronian rhetoric and scholastic thought, and only in its methods of presentation is it Ramist, the more recent work of McKim has demonstrated fairly clearly that Perkins was indeed imbued with Ramist logic and method.[30] Miller was correct in identifying Perkin's words 'axiomaticall, or syllogisticall, or methodicall' in this work on preaching as a reference to Ramism. Miller notes:

> 'The Puritan form of the sermon, which was first advanced by Perkins and then expounded in Puritan manuals, was altogether congenial to Ramist ways of thinking, and hence there is good cause to suppose that Perkins arrived at it by pondering the question in the light of Ramus' logic and rhetoric.'[31]

For those who followed Perkins and the 'Puritan Plain style' the sermons of Andrewes were simply a violation of logic, mis-placed rhetoric, an unwarranted display of human wisdom, and aimed only at the educated. The fact that Andrewes's sermons were preached at Court to a high proportion of well educated people, including a King-theologian, made no difference to the overall verdict.

What, then, was the result of the 'Plain style' (regardless of whether we have Ramist versus Aristotelian logic and rhetoric) as advocated by Marshall in the Westminster *Directory*? It is perhaps best illustrated by reference to a sermon of Marshall himself.

Marshall was born at Godmanchester, Huntingdonshire in 1594, and had studied at that noted 'hotbed' of Puritanism, Emmanuel College, Cambridge, graduating B.A. in 1616, and M.A. in 1618, and gained his B.D. in 1629. He became a private tutor, and then lecturer at Wethersfield, Essex, and later Vicar of the adjoining parish of Finchingfield. He gained a reputation as a good preacher, but although a conformist, did not disguise his presbyterian sympathies. He preached before the House of Commons during the Short Parliament, and fully supported the Parliamentary cause. He advocated a reformed episcopacy, and his name supplied the first two letters of *Smectymnus*, the reply to Joseph Hall's *Humble Remonstrance*. During the Civil War he was one of the chaplains to the regiment of Robert Devereux, the third Earl of Essex. He became a strongly convinced Presbyterian, and a vocal member of the Westminster Assembly, and not without influence on members of the Long Parliament. In 1651 he had left Finchingfield to become town preacher at Ipswich. He died of consumption on 19th November 1655 and was buried in the South Aisle of Westminster Abbey. His remains were removed on 14th September 1661 and cast into a pit 'at the back door of the prebendary's lodgings in St Margaret's Churchyard'.[32]

Marshall was one of group of regular preachers before the Long Parliament, both to the Commons and the Lords. Amongst this group he was preeminent, and was regarded in his own circles as an outstanding preacher. His most famous sermon was entitled *Meroz Cursed*, preached before the House of commons on 23rd February 1641/2, and published several times. However the example selected here was preached after the publication of the *Directory*, and having been preached before the Lords in the Abbey, it is something akin to a Puritan counterpart to the Court sermons of Andrewes. Entitled *A Two-edged Sword*, it was repreached on 28th October 1646 and entered in the Stationer's Register on 17th November 1646.[33] The King had surrendered, and Parliament was considering standing down the army.

Marshall begins his sermon with the text – Psalm 8.2, which he suggests is governed by the key to the whole psalm, which is verse 4. He proceeds to an analysis of the text, namely the identity of the 'Babes and Sucklings', and the dignity which they have. Their identity is illustrated by Matt. 21.9, Heb. 2.6–7, 1 Cor. 15.25, Phil. 2.6–7 and Psalm 81. Before this distinguished audience Marshall is quite happy to quote the occasional Latin word. Thus explaining the significance of Psalm 81 he says:

> 'it is a Psalme upon Gittith, the word from whence it is derived, signifies a Winepresse; and they conceive that this Psalme, and the rest which beare this Title, were usually sung *vindemiarum*, or *torcularium tempore*, at the time of treading their Winepresses, which was about the feast of Tabernacles, the feast which typified the Incarnation of Jesus Christ.'

The conclusion is that the Babes and Sucklings are the Lord Jesus Christ and his Seed, or the Church Militant, whereas the enemies are the Church Malignant – satan and his children as identified in Psalm 44.

Marshall turns to examine the words 'strength' with reference to the LXX, 'still or quell', appealing to the Latin roots, and 'mouth'. From this he develops two 'Instructions' or 'Doctrines':

> 'That though it bee very unlikely to flesh and blood, to sense and reason; yet Christ and his seed have sufficient strength wholly to rout and destroy all their enemies.
>
> That all that power and strength which Christ and his followers are endued with, proceeds out of their mouth.'

The first doctrine has two branches: sense and reason suggest that Christ and his seed will not prevail; but secondly they do in fact have sufficient strength to prevail. The first branch is shown to have no substance by reference to Jer. 31.22, Isaiah 41.14–16, Psalm 22.6 and Luke 10.3. A reminder of the Civil War context of this sermon is given in the description of Christ as 'head and Captain-generall of the Party'. Christ prevailed, and his cause prevailed in the past – the disciples who were only fishermen, subdued the world; Athansius prevailed over the 'Arrian world', and Luther too. Human reason underestimates God's hidden power, such as in the case of the spiritual hosts which were with Elisha.

The second branch is that despite reason, scripture shows that God does give them strength, as shown in Gen. 3.15, Matt. 16.18, Isaiah 54.17, 41.14, Micah 4.13, and confirmed by the resurrection, and that hitherto the Christian Church has prevailed against its enemies. The Babes and Sucklings prevail because it is God's design (the eternal decrees), his heart is with them, and his almighty power. The 'Uses' of the first branch is that it is to be expected that only a minority will support the Christian cause – 1 Cor. 1.27, John 7.48. Christ and his saints are like David against Goliath. With his own 'needful and seasonable' times in mind Marshall exhorts:

> 'Indeed when the Church is smiled upon, and countenanced by Kings and Princes, it's no marvaile though wise, rich, and great men doe joyne with it; but when warres and persecutions are raised against it, which hath most-what been the Churches lot hitherto, wonder not though wise men withdraw from it, when they see nothing but ruine attend them who take with this side; and this is the very reason of their withdrawing, and this also abundantly satisfies mee in our present trouble, where'in we have had so many Lords, so many Gentlemen, so many Learned men, so many great and rich men to have deserted the cause that the Parliament was engaged in.'

The uses of the second branch is that everyone who gives up his name to Christ becomes a soldier of Christ, and the Church will succeed. Each soul will, and all the Babes and Sucklings. In this section of the sermon Marshall again is happy to quote in Latin in reference to the Romans never losing a battle.

The second doctrine is that the Babes and Sucklings prevail by

what comes from their mouths. He proceeds to discuss Psalm 6.8,
18, Ep. 4.7–11, Acts 2.3 and Rev. 11.56; 12.11. In the explanation
of the latter we find use of the scholastic distinction between the
meritorious and instrumental causes.

Five things proceed from the mouth of the Babes and Sucklings
— Preaching, confessing the Name, Praising, Praying and
Covenanting – and each of them is expounded with examples.
The 'Reasons' are that God has founded the strength, or appointed
it. An objection might be that if this is so, why do Christians take
up human arms? They do so because they need to defend themselves, they are human as well as saints, and it is the right of
freemen. Thus it was permissible for Parliament to take up arms.

The Use is that many Christian words (weapons) have been
used, and the enemy has been scattered. Secondly, although it is
being debated as to whether or not the army should be disbanded,
the weapons of Christians must be retained. Soldiers to spread the
gospel are needed. The House of Lords needs to assist in this
matter. The power they have is from the Lord and should be used
so as to make it efficient. They must have a mouth which is sanctified, and it must be furnished from the store-house of Christ's
merit and a sanctified heart. And so Marshall ends abruptly:

> 'Consider what I have said, and the Lord give you under-
> standing in all things: And I shall end.'

In this sermon Marshall occasionally shows his scholarship, as in
reference to the LXX, to Latin roots and Latin quotes. The odd
scholastic term, revived and pressed into use by Reformed
Orthodoxy, appears here and there. But there is no word play so
loved by the metaphysicals and no careful analysis of words. We
have very plain logic, which may not be especially Ramist, but
which when set out in chart form (pp. 108–9) conforms almost
perfectly to the instructions Marshall gives in the *Directory*, though
this would be true of many other Puritans, such as Thomas
Watson's *God's Anatomy upon Man's Heart*, 1648.

Perhaps partly inspired by T. S. Eliot's extravagent praise of
Andrewes's sermons (not altogether uncoloured by his Anglo-
Catholicism), there has been in recent decades renewed interest in
both his sermons and other writings.[34] It would be tempting to

conclude that the apparent neglect of authors of the 'Puritan plain style' represents the just desserts of all such inferior and inelegant prose. In fact, at least from the point of view of style, the truth is rather different. As the chart of Marshall's sermon illustrates, this style was in fact a highly elaborate form of discourse – indeed, almost an art form – and perhaps left a greater legacy than the metaphysicals. Sasek pointed out:

> Puritan 'plain style', as it is universally called, was a successful competitor with the richness and complexity of Donne and Browne and a precursor of the relative austerity, but increased lucidity, of Dryden and his contemporaries.[35]

They substituted one art form for another. Yet if the 'plain style' helped end the metaphysical sermon, it would itself lead towards and yield to the later styles of South and then Tillotson which if intolerably tedious and dull now, were regarded as masterpieces in their day. Styles of preaching change, and rather more swiftly than prayer styles and liturgical structures, so that a Word in Season soon reaches its sell-by-date. The type of liturgy advocated by the *Directory*, although not without metamorphosis, lived on in Presbyterian circles well into the last decades of the nineteenth century.[36] In contrast the section 'Of Preaching of the Word of God' was obsolete within little more than a generation.

A
Tvvo-edged Svvord
OUT OF
THE MOVTH
OF
BABES,
TO
Execute vengeance upon the Enemy and Avenger.

Prefented in a Sermon to the Right Honou-
rable the Houfe of Lords affembled in Parliament,
in the Abbey-Church at *Weftminfter*, *Octob.* 28. 1646.
the folemn day of their Monthly *FAST*.

By STEPHEN MARSHALL *B. D. Minifter of
Gods Word at* Finchingfield *in* Effex.

Efa. 41. 14, 15. *Feare not thou Worme Jacob, thou fhalt threfh the Moun
taines, and beat them to duft.*
Jer 31. 22. *The Lord hath created a new thing in the earth, a Woman fhall
compaffe a Man.*
Revel. 11. 5. *If any man will hurt them, fire proceedeth out of their mouth
and devoureth their enemies.*

London, Printed by R. *Cotes* for *Stephen Bowtell*, at the Bible
in *Popes-head-alley*, 1646.

STRUCTURE OF MARSHALL'S SERMON 'A TWO-EDGED SWORD'

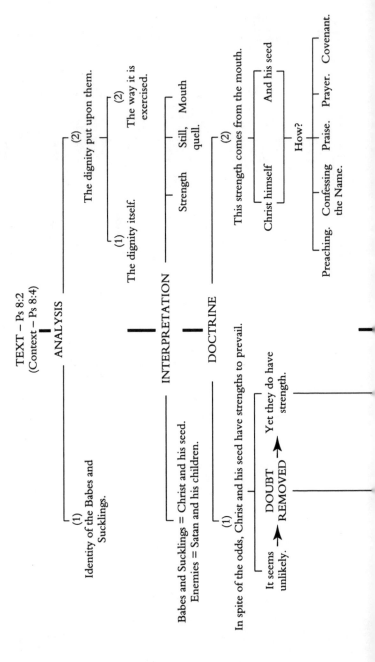

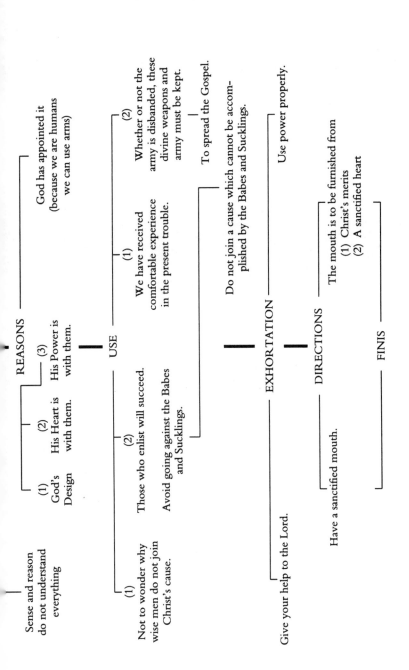

NOTES

1. A. F. Mitchell, *The Westminster Assembly* (London 1883) pp. 111–2. See also John H. Leith, *Assembly at Westminster* (Atlanta 1973) Robert S. Paul, *The Assembly of the Lord* (Edinburgh 1985).

2. For further discussion, Bryan D. Spinks, *Freedom or Order?* The Eucharistic Liturgy in English Congregationalism 1645–1980. (Allison Park 1984). Chapter 2. Being an ecumenical body it could be described as a joint liturgical group.

3. Horton Davies, *Like Angels from a Cloud. The English Metaphysical Preachers 1588–1645* (San Marino 1986); William Haller, *the Rise of Puritanism* (New York 1938); Perry Millar, *The New England Mind* (New York 1939, Boston 1970).

4. Miller, *op.cit.*, pp. 332–3.

5. Davies, *op.cit.*, pp. 50ff.

6. Edward R. Gane, 'The Exegetical Methods of Some Sixteenth-Century Anglican Preachers: Latimer, Jewel, Hooker and Andrewes', *Andrews University Seminary Studies* 17 (1979), pp. 23–38, 169–188; 'The Exegetical Methods of Some Sixteenth-Century Puritan Preachers: Hooper, Cartwright, and Perkins', *Andrews University Seminary Studies* 19 (1981), 21–36, 99–114. See also Richard A. Muller, *Post-Reformation Reformed Dogmatics*. Vol. 2 Holy Scripture: The Cognitive Foundation of Theology. (Grand Rapids, 1993).

7. Davies, *op.cit.*, p. 22.

8. Nicholas Lossky, *Lancelot Andrewes The Preacher (1555–1626)* (Oxford 1991).

9. *Ninety-Six Sermons by Lancelot Andrewes*, Library of Anglo-Catholic Theology, Vol. 1. Oxford and London 1874, pp. 91–2 (Christmas Day 1611).

10. *Ibid.*, p. 145 (Christmas 1614).

11. *Ibid.*, Vo. 2 (1841 edition), p. 376 (Easter Day 1616).

12. W. Fraser Mitchell, *English Pulpit Oratory from Andrews to Tillotson* (London 1932), p. 162.

13. T. S. Eliot, *For Lancelot Andrews*. Essays on Style and Order (London 1928/1970), pp. 11, 15.

14. Cited in F. J. Powicke, *A Life of the Rev. Richard Baxter* (London 1924), p. 283.

15. Edward Reynolds, Epistle Dedicatory to Seven Sermons on the Fourteenth Chapter of Hosea in *Works* III quoted in Lawrence A Sasek, *The Literary Temper of the English Puritans* (Baton Rouge 1961), p. 51–52.

16. William Perkins, *Of the Calling of the Ministerie*, 1618 p. 430.

17. T. H. L. Parker, *Calvin's Preaching* (Edinburgh 1992) p. 137.

18. Henry King, *An Exposition Upon the Lord's Prayer* (London 1628), p. 46.

19. Wolfgang Musculus, *In Epistolam Apostoli Pauli ad Romanos* (Basel 1555); see also *Commonplaces of Christian Religion* (London 1578).

20. Miller, *op.cit.*, p. 336; J. W. Blench, *Preaching in England in the late Fifteenth and Sixteenth Centuries*, Basil Blackwell: (Oxford 1964), p. 111 suggests that Andrews reached this form quite independently of Keckermann, but his work confirmed Andrewes in his method.

21. ed. I. Breward, *The Work of William Perkins*, Courtenay Library of Reformation Classics (Abingdon 1970); 'The Significance of William Perkins', in *Journal of Religious History* 4 (1966–7), pp. 113–28; R. T. Kendall, *Calvin and English Calvinism* (Oxford 1979), pp. 52–54.

22. *Works* 3 Vols, (London 1616–18), vol 2. p. 646.

23. *Ibid.*, p. 673.

24. *Ibid.*, p. 670.

25. *Ibid.*, p. 670.

26. *Ibid.*, pp. 670–1.

27. Quoted by Miller, *op.cit.*, p. 334.
28. Miller, *op.cit.*, passim. Walter J. Ong, *Ramus. Method, and the Decay of Dialogue* (Cambridge Massachusetts 1958).
29. Miller, *op.cit.*, p. 338.
30. Wilbur S. Howell, *Logic and Rhetoric in England 1500–1700* (New York 1956); Donald McKim, *Ramism in William Perkins' Theology*, (New York/Berne 1987); 'William Perkins' Use of Ramism as an Exegetical Tool', in William Perkins, *A Cloud of Faithful Witnesses: Commentary on Hebrews 11* ed. Gerald T. Sheppard, Pilgrim Classic Commentaries, vol. 3 (New York 1990) pp. 32–45.
31. Miller, *op.cit.*, p. 339.
32. DNB; E. Vaughan, *Stephen Marshall. A Forgotten Essex Puritan* (London 1907). Vaughan noted: 'No monumental record exists to tell his fame, either at Westminster or in that quiet country parish where his very name is almost forgotten'. The Church of England is rarely kind to its sons who ruffle its feathers, however outstanding their contribution.
33. ed. R. Jeffs, *The English Revolution. I. Fast Sermons to Parliament*, Vol. 25 Oct–Dec. 1646 (London 1971). For a general survey of such sermons, John F. Wilson, *Pulpit in Parliament*. Puritanism during the English Civil Wars 1640–1648 (Princeton N.J. 1969).
34. In addition to Lossky, see Marianne Dorman's edition of some of the Liturgical Sermons, (Edinburgh 1992), and A. M. Allchin's essay in ed. G. Rowell, *The English Religious Tradition and the Genius of Anglicanism* (Wantage 1992) pp. 145–64. Mention may be made of Paul Welsby's book of 1958.
35. Lawrence A. Sasek, *Ibid*, p. 39.
36. See, for example, its survival in Ireland, R. Buick Knox, 'The Doctrine and Practice of Worship in the Irish Presbyterian Tradition' in *Record* (The Church Service Society) 27 (1994) pp. 9–21.

7

'Human Nature Honoured': Absolution in Lancelot Andrewes

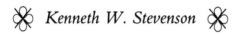 *Kenneth W. Stevenson*

' ... Christ, to Whom alone this commission was originally granted, having ordained Himself a body, would work by bodily means, and having taken the nature of a man upon Him, would honour the nature He had so taken.' [1]

The occasion

When Lancelot Andrewes died in 1626, the new King, Charles I, instructed William Laud and John Buckeridge to publish a selection of Andrewes' sermons. The choice of editors was an appropriate one, for both were admirers of Andrewes, Laud being Bishop of London, and Buckeridge (then Bishop of Rochester but now of Ely) had preached the sermon at Andrewes' funeral. Accordingly, ninety-six duly appeared in 1629. It was by no means the first appearance of Andrewes the preacher in print, nor was it to be the last. But the '96' have a prominence which the others lack. [2]

They consist mainly of the sermons Andrewes preached before the Court at the major festivals and commemorations: seventeen at Christmas, fourteen for Ash Wednesday and Lent, three on Good Friday, eighteen on Easter Day, fifteen for Whitsunday, eight on the annual commemoration of the Gowries (an alleged attempt to assassinate King James on August 5th, 1600), and ten on Gunpowder Plot day (November 5th). It says something for Andrewes' reputation that four of these sermons (those for 1622 on Ash Wednesday, Easter, Whitsun, and the Gowries) were never actually preached – only prepared for the occasion, but not delivered due to failing health.

Appended to these sermons for special occasions is a selection of eleven others, most of which were delivered at Court. It is the fourth that is the main subject of this investigation. Preached on the first Sunday after Easter, 1600, it is based on a text taken from the Gospel for the Day: 'whosesoever sins ye remit, they are remitted unto them; and whosesoever ye retain, they are retained.' (John 20.23)[3]

Before looking at its argument in detail, a word needs to be said about its place in Andrewes' life and ministry. By the year 1600, Andrewes was a well-known figure in London society. His career as an academic at Cambridge and his renown as a preacher had brought him to the attention of Francis Walsingham, Queen Elizabeth I's Secretary of State, and in 1589 he was given the living of St Giles', Cripplegate, as well as the prebendal stall of St Pancras in St Paul's Cathedral which by tradition had attached to it the role of penitentiary. Andrewes decided to revive this latter tradition, and to use both these responsibilities as a base for his preaching and pastoral ministry. In a memoir on the Church of England written for the young Prince Henry, Sir John Harington describes the way in which Andrewes conducted his duties as a penitentiary:

> 'While he held this place, his manner was, especially in Lent time to walk daily at certain hours in one of the aisles of the church, that if any came to him for spiritual advice and comfort, (as some would, though not many,) he might impart it to them. This custom being agreeable to the Scripture and Fathers, expressed and required in a sort in the Communion Book, not repugning the XXXIX Articles, and no less approved by Calvin in his Institutions, yet was quarelled with by divers (upon occasion of some sermons) as a point of Popery.'[4]

Between these lines we can read something of the motivations and attitudes of the time; Andrewes' repeated defence of the role of spiritual director, the place of that ministry as vindicated ('in a sort') in one of the Prayer Book exhortations before Communion, and the popular response. We shall meet this again.

Andrewes was an aspiring cleric. In 1597 he was appointed a prebendary of Westminster Abbey, an office that would have brought him even nearer the centre of life. When the deanery fell vacant in 1601, he was promoted to it above the heads of his senior colleagues on the chapter. And when, on Elizabeth's death, James VI of Scotland came south as King James I of England, he struck up a deep relationship with Andrewes that finds expression in the directions concerning the coronation: Andrewes as 'Abbot of Westminster' (the old title!) was to have sole responsibility for preparing the King for the solemn rite the night before; he was to walk on the right hand of the monarch and look after him throughout the service (even though the King was to be supported by two bishops); and he it was who would deliver the cup at the communion.[5] We may surmise that these procedures either arose out of an already-existing friendship or led into one. At any rate, monarch and cleric remained close throughout the entire reign. Further promotion came Andrewes' way. He became Bishop of Chichester in 1606, Ely in 1609, and, finally, he took over the senior see of Winchester in 1619. Although he preached before the Court during Elizabeth's reign, the only recorded sermons on special occasions in the liturgical year contained in the '96' were delivered in Lent and Good Friday. By contrast, all the Christmas, Easter, Whitsun, Gowries and Gunpowder preachments were given by him as a diocesan bishop before King James. Indeed, such was his standing at Court that James took him north in 1617 for the celebration of the fiftieth anniversary of his coronation as King of Scotland – hence the twelfth Easter Day sermon in Durham Cathedral, and the tenth Whitsun sermon in the Chapel Royal at Holyrood, in Edinburgh.

The Sermon on Absolution
In his lengthy funeral oration, Buckeridge remarked thus of Andrewes' attitude to the preparation of sermons:

> 'He was always a diligent and painful preacher. Most of his
> solemn sermons he was most careful of, and exact; I dare say
> few of them but they passed his hand, and were thrice revised,
> before they were preached; and he ever misliked often and

loose preaching without study of antiquity and he would be
bold with himself and say, when he preached twice a day at
St Giles', he prated once ...'[6]

If we compare these thoughts with the sermon on absolution, we
are in for few surprises. It is intricately set out, with neat divisions
and subdivisions, copious margin-references to the Bible, and a
lively, sharp style. By Andrewes' standards, it is perhaps a little
longer than usual. He clearly has much to say. Indeed, although it
has three main sections, he only gets to the last near the end – 'time
hath overtaken me'[7] As we shall see, Andrewes' thought was to
integrated that he was able to express the same ideas afresh in later
preaching without any sense of repetition. But we may note on
this occasion the desire to get as much of his message across, and
perhaps suspect a hasty final page.

What does the sermon say?[8] He begins with a customary introduction, in which he describes the text (John 20.23) as words
spoken by the risen Christ 'at his epiphany, or first apparition after
he rose from the dead.' He insists that they contain a 'commission',
a gift to the apostles after his resurrection, a promise from him to
the Church. In characteristic style, he goes on to base this promise
and commission in the Trinity:

> 'To the service and ministry of which divine work a commis-
> sion is here granted to the Apostles. And first, they have here
> their sending from God the father, their inspiring from God
> the Holy Ghost, their commission from God the Son; that
> being thus sent from the Father, by the power of the Holy
> Ghost, in the person of Christ, they may perform the office
> or, as the Apostle calleth it, the embassage of reconciling
> sinners unto God, to which they are appointed.'[9]

Andrewes draws attention to the three main divisions of the
sermon: the power of absolution, the matter or subject, and the
promise of ratifying of it. And he spends a great proportion of the
sermon on the power, which he rests firmly and ultimately in
Christ. (In my own copy of the '96', one of the first editions, this
sermon has the running title, 'of the power of absolution'.) The
terms of remitting and retaining are the result of Jesus' ministry in

the synagogue at Nazareth (Luke 4.18), which leads him to liken sins as a form of imprisonment, from which forgiveness sets us free. 'The mind of the Holy Ghost ... is to compare the sinner's case to the estate of a person imprisoned.'[10] The power for remitting sins, however, comes from God alone. But because it is God's forgiveness, ministers are required to express this ministry. Andrewes neatly distinguishes between the 'ye remit' (what the priest says) and 'they are remitted' (what God does):

> '... thus the case stands between them: *remittuntur*, which is God's power, is the primitive or original; *remiseritis*, which is the Apostles' power, is merely divided. That in God, sovereign; this in the Apostles, dependent. In Him only absolute: in them, delegate. In Him imperial, in them, ministerial.'[11]

Andrewes is here walking a theological tight-rope (in this case the authority of absolution) for in two pithy sentences that are strongly reminiscent of Hooker's theological approach, he quickly explains the source of this authority:

> 'Partly this, that there should be no such difficulty to shake our faith, as once to imagine to fetch Christ from heaven for the remission of our sins.
>
> 'Partly also, because Christ, to Whom alone this commission was originally granted, having ordained Himself a body, would work by bodily things; and having taken the nature of man upon Him, would honour the nature He had so taken.'[12]

The Apostles heard this commission, and therefore it is to them and their successors, that the commission is given. And it is at this point that Andrewes prepares the ground for what is perhaps the most original aspect of the sermon. He begins to distinguish between authority and knowledge, regarding both as essential to ministerial office:

> 'Now all Christians are not so sent, nor are all Christians inspired with the grace or gift of the Spirit that they were here. Consequently, it was not intended to the whole society of Christians. Yea I add, that forasmuch as these two, both these two, must go before it, 1. *Missio*, and 2. *Inspiratio*, that

> though God inspire some laymen, if I may have leave so to
> term them, with very special graces of knowledge to this end,
> yet inasmuch as they have not the former of sending, it
> agreeth not to them, neither may they exercise it until they
> be sent, that is, until they have their calling thereunto.'

Here, Andrewes is making a distinction between what we would
nowadays call ministerial and charismatic office. He is less unyielding than at first sight appears; for he goes on to affirm that because
'the grace of God is not bound but free ... if at any time He vouch-
safe it by other that are not such, they be in that case *Ministri neces-
sitatis non officii*, "in case of necessity Ministers, but by office not
so."' [13] Understanding the pastoral character of absolution, he states
that three parties are required: the sinner, God, and the priest. But
in what context? Andrewes adopts a favourite technique in
working out his theology and sets absolution in the wider context
of Christian life. He lists four other ways in which forgiveness
is proclaimed and imparted: by baptism, by the eucharist, by
preaching, and by prayer. In each of these, the minister is required
in some way, so that there is nothing special or unique about
absolution. [14]

So far he has been gradually building up his argument. Now he
reaches a vital stage in the sermon, with the tell-tale 'not to hold
you long', whereby he provides his own interpretation of the
traditional 'power of the keys' (Matthew 16.19):

> 'Whereunto our Saviour Christ, by His sending them, doth
> institute them and give them the key of authority; and by
> breathing on them and inspiring them doth enable them, and
> give them the key of knowledge to do it well; and having
> bestowed both these upon them as the stewards of His house,
> doth last of all deliver them their commission to do it, having
> so enabled them and authorized them as before.' [15]

It is in the contrast between authority and knowledge that much
of the rest of the sermon rests. Having recognised the inbuilt gift
of knowledge which many people have (his reference to 'laymen,
if I may have leave so to term them'), Andrewes insists that these
two aspects belong together. There is no point, he would argue, in

having a church full of two distinct groups of people – those with authority, and those with knowledge. Therefore, the ministerial office is one that requires discernment and experience, not just a sudden call that people may feel within themselves.

Andrewes now moves swiftly into the second division of the sermon – the subject, which is sin. But instead of listing different types, he looks in the other direction, just as any experienced father-confessor would to a grieving penitent – the love and mercy of God. He forgives without exception, until seventy times seven (Matthew 18.22), or countless debts (Luke 7.41). No one is beyond the forgiveness of God. But in the ministry of forgiveness, a knowledge and understanding of human frailty is needful, and once again, the two keys enter the picture:

> 'Many sinners there be, and many sins may be remitted, but not to any, except they be of this *quorum* (= whose). In which point there is a special use of "the key of knowledge," to direct to whom, and to whom not; since it is not but with advice to be applied, nor "hands hastily to be laid on any man," as the Apostle testifieth; which place is referred by the ancient writers to the act of absolution, and the circumstance of the place giveth no less. But discretion is to be used in applying of comfort, counsel, and the benefit of absolution.'[16]

It is interesting that he here refers to the laying-on of hands – not for the only time, as we shall see.[17]

He now goes on to enunciate two principles. The first is that the penitent should be a member of the Church, which is the recipient of the grace of God, flowing down as if through the 'conduit-pipes' (a favourite image in Andrewes). There seems no use in giving absolution to someone who is cut off from, or uninterested in, the wider church community. 'The power of the keys reacheth not' those who are outside the Church.[18] Secondly, they should be repentant, which means that they should actually desire forgiveness and feel the weight of their sins. Repentance is not a passive state, but an active one, a turning towards God for what he alone can grant, and wants to grant. Some sinners do not grieve, whereas others will not let their sins go:

'In which very point (of sorrow for sin) there is an especial good use of the key of knowledge, for counsel and direction ... to advise both what works are meet and also what measure is to be kept, "the key of knowledge" will help to direct, and we may have use of it if we mean to use it to that end.'[19]

And he concludes this part of the sermon with another flash of human perception:

'For most usual it is for men at their ends to doubt, not of the power of remitting of sins, but of their own disposition to receive it; and whether they have ordered the matter so that they be within the compass of God's effectual calling, or, as the text is, of the *quorum* to which it belongeth.'[20]

Rushing into the third and final division of the sermon, which is a scant few summarised paragraphs, Andrewes briefly discusses the ratifying of forgiveness, by pointing to four salient features; the order to forgive (on earth, so in heaven); the present tense (no delay); the manner (Christ's act, the Church as his agent); and the certainty (it is fact, not vague wish). 'And all to certify us that He fully meaneth with effect to ratify in heaven that is done in earth, to the sure and steadfast comfort of them that shall partake it.'[21]

The Aftermath

What was the general reaction to this closely-argued and carefully-prepared sermon? Although the apparent subject of the discourse is absolution and forgiveness in general, the actual discussion concerns the theology and practice of private confession. The rite in question appears in the Prayer Book, in the order for the Visitation of the Sick, to which an exhortation before Communion gives implicit reference when urging those troubled in spirit to make their confession privately in the presence of a priest. In the nineteenth century edition of Andrewes' works published by the *Library of Anglo-Catholic Theology*, some biographical details are given to the sermons, all of them either favourable comments or straight descriptions of events surrounding them. All, except for one case – the sermon on absolution. In a letter from Rowland Whyte, a courtier, to Robert Sydney, a hero in the Dutch campaigns, and the main channel of communication between the Court and the Earl of Essex during his rebellion, Whyte notes the following:

> 'Dr Andrewes made a strange sermon at court on Sunday; his text was the xx chapter of the Gospel St John the 23rd verse, touching the forgiveness of sins upon earth. That contrition without confession and absolution and deeds worthy of repentance, was not sufficient. That the ministers had the two keys of power and knowledge delivered unto them; that whose sins soever they remitted upon earth, should be remitted in heaven. The court is full of it, for such doctrine was not usually taught here. I hear he was with Mr Secretary about it, it may be to satisfy him.' [22]

Whyte presents a concise summary of the argument of the sermon, which probably means that he himself heard it. He touches the main points of what Andrewes was trying to say. The sermon was based on a text, it insisted that an individual contrite heart was not enough, that the keys of authority and knowledge are given to clergy, who can then remit sins by absolution. One can feel through Whyte's letter a fear of 'popery', a sense that individual religion, that bugbear of popular Protestantism at its worst, proved an obstacle for at least some of the hearers to take in the sermon and appreciate it. And one can also feel the power of lay opinion in the rumour (which may well have been true) that Andrewes was either summoned by the Secretary of State, or else voluntarily went to see him. This office was by now held by Robert Cecil, the second son of William Cecil, Lord Burghley, the legendary first minister to Elizabeth for many years. Cecil was not as religious a man as his father, but by 1600 he had enormous influence. A ballad written a year later contained the words:

> 'Little Cecil trips up and down
> He rules both court and crown.' [23]

It is doubtful if Andrewes gave way in any manner to lay pressure on his theological views. He had already come out somewhat strongly against the 1595 'Lambeth Articles', because, among other things, he feared the effect of predestination on peoples' view of the nature of the Church. Now in this sermon he seemed to some to be leading the Church back to before the Reformation, when in fact he was providing a studied defence of the Prayer Book position, where absolution is given at Morning and Evening Prayer in a declaratory form, at Holy Communion in a precatory form, and in the Visitation of the Sick, in a direct version based on the mediaeval 'ego absolvo te' formula. But, of course, he does not cite the Prayer Book (he seldom does in his preaching in any case), preferring to base his arguments on his unique blend of scripture, tradition, and reason.

Andrewes' sermon doubtless became the talk of the court – and beyond. But two factors need to be borne in mind, just to show the enduring quality of his ministry. The first is that he was back at court that same year, on the Sunday before Advent, preaching on a text from the lesson for the epistle, 'This is the Name whereby they shall call Him, The Lord our righteousness' (Jeremiah 23.6)[24]. In this particular sermon, Andrewes is no less controversial in his insistence on what has been called 'the two righteousnesses', a theme which is discussed – together with a comparison with Hooker – by Nicholas Lossky in his magisterial study of the theology of Lancelot Andrewes.[25] In it, Andrewes walks another tight-rope, insisting that all our righteous deeds are in the end God's but distinguishing between the righteousness which comes directly from God's action in Christ, and our own propensity towards righteousness, which we have in spite of our fallen human nature.[26]

For the other factor, we need to turn to the second principal collection of his utterances, the Apospasmatia Sacra (= 'holy fragments'), a selection of lectures mainly on the first four chapters of Genesis which he gave at St Paul's and St Giles', before his elevation to the episcopate.[27] In a lecture delivered in St Giles' on April 2nd 1600, only three days after the famous sermon at court on absolution, Andrewes took as his text, 'Repent and be baptized' (Acts 2.37), in which he returns to some of the themes in the earlier sermon. One is the effect of sin upon the memory ('for the remembrance of it stings the conscience so as it cannot be quiet'). The other is the need for repentance to issue forth in the desire for forgiveness and amendment of life:

'It is not enough to be pricked in the heart for sin past, but we must do something. And he speaks first by way of precept, Repent, and that is, rest not in that passive part, but know that when you are pricked in your hearts, repentance must be showed in your life.' [28]

It is hard to avoid the conclusion that, if this was not already a firm part of Andrewes' theology, in all its consistency, it might also have been introduced into the discourse as a response to the controversy stirred up by the absolution sermon. But it would in any case make sense of Harington's reference to 'some sermons' (i.e. more than one) which provoked unfavourable comment because of the position he took on absolution.

In a subsequent sermon at St Giles', which occurs in the collection very soon after the one just quoted, but which is unfortunately undated, we come across the theme which dominates the absolution sermon, and to which Whyte also makes mention in his letter to Sydney, namely the keys of authority and knowledge:

'And it is knowledge that must discern between good and ill; evil things may go under the shew of good; and therefore we must have knowledge to unmask them. So the doctrine of repentance, being a good thing, hath a shew of will, and, without the grace of knowledge, men are hardly brought to believe it. As there is *prudentia carnis* (= wisdom of the flesh) (Romans 8.6), and *prudentia saeculi* (= wisdom of this age) (1 Corinthians 3.19), so there must be a spiritual knowledge and wisdom, to discern them, and to measure what is good ... Knowledge is lame without power, and power is blind without knowledge; for knowledge is the lighting of the eyes of the mind.' [29]

We shall return in a moment to the *Apospasmatia Sacra* when it comes to evaluating the special features of the absolution sermon. In the mean time, we take note of the likelihood that Andrewes was in some way either defending the views expressed in that famous sermon in subsequent preachments delivered in the more modest environment of St Giles', or else systematically working through his own course of Christian doctrine. Whichever be the case, it is truly remarkable to see the close juxtaposition of the ideas, complete with their penetrating psychology: to the court, a sermon distinguishing between the keys of authority and knowledge, to the congregation at St Giles' probably quite soon after, a lecture which warned that 'knowledge is lame without power, and power is blind without knowledge.'

The sermon in the context of Andrewes' other preaching
It is now appropriate to look at the main theological features of the sermon as these can be compared with the rest of his preaching. The repertoire is so vast that it is only possible to take a few examples, and these will also serve to point to the special emphases in Andrewes' whole theology.

For a start, Andrewes sets his explorations in the context of Trinitarian theology. In the theological climate of today, Andrewes produces a unique blend of the 'economic' and 'immanent' approaches to the operation of the deity. When he says of the apostles' being sent from the Father, inspired by the Spirit, and commissioned by the Son, he is in line with those intricately-argued Whitsun sermons which repeatedly expound the doctrine of the Trinity in terms both transcendent and rooted in human experience. A similar example, also worked out from a simple scripture text – in this case, the narrative of the baptism of Christ (Luke 3.21–22) – is to be found in the Whitsun sermon for 1615, also near the start, where Andrewes seems to cut through a certain degree of doctrinal red-tape in an iconographic brush-stroke with the words, 'here is the whole Trinity in person. The Son in the water, the Holy Ghost in the dove, the Father in the voice.'[30]

Similarly, we can see the same insight into the deification of human nature by the incarnation and redemption. This is a favourite theme in Andrewes, to which both Allchin and Lossky have drawn attention. The examples that could be given are legion, but perhaps the one which balances the honouring of human nature that we have noted n the absolution comes from the Christmas 1609 sermon: 'We made the sons of God, as He the Son of Man; we made partakers of His divine, as he of our human nature.'[31]

Andrewes is – as we have seen – strong on ministerial office in the Church, and the need for call to be balanced by authority imparted. In his final Whitsun sermon (1622), prepared but never delivered, he is more pointed:

> 'Well in those two they have somewhat yet; either a calling without a gift, or a gift without a calling. What say you to them that have neither, but fetch and run for all that, and leap quite over gift and calling, Christ and the Holy Ghost both, and chop into the work at the first dash? ...Good Lord what the poor Church suffers in this kind!'[32]

Perhaps these words reflect overtly what lies under the surface of what he preached twenty years earlier in the absolution sermon concerning the various problems facing the church on the ground. There are also certain expressions and themes germane to absolution that are repeated later on in Andrews' sermons. In 1617, in Durham Cathedral on Easter Day, he preaches that repentance is the virtue of Christ's resurrection, raising the soul to new life; and later that year, at Whitsun in the Chapel Royal at Holyrood, he describes sin as an imprisonment, from which freedom is granted by the turning of the keys of hell and death.[33] In the absolution sermon, we have noted how Andrewes identifies the laying-on of hands with the forgiveness of sins. In the Whitsun sermon for 1612, he lists the 'offices' of the Holy Spirit, among which is that we are 'by Him after renewed to repentance, when we fall away, by a second imposition of hands.'[34]

But of all the truths enunciated in the absolution sermon, perhaps two stand out most prominently, because of the quiet force with which Andrewes speaks of them. The first is the need for what we would nowadays call spiritual direction. In the Whitsun sermon for 1611, Andrewes laments those who leave things until it is conveniently late in life:

> 'Our manner is, we love to be left to ourselves, in our considerations to advise with flesh and blood; thence to take our direction, all our life: and, when we must part, then send for Him, for a little comfort, and there is all the use, we have for Him. But he that will have comfort from Him, must also take counsel of Him; have use of Him as well against error and sinful life, as against heaviness of mind.'[35]

The second is the question of the power of the keys. The traditional identification of these keys is the gates of heaven and hell
(Matthew 16.19), corresponding to the power to remit and retain.
And these appear in one form or another in later sermons, for
example in 1616 at Whitsun, 1617 again at Whitsun, and in 1618
at Easter.[36] But where does Andrews get his notion of the 'key of
knowledge'? The answer lies in a sermon tucked away at the very
back of the *Apospasmatia Sacra*, which is dated October 13th 1590,
and which has the margin note: 'Place this in the beginning of the
book next before the sermon upon Gen. 1.2. For this was the
Bishop's first Lecture in Saint Paul's, preached as an Introduction
to his following discourse upon the four first chapters of Genesis.'[37]

It is a typical Andrewes sermon, whose text is Luke 12.52, the
warning of Jesus to the Pharisees for distorting the key of knowledge. Its opening words are a telling sentence, which we may
without much hesitation regard as a theme dear to Andrewes'
heart, given the context of the sermon in question: 'Knowledge of
holy things is compared by our Saviour Christ to a key.' There
follows a carefully-worked out discussion of discernment in the
books of the Bible, with particular reference to the careful study of
the beginning of the Old Testament. Knowledge is central to the
creation and fall of the human race, as evidenced by his subsequent
lecture on Genesis 2.17, delivered on June 19th in the following
year. In it, Andrewes demonstrates the spiritual qualities of a
knowledge which is what we would nowadays call experiential
and disciplined, as well as showing a true discernment of spiritual
truth.[38] Andrewes does not leave the human race in a state of rejection and depravity. With a careful commixture of New Testament
texts, he places us back in the arms of God's mercy, with the capacity to know, albeit in a stumbling manner, what is God's will – and
to try to perform it.

One final point needs to be made about Andrewes' sacramental
theology, which is that in it everything is connected to everything
else. We saw in the absolution sermon how he listed the four other
ways in which forgiveness could be known and experienced –
baptism, eucharist, preaching, and prayer; and then absolution
itself enters the picture. So he sees, again and again, the connections between the sacraments and the sacramental rites (however

they are to be termed). It is significant that several of the connections we have made have been with the Whitsun sermons, for Andrewes' theology of the Spirit again and again lies at the foundation of what he has to say about God, the Church, the sacraments, and the way in which these meet and interplay with the human condition. It is a refreshing way of avoiding a cold and mechanistic sacramental theology. All our striving for God is in the power of the Spirit, and that includes forgiveness, breathed on the apostles – and their followers – by nothing less than the risen, Spirit-filled Lord himself. The 1612 sermon, referred to briefly above, contains a paragraph which makes this point fully:

> 'A third necessity there is we receive Him (i.e. the Holy Spirit), for that with Him we shall receive whatever we want, or need to receive, for our soul's good. And here fall in all His offices. By Him we are regenerate at the first in our baptism. By Him after, confirmed in the imposition of hands. By Him after, renewed to repentance, "when we fall away," by a second imposition of hands. By Him taught all our life long that we know not, put in mind of what we forget, stirred up in what we are dull, helped in our prayers, relived in "our infirmities", comforted in our heaviness; in a word, "sealed to the day of our redemption," and "raised up again in the last day." Go all along, even from our baptism to our very resurrection and we cannot miss Him, but receive Him we must.' [39]

Comparison with the Preces Privatae

The *Preces Pivatae* (= 'Private Prayers') of Lancelot Andrewes provide a unique mirror into the inner life of one of the most remarkable figures of his time. Never intended for publication, they were by origin personal and private in character. In his edition, F. E. Brightman gives a 'Cranmerian' translation of the prayers (it should be noted that they were prayed by Andrewes in the original languages, Latin, and, where appropriate, Greek and Hebrew), together with copious sources, and quotations from the sermons. It is living proof of the integration of the man's preaching with his praying.

There are, however, precious few direct references to material which parallels the absolution sermon. In his biography of Andrewes, Welsby makes the curious criticism that his prayers are excessively penitential, a charge which Lossky rebuts firmly, on grounds that Andrewes' piety reflects that of the devout of every age.[40] It is significant that all three references to the power of the keys come in prayers of thanksgiving for life in the Church and the community of the redeemed:

> 'who hast opened to me a door of hope,
> when I confess and ask,
> by the power of the mysteries and the keys.'

In the other two, there is a simple thanksgiving 'for the keys', but the third is longer:

> '... supplying unto me good hopes
> touching the remission of them (= sins),
> through penitence and the works thereof,
> by the power of the thriceholy
> keys and sacraments
> that are in thy Church.'

Other references to forgiveness are of a more general nature, such as the eucharist as the forgiveness of sins, and two biblical texts used in the absolution sermon.[41] It is clear from all these references that Andrewes sees the place of forgiveness within the context of God's loving mercy, mediated through the ministry of the Church, through prayer and sacrament. As to Andrewes' own private practice, there is no direct evidence. In his prayers for use with the sick, he provides an opportunity for a general confession of sin; and in his 1625 Visitation Articles in the Winchester diocese, he inquires into whether local clergy exhort the troubled and disquited to open their grief and receive absolution before Holy Communion.[42] From this evidence, as well as from the sermon on absolution, the repeated calls from the pulpit for a wider use of the custom, and what he has to say in the *Preces Privatae*, both in his general penitential prayers and his references to 'the power of the keys', it is safe to assume that he did himself avail himself of the practice of private confession and absolution.

We know that he was sought after by others, including King James, for spiritual counsel. If we put the form of private confession and absolution contained in the Prayer Book alongside some of his other observations (e.g. the importance of priestly discernment, and the gesture of the laying-on of hands), we may gain an accurate picture of how he ministered to other people, and how he expected to be ministered to himself.

Wider Evaluation

In the context of his time, Andrewes was working out a creative synthesis of tradition, in a climate in which religion was even more politically-debated than it is in some quarters today. He did not hold – as did the late mediaeval Catholic Church – that communion should be preceded by private confession. Nor did he hold that the priest effected the absolution. On the other hand, he refused to go down the road of detailed, corporate examination of the faithful before communion, as some Puritans. He was trying to steer a middle course and in line with others of his ilk was keen to commend this ministry to a wider public in order to help them to see it in a new light: this sermon is utterly consistent with the prebendary of St Paul's who (as we noted earlier) would walk up and down St Paul's during Lent as penitentiary.

As far as official attitudes to this rite are concerned, we need look no further than *The Book of Homilies* (1562), where, in the homily on repentance, there is a lengthy discourse of a general kind on the merits and functioning of repentance and forgiveness, laced with copious Scriptural references, as well as citations to the Fathers. Interestingly, it also refers to 'auricular confession' (an expression Andrewes seems deliberately to avoid). But here the homilist carefully rejects it as in any way mandatory, emphasising its optional character, in line with the Prayer Book itself. Those who 'find themselves troubled in conscience' are to go to a 'learned curate or pastor : that they may receive at their hand the comfortable salve of God's word.' This latter might conceivably refer to the practice of hand-laying at absolution, though this seems unlikely, particularly as there is no rubric to that effect in the rite itself.[43]

As to the specific issue of the 'I absolve thee' formula for absolution, it was the subject of Puritan objection four years later at the Hampton Court Conference in 1604, which Andrewes (still Dean of Westminster) attended in an official capacity. Voices were also raised against it in the House of Lords Committee in 1641, and after the Restoration at the Savoy Conference in 1661. The nature of the objections concerned its declaratory form, though many Puritans disliked the other absolutions in the Prayer Book also.[44]

In a recent essay, Geoffrey Rowell examined the place of the Anglican tradition from the Reformation to the Oxford Movement in the area of confession and absolution.[45] It is well-known that all the Reformers maintained that the power of the keys was delivered to the Church. The question remains, in what way? Luther kept the practice of private confession, but insisted, like the Anglican reformers, that it should be optional only. The penitent confesses, and then receives absolution in a direct 'I declare to you' form. This practice persists, with a laying-on of hands, in parts of the Lutheran world to this day. Indeed, the rite in question can be celebrated either in private, or else publicly, as a preparation for Communion, the pastor going along the altar-rail laying hands on pairs of penitents in turn. The private context does require discernment, and it is interesting to note how the Elizabethan Thomas Becon stressed the need for wisdom and discretion on the part of the minister, and the importance of the penitent coming to greater self-knowledge.[46] Other writers of the time stress these aspects, too.

The resemblance, however, between Hooker's basic approach and Andrewes' is striking. Both base their arguments on scripture, both emphasise the fact that confession in this manner is not to be imposed on all and sundry, though it is clearly helpful for many who are troubled, and both insist on the fact that the authority to forgive – in whatever context – has been entrusted to the Church. As Hooker himself observes of ministerial office: 'whether we preach, pray, baptise, communicate, condemn, give absolution, or whatsoever, as disposers of God's mysteries, our words, judgements, acts and deeds, are not ours but the Holy Ghost's.'[47]

Both John Cosin and Jeremy Taylor provide forms for confession and absolution, Taylor – following Andrewes – taking care to encourage the sick person to make as detailed a confession as possible.[48] Bramhall follows Andrewes directly in an eloquent passage in which he, first of all, lists the other contexts in which forgiveness is known (baptism, eucharist, preaching, and prayer), and then he draws a contrast between the place of the clergyman in relation to God: 'God remits sovereignly, imperially, primitively, absolutely; the Priest's power is derivative, delegate, dependent, ministerial, conditional.' Both these insights are lifted straight from the corresponding passages of the Andrewes absolution sermon.[49] Rowell draws attention to Newman's first recorded experience of giving absolution privately to a student at Oxford in March, 1838. He used the Prayer Book form from the Visitation of the Sick, but with the laying-on of hands at the absolution.[50] Newman held Andrewes in deep respect, and one wonders if his practice here was influenced by him.

Like the other Reformers in their various ways, Andrewes rejects the late mediaeval theology and practice of confession,[51] but is there a parallel with Orthodoxy? At first sight, such a question may seem far-fetched, but Andrewes' learning was vast, and it is indeed doubtful whether he would have made so much of this aspect of Christian life for his own preaching and ministry without being himself informed of Orthodox thinking and custom, particularly given his deep knowledge of that tradition as a whole.[52]

In fact, in the absolution sermon are to be found four of Orthodoxy's foundational elements: forgiveness as the deification of humanity (Christ taking on himself human nature ...); God as the sole agent of absolution; the importance of seeing absolution in terms of reconciliation within the Church; and, finally, in the repeated references to the keys of authority and knowledge we can detect the popular Orthodox practice, already long established in Andrewes' time, of going to a religious for spiritual counsel (knowledge), followed by absolution with the laying-on of hands, from a priest (authority). That Andrewes is keen to draw these 'keys' together in a suitably instructed and humanly sensitive priesthood should not detract from his acute awareness of these two distinct but overlapping aspects inherent in the task of making forgiveness real for those who avail themselves of this minstry.

Conclusion

How successful was Andrewes? At one level, his 1600 sermon on absolution can be dismissed as yet one more cleric exhorting the faithful to wake out of their comfortable, privatised religious slumber! To read the sermon and then to read Whyte's letter to Sydney is, in a sense, no surprise. The majority of Anglicans, to say nothing of Presbyterians, Lutherans, and others, still grate their teeth when a practice that they neither understand completely nor particularly want to like is held up to them by an enthusiastic expert. But the problem continues to belong to the whole of the Western Church today, not least when we consider the gradual decline of the practice of private confession in the Roman Catholic Church.

How does one inculcate in people a sense of personal discipline without putting in its place something which appears both severe and unyielding? It is interesting that the first point made by Whyte in his letter concerns the insufficiency of simply wallowing in our own sinfulness and doing nothing about it – as if this caused more of a stir than what Andrewes had to say about the nature of absolution itself. By all accounts, Andrewes, who was an awesome but a gentle and likeable man who had a particular gift for friendship, stood firmly by what he said, and made sure that the same message was given on later occasions. And as for the real aftermath of the sermon, one has to bear in mind that much effective pastoral ministry is of necessity hidden.

In our own very different world, with its own particular propensities for privatising religious experience, Andrewes' particular insights deserve to be reappropriated. We may summarise them as follows:

1. Absolution, the power to forgive, has been imparted to the Church by the Risen Lord, breathing the Spirit on the disciples in a dramatic encounter for all time. It therefore invades a whole terrain of human experience, which includes peoples' needs, whether these are overtly expressed, by those who come forward for private confession; or have to be decoded, in the case of those who rely from conviction (or out of shyness) on the corporate act of confession in the Christian assembly, but who are still helped by pastoral care. Perhaps the moves to break down the barriers that lie between 'private' and 'corporate' religious experience at the

moment will bear fruit. There was a growing Puritan trend to examine, publicly, those who intended to receive communion, which was another reason for Andrewes to draw from the Prayer Book, and the tradition represented by it, another way of forgiveness that was pastorally more edifying.[53] One can easily read between the lines of the absolution sermon a desire to see this entire area 'whole', instanced particularly by his determination to connect repentance and forgiveness with the sacrament where they ultimately belong – baptism. Indeed, Andrewes' pneumatology here is a classic example of the way in which the traditional Catholic-Protestant divide can be breached by a dynamic theology of the Trinity.[54]

2. The two keys of authority and knowledge are a vital foundation for the effective ministry of this part of the Christian gospel, and in this respect, Andrewes' unique synthesis makes sense of the necessary balance between 'charism' and 'office'. It is not a ministry in which to dive into human problems, come what may. Moreover, the essentially personal nature of what he is describing argues towards the retention of the direct 'I absolve you' form, so long as it is clear that God is the ultimate source of all forgiveness.[55] For those concerned that absolution in the context of privacy should be as personal in style as at all possible can be helped by the clarity of Andrewes' discussion of the intimate connection between God the forgiver, the penitent seeking forgiveness, and the priest as the one expressing and conveying that forgiveness. It could be that what Andrewes recognises as the gifts of 'certain laymen' is an interesting throw-forward to a later century – ours – in which ministry often operates in a different and less hierarchical manner.

3. Andrews provides, as always, a divine anthropology for the human environment he is attempting to reach, and he expresses it through the medium of a theology that is at once liturgical, mystical, and systematic. It is not a human race revelling in existential angst, but one that takes self-knowledge seriously, and with a sense of proportion. Moreover, the human race which we find here is not the fruit of an individualistic isolationism, for Andrewes' vision is about a Church made up of a vast and varied array of redeemed sinners – who live thankful lives. The Trinity hover together, and offer the foundation, the Father sending, the Spirit inspiring, the

Son commissioning. The sacraments and their accompaniments commingle, rich with overflowing 'conduit-pipes', enriching human experience by healing wounds, releasing the captives, and binding up the broken-hearted. And in the centre stands Christ, who 'having taken the nature of a man upon Him, would honour the nature he had so taken.'[56]

NOTES

1. See *The Sermons of Lancelot Andrewes* V (Library of Anglo-Catholic Theology) (Oxford: Parker, 1843) p. 90 (whole sermon, pp. 82–103). Referred to hereafter as *Absolution*. The sermon was also printed, with some appended notes, in *Tracts from the Anglican Fathers: The Prayer Book* (Volume 1) (London: Painter, 1841) pp. 113–141.
2. See *The Sermons of Lancelot Andrewes* I–V (Library of Anglo-Catholic Theology) (Oxford: Parker, 1841–1843) (= *Sermons*, followed by volume number).
3. On the theology of Lancelot Andrewes, see the following: Nicholas Lossky, *Lancelot Andrewes the Preacher 1555–1626: The Origins of the Mystical Theology of the Church of England* (Oxford: Clarendon Press, 1991); A. M. Allchin, 'Lancelot Andrewes', in Geoffrey Rowell (ed.), *The English Religious Tradition and the Genius of Anglicanism* (Wantage: Ikon Books, 1992) pp. 145–164; A. M. Guite, 'The Art of Memory and the Art of Salvation', Durham University Ph.D. thesis, 1993, pp. 109–174 (on Andrewes); and Kenneth Stevenson, *Covenant of Grace Renewed: A Vision of the Eucharist in the Seventeenth Century* (London: Darton, Longman and Todd, 1994) pp. 39–66, and *passim*. The classic and indispensable tool for the study of this whole area is still the magisterial work, H. R. McAdoo, *The Spirit of Anglicanism: A Survey of Anglican Theological Method in the Seventeenth Century* (London: A and C Black, 1965).
4. See John Harington, *A Briefe View of the State of the Church of England* (London: Kirton, 1653) p. 144 (whole section on Andrewes, pp. 141–147, under Bishops of Chichester, as Harington completed his work in 1608). Reprinted in *Lancelot Andrewes: Minor Works* (Library of Anglo-Catholic Theology) (Oxford: Parker, 1854), pp. xxxv–xxxviii. See also, in general, Paul A. Welsby, *Lancelot Andrewes: 1555–1626* (London: S.P.C.K., 1958).
5. See Christopher Wordsworth (ed.), *The Manner of the Coronation of King Charles the First* (Henry Bradshaw Society II) (London, 1892), pp. 110, 111, 112, 131, 133, 134.
6. *Sermons* V pp. 295f (whole sermon, pp. 259–298). This sermon was usually printed at the end of the early editions of the '96'.
7. *Absolution* p. 101.
8. See above n.1.
9. *ibid*. p. 84.
10. *ibid*. p.85.
11. *ibid*. pp. 89f.
12. *ibid*. p. 90. Compare these grounds for belief in Christ's presence with Richard Hooker's memorable assertion that 'God has deified our nature, though not by turning it to himself, yet by making it his own inseparable habitation', *Laws of Ecclesiastical Polity* V 54.5. See also Stevenson, *Covenant of Grace Renewed*, pp. 25ff. for a discussion of Hooker's sacramental theology in the context of Christology.
13. *ibid*. pp. 92f.

14. *ibid.* pp. 94.f
15. *ibid.* p. 96.
16. *ibid.* p. 97. Andrewes gives no citations to his 'ancient writers', but he will have been aware of the practice of canonical penance as described, for example, in Cyprian *Epistulae* 15 and 16, and Tertullian *De Paenitentia* 9; see Kenneth Stevenson, 'The Origins and Development of Ash Wednesday', in Kenneth Stevenson, *Worship: Wonderful and Sacred Mystery* (Washington: Pastoral Press, 1992) pp. 159–187.
17. See below n. 34.
18. *ibid.* p. 98. On 'conduit-pipes', see Stevenson, *Covenant of Grace Renewed*, p. 51 and nn. Henry Bullinger attacks the way 'the common sort of priests and monks' liken the sacraments to 'instruments, pipes, certain conduits of Christ's passion, by which the grace of Christ is conveyed and poured into us'; see *The Decades of Henry Bullinger* (Parker Society V) (Cambridge: University Press, 1852), pp. 296f. The *Decades* were made a text-book for the examination of the inferior clergy in 1587. I am indebted to Gordon Jeanes for drawing my attention to this. Andrewes is clearly running in the face of the unofficial 'official-line' of a previous generation. In this respect, he is following Hooker, *Laws of Ecclesiastical Polity* V 67.5 ('conducts of life and conveyances of his body and blood'); see Stevenson, *ibid.*, p. 28.
19. *ibid.* p. 100. Cf. the theme of repentance in the Ash Wednesday sermons, where a similar emphasis is made, see Lossky, *op.cit.* pp. 127–148.
20. *ibid.* p. 101.
21. *ibid.* p. 103.
22. See *Minor Works* p. lxii; referred to in Lossky *op.cit.* p. 15.
23. Quoted in Paul Johnson, *Elizabeth: A Study in Power and Intellect* (London: Weidenfeld and Nicolson, 1974) p. 41. Harington refers to Andrewes on one occasion being summoned by his patron (who was Walsingham), in the hope that Andrewes might temper his theological views with some judicious Puritanism, which Andrewes refused to do; see Harington, *op.cit.* p. 143.
24. *Sermons* V pp. 104–126.
25. See Lossky, *op.cit.* pp. 262–272; see also Stevenson, *op.cit.* pp. 26f and 50f.
26. Easter Sermon 18 (1624), *Sermons* III pp. 98f.
27. *Apospasmatia Sacra: or a collection of posthumous and orphan Lectures: delivered at St Pauls and St Giles his Church* (London: Hodgkinson, 1657). Some scholars have questioned how far these printed texts reflect what Andrewes preached, but the consensus seems to be emerging that they are authentic; Allchin's essay (see above n. 3) is based on some of them.
28. *ibid.* pp. 603, 606. For Harington's reference to 'upon occasion of some sermons', see above n. 4.
29. *ibid.* p. 630.
30. *Absolution* p. 84; cf. Whitsun 1 (1606), 3 (1610), 4 (1611), 5 (1612), 8 (1615), 9 (1616), 10 (1617), 11 (1618), 14 (1621), and 15 (1622), *Sermons* III pp. 113, 147, 163, 185, 242, 262, 284, 304f., 362, 378. On the question of Trinitarian theology, see, for example, Colin E. Gunton, *The Promise of Trinitarian Theology* (Edinburgh: T and T Clark, 1991); and Jürgen Moltmann, *The Spirit of Life: A Universal Affirmation* (London: S.C.M., 1992). An important foundational study in this regard is, of course, Geoffrey Wainwright, *Doxology: The Praise of God in Worship, Doctrine and Life – A Systematic Theology* (London: Epworth, 1980) pp. 15–146. The common misconception that the Reformers lacked interest in Trinitarian theology has been exposed in the recent essay by Christoph Schwöbel, 'The Triune God of Grace: Trinitarian thinking in the theology of the Reformers', in James M. Byrne (ed.), *The Christian Understanding of God Today* (Dublin: Columba Press, 1993) pp. 49–64, from which it is clear that Andrewes stands in good company, sharing a love of the Fathers, and the theological agenda (as he saw it) of his day.

31. Christmas 4 (1609), *Sermons* I p. 59. On this issue, see A. M. Allchin, *Participation in God: A Forgotten Strand in Anglican Tradition* (London: Darton, Longman, and Todd, 1988) pp. 7–23; and Lossky, *op.cit. passim.*

32. Whitsun 15 (1622), *Sermons* III p. 396.

33. Easter 12 (1617), *Sermons* II pp. 399ff.; Whitsun 10 (1617), *Sermons* III p. 296.

34. *Absolution* p. 97; cf. Whitsun 5 (1612), *Sermons* III p. 191.

35. Whitsun 4 (1611), *Sermons* III p. 177.

36. Whitsun 9 (1616), *Sermons* III pp. 261f; Whitsun 10 (1617), *Sermons* III p. 296; Easter 13 (1618), *Sermons* II pp. 426f.

37. *Apospasmatia* p. 657 (whole lecture, pp. 657–660).

38. *ibid.* pp. 187–192.

39. Whitsun 5 (1612), *Sermons* III p. 191; also Whitsun 4 (1611), *ibid.* p. 170. Lossky's discussion of the Whitsun sermons is perhaps the most penetrating and original part of his study, see *op.cit.* pp. 208–288.

40. See Welsby, *op.cit.* pp. 264ff.; cf. Lossky, *op.cit.* p. 7 n. 1, and also p. 139.

41. F. E. Brightman, *The Preces Privatae of Lancelot Andrewes, Bishop of Winchester* (London: Methuen, 1903), pp. 37.6, 213.7, 225.5, 122.31, 150.7ff., 160.25ff., for which see also Brightman's notes.

42. See *Minor Works* pp. 210ff. (prayers with the sick), p. 131 (1625 Visitation Articles).

43. See *Certain Sermons or Homilies Appointed to be read in Churches in the time of Queen Elizabeth of famous Memory* (1562) (London: S.P.C.K., 1843) p. 577 (whole homily, pp. 560–586). I am indebted to Colin Buchanan for drawing my attention to this.

44. See Edward Cardwell, *A History of Conferences and Other Proceedings connected with the Revision of the Books of Common Prayer* (Oxford: University Press, 1840) pp. 173f. (Hampton Court), 276 (House of Lords Committee), and 331f. (Savoy). When the objection was raised at Hampton Court before the King, he asked to be shown the text; after looking at it, he was satisfied with its character. (One wonders if Andrewes himself, already confidant of the King, had a hand in this.) On the absolution here, see F. E. Brightman, *The English Rite* II (London: Rivingtons, 1915) pp. 828f.: it is interesting to note that 1549 appends to the rubric on the absolution itself that 'the same form of absolution shall be used in all private confessions', an indication of the survival of the practice itself; this was deleted in 1552 and not restored thereafter. (The 1604 Canons make reference to the power of the keys in relation to excluding notorious offenders from Communion (Canon 26), and to absolving them (Canon 65), see *The Constitution and Canons Ecclesiastical and the Thirty-Nine Articles of the Church of England* (London: S.P.C.K., 1843), pp. 14f., 36f.)

45. Geoffrey Rowell, 'The Anglican Tradition: from the Reformation to the Oxford Movement', in Martin Dudley and Geoffrey Rowell (edd.), *Confession and Absolution* (London: S.P.C.K., 1988) pp. 91–119.

46. Rowell, 'The Anglican Tradition', p. 93.

47. Hooker, *Laws of Ecclesiastical Polity* V, 87.8. Rowell discusses the detailed treatment in *Laws* VI, 4.3 and 15, and 6.1–13; see 'The Anglican Tradition', pp. 97–100.

48. See Peter Stanwood and Daniel O'Connor, *John Cosin: A Collection of Private Devotions* (Oxford: Clarendon Press, 1967) pp. 235f. For Jeremy Taylor, discussed by Rowell, 'The Anglican Tradition', pp. 100f., see *Holy Dying* (London: Longmans, 1850) pp. 508ff. (Chapter 5, Section III).

49. Quoted by Rowell, 'The Anglican Tradition', p. 102. See *The Works of John Bramhall* V (Library of Anglo-Catholic Theology) (Oxford: Parker, 1845) pp. 213–4. Bramhall, however, uses Andrewes' list of baptism, eucharist, preaching and praying (though the latter two are inverted); cf. *Absolution* pp. 94f (see above n.14). He reproduces almost word for word the passage quoted from Andrewes on God's authority compared with the priest's, *ibid.* pp. 89f. (see above n. 11).

50. Rowell, 'The Anglican Tradition', pp. 108f.
51. For a recent study of mediaeval Catholic piety and practice, see Alexander Murray, 'Confession before 1215', in *Transactions of the Royal Historical Society* (Sixth Series III) (London: Royal Historical Society, 1993) pp. 51–81.
52. The literature on the Byzantine rite of penance is sparse: see Frans Van de Paverd, 'La penitence dans le rite byzantin', in *Questions Liturgiques* (1973) pp. 191–203; and also Paul Meyendorff, 'Penance in the Orthodox Church Today', *Studia Liturgica* 18 (1988) pp. 108–111.
53. For a discussion of public penance and reconciliation in the Reformed (and Puritan) traditions, see Bryan D Spinks, 'A Seventeenth-Century Reformed Liturgy of Penance and Reconciliation,' *Scottish Journal of Theology* 42 (1989) pp. 183–197.
54. See John Gunstone, *Pentecost Comes to the Church: Sacrament and Spiritual Gifts* (London: Darton, Longman, and Todd, 1994) chapters 14–16 (counsel and comfort) and 20 (forgiveness). I am indebted to Christopher Cocksworth for drawing my attention to this work.
55. See above n. 44. On the recent debate in the Church of England, see Gordon Jeanes, 'The formula of absolution "ego absolvo te" – a discussion of its function and proposals for its emendation', a paper submitted to the Liturgical Commission of the Church of England, April 1994. On the revision of the Roman rite, see Annibale Bugnini, *La riforma liturgica* (1948–1975) (Bibliotheca Ephemerides Liturgicae "Subsidia" 30) (Roma: Edizioni Liturgiche, 1983) pp. 646–664, esp. pp. 649ff., where he recounts the unsuccessful attempt by the revisers to gain approval for the official text to contain an absolution formula in which God is the performing agent. At the time of writing, the Liturgical Commission of the Church of England is preparing draft rites of reconciliation of both a collective and an individual character; of the two private rites, one has a declaratory 'I-formula' of absolution which has been drafted in order to express the life-giving power of the Spirit, as well as the sense of release from the bonds of sin – two salient features of the Andrewes sermon.
56. See above n. 1.

8

The Wesley Hymns on the Lord's Supper (1745) in History and Eucharistic Theology

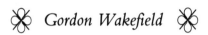 *Gordon Wakefield*

THE CHRISTIAN faith has been sung from the start. There have always been hymns in Christian worship, as is evidenced in the New Testament. Paul exhorts the Colossians, 'With psalms and hymns and spiritual songs sing from the heart in gratitude to God'. (Col. 3:16b; cf. Eph. 4:19) Discursive prose is not adequate to the Gospel. And in spite of the tragic element in Christianity, not least in the continuing centuries which seem to render so much of Christ's ministry void, there has always been and still remains, a lyricism past power of propositions. This is evident in the prolific writings of the late Hans Urs von Balthaser, full of the kenotic mystery of the Passion as they are. Singing may also unite a congregation, though, not always if the tunes are unknown, the words changed from the original, the sentiments alien. Dietrich Bonhoeffer wrote words with which John Wesley would have agreed, 'There is no place at the service of worship where vanity and bad taste can so intrude as in the singing'. Yet 'The heart sings because it is overflowing with Christ', a sentence which will remind Methodist of a Wesley hymn:

> My heart is full of Christ
> And longs its glorious matter to declare.[1]

Why do Christian sing when they are together? The reason is, quite simply, because in singing together it is possible for them to sing and pray the same Word at the same time ...

It is not you that sings, it is the Church that is singing, and you, as a member of the Church, may share in its song. Thus all singing together that is right, must serve to widen our spiritual horizon, make us see our little company as a member of the great Christian Church on earth, and help us willingly and gladly to join our singing, be it feeble or good, to the song of the Church.

Wesley would emphasis, recurrently, that the Church is not only the company on earth. We join with the whole company of heaven. As a Hymn on the Lord's Supper has it:

> The Church triumphant in thy love,
> Their mighty joys we know;
> They sing the Lamb in hymns above,
> And we in hymns below.
>
> Thee in thy glorious realm they praise,
> And bow before thy throne;
> We in the kingdom of thy grace,
> The kingdoms are but one.[2]

In the Catholic tradition, hymns belong to the Office, especially the great Canticles of Scripture and the *Te Deum* in the West, often in plainsong, but there is a tendency to regard them as intrusions in the liturgy apart from the *Kyries*, the *Gloria in Excelsis*, the *Sanctus*, and the *Agnus Dei*. They have been inserted somewhat uneasily from the nineteenth-century onwards in response to popular demand, possibly created by their predominance in evangelicalism including Methodism, though the influence of Keble's *The Christian Year* must not be discounted, product of a conflict within himself between romanticism and mistrust of enthusiasm. They seem to be used chiefly to cover movement, as introits, or at the offertory, or as opportunity to consume what is left of the elements, though, significantly for our subject, they now often have place in parish worship as devotions at the communion of the people, to edify and offer praise during the period of waiting. Some, like the eminent man of letters, C. S. Lewis, simply do not like hymns, (W. H. Auden loved them), while one feels that many pure liturgists regard them as an embarrassment, reducing worship to 'Songs of Praise', caricatured as the 'hymn sandwich'. Added to which, the traditional hymns seem threatened by modern songs and choruses, some mantra-like, which may be more congenial to the young than the poetic and musical expressions of classical theology.

It is in the evangelical tradition and among the sects that hymns have been indispensable expressions of people's praise. Chorales are at the heart of Lutheranism and there could have been no Bach without Luther. The persecuted have sung to affirm faith amid all griefs, when reason would have denied God, as did the Jews in the death-trains on the way to Auschwitz, celebrating the day when they would feast upon Leviathan. In the sixteenth-century, the Amish Mennonites, refugees to the new world from persecution in the old, produced one of the earliest hymn books. Admittedly, they rejected Catholic organisation and sacramental theology and embraced a wide range of doctrine from the Trinity to Unitarianism. Much of the hymnody of the persecuted and under-ground was in the tradition of Bernard of Clairvaux, and of an intense Jesus-piety. The German Pietists of the seventeenth-century and after were no sect but a movement of mystical and evangelical religion in reaction to Lutheran scholasticism. They were, however, in the Bernardine tradition, as instanced in the hymns of Paul Gerhardt (1617–76), which helped to sustain Dietrich Bonhoeffer in prison in our own century. They owed much to the English Puritans, whose devotions were more tender than might be supposed, and influenced John Wesley and the Methodists, largely through the Moravians.

There were Protestants, and indeed some far back in Augustine's day, who deplored music in worship as a sensual distraction, while others believed that to sing composed hymns was as misguided as to read prayers. Hymns should be immediate, spontaneous expressions of the Spirit. But Protestantism generally came to take seriously the precedent of Christ and his disciples at the end of the Last Supper, 'When they had sung a hymn, they went out to the Mount of Olives' (Mark 14.26). This was scrip-tural warrant. This is why Cranmer felt that his 1552 Communion Service should conclude with a hymn and why, in default of any gift for writing hymns himself and because Psalms and Canticles were used earlier in the full service of Matins, Litany and Communion, he transferred the *Gloria in Excelsis* to its unique Anglican place at the end, not the beginning, of the Eucharist. W. H. Frere believed that this 'makes a more balanced service than the Latin one is, one which comes to a climax, as no other rite does, of an uplifting kind, and ends with a chorus of praise'. (Not a sentiment Cranmer's detractors would allow themselves.) Frere would have regretted the return of the Gloria to its traditional position in more modern revisions.[3] At the end of the seventeenth century, the Baptists, Benjamin Keach and Joseph Stennett, under the authority of the same scripture, were convinced that hymns were appropriate to the Sacrament. Against some opposition the latter published, in 1697, the first collection of Hymns on the Lord's Supper. Isaac Watts was to follow with communion hymns, one overwhelmingly great, to be sung world-wide, 'When I survey the wondrous cross', another now found in Anglican as well as Free Church books, 'Nature with open volume stands'. Both very much regard the Supper as a shewing forth of Christ's death, though they view the sacrifice of Christ, the work of God, in the context of 'the whole realm of nature'. This is seen in Stennett's undistinguished stanzas.

> Lord, all the works thy hand has formed
>   In earth and heaven above
> And all thy tracks of providence
>   Show thee a God of love.
>
> But thy surprising acts of grace
>   To Adam's guilty seed
> Loudly proclaim to all the world
>   That God is love indeed.

From the beginning, in 1738, of the Methodist Revival, part, it must not be forgotten, of the wider Evangelical Revival, which owed its inception to George Whitefield two years earlier, the more hospitable Parish Churches were used by Methodists. Their own buildings came a little later. The churches could be thronged at Methodist Communion Services. Admission was controlled, but there is reliable evidence that in some places congregations numbered more than one thousand. At St Patrick's Cathedral, Dublin, they have still communion vessels which had specially to be made to accommodate the Methodists. Communion became a focus of fellowship, a 'confirming ordinance' and a 'converting ordinance'. John Wesley justified the last, not only by what actually happened in the revival, but by the fact that the disciples themselves were unconverted when the Eucharist was instituted and they first received it on the betrayal night.

Communicants came and knelt at the altar rails. The Reformed custom of receiving in their pews as though seated at table – deplored in the previous century by George Herbert as claiming apostolic status rather than approaching as penitents – was not followed. Distribution in both kinds took a very long time, especially if communion was not continuous but 'in tables', which became the Wesleyan custom and still remains, though larger attendances at communion have resulted in some places in what is regarded as the Anglican custom. Services could last for five hours.

The services would not be choral in the Cathedral sense nor use settings of the Mass. This would be contrary to the eighteenth-century Church of England ethos as well as to that of the revivalist atmosphere, in which the Tractarian divines of the next century would have been altogether ill-at-ease, and perhaps Wesley too by instinct, since he believed that the Sacrament was the most awesome of services and to be approached with the utmost reverence. To fill the time of waiting, avoid distractions and contain enthusiasm, which, left to itself, might have found unedifying expressions, the Wesleys, chiefly Charles, the prolific hymnographer, wrote a series of hymns. They were published in 1745 and became best-sellers, going through ten editions by 1794, above all other Wesley collections. The hymns would also be used at private services of Communion where there might be fewer than forty present. Dr Bowmer has claimed that this introduction of hymns did much to prepare for the revival of choral communion services usually attributed to the Oxford Movement.[4] As well as keeping rapture within bounds, they relieved by liveliness and joy the dreariness of much eighteenth-century liturgy, both Church of England and Nonconformist.

The *Hymns on the Lord's Supper* are prefaced with an abridged version of a seventeenth-century treatise, *The Christian Sacrament and Sacrifice* (1672) by Daniel Brevint (1616–95).[5] He was a Jersey-man and an exile in France during the Commonwealth, where his Anglicanism was strengthened both against Rome and French Protestantism. He, already a French Reformed Pastor, his degree incorporated at Oxford, after some dispute, received Anglican orders in Paris, and became chaplain to Marshall Turenne's wife and daughter for whom *The Christian Sacrifice and Sacrament* was written in French. Charles II met him in Paris and on his return to England at the Restoration, he was given the living of Brancepeth in Durham and made a Prebendary. He became Dean of Lincoln in 1681. It is significant that the Wesleys were Lincolnshire men from Epworth Rectory. They may have been familiar with their late Dean's work through proximity.

Brevint's treatise belongs to the rich genre of Caroline euch-aristic devotion. Brevint was fiercely anti-Roman but there is nothing here of Zwinglianism or the 'real absence' as in Dod-dridge's eighteenth-century work, *The Rise and Practice of Religion in the Soul*, or of the Eucharist as a simple fellowship meal. Brevint believes in the Real Presence of Christ in the Sacrament. It is Christ he meets there 'not a bare *representation* or *remembrance*',[6] but, like Hooker in Book V of *The Laws of Ecclesiastical Polity*, he is agnostic about the mode.

> I come then to God's Altar, with a full persuasion that these words, *This is my body*, promise me more than a *figure*; that this holy banquet is not a bare *memorial* only, but may actu-ally *convey* as many blessings to me, as it brings curses on the profane receiver. Indeed, in what manner it is done, I know not; it is enough for me to admire. *One thing I know*, said the blind man of our Lord, *He laid clay upon my eyes, and behold I see.*[7]

The bread of the Eucharist is like the clay of the miracle. Above all, Brevint's doctrine of the Eucharistic Sacrifice shows an under-standing, praised by Waterland in the next century, which might have saved much Reformation controversy. In some ways, he echoes fifth century Theodore of Mopseuestia and anticipates twentieth-century Casel and de la Taille. '... this sacrifice, which by a *real* oblation was not to be offered more than once, is, by a devout and thankful commemoration to be offered up every day.'[8] Stevenson thinks that Brevint, given his origins in the Reformed Church, may well have owed something to the High Calvinist treatise of Philippe du Plessis-Mornay of Saumur, 'On the institution, use and doctrine of the sacrament of the holy eucharist in the ancient church' (1598). Many of his expressions and phrases are found in Brevint, 'in the insistence of the vivid character of the memorial, the centrality of the cross, and the biblical language of sacrifice that make an integral connection between ourselves and Christ.'[9] It is something of an irony that through the Anglican Brevint, the Wesleys, so vehemently opposed to Calvinism as they experienced it, should have assimilated something of its eucharistic tradition.

Brevint's influence on the Wesley hymns must not be disregarded as has been a tendency of some Methodist scholars, in a desire to claim their originality. Sometimes they are treated without reference to Brevint. Many of the hymns are paraphrases of *The Christian Sacrament and Sacrifice* though two are unhappy bowdlerisations of George Herbert's 'The Invitation' and 'The Banquet'. The hymns follow Brevint's divisions of the subject, though reduced from eight to six, in effect five – John Wesley had a positive lust for abridgement – and make his theology their own.[10]

Wesley's organisation is this:

I   As (the Lord's Supper) is a Memorial of the Sufferings and Death of Christ.
II   As it is a Sign and Means of Grace (the longest section).
III The Sacrament a Pledge of Heaven.
IV   The Holy Eucharist as it implies a Sacrifice.
V   Concerning the Sacrifice of our Persons.
VI   After the Sacrament. (There is no corresponding section in Brevint).

The Memorial

Ought not then one who looks on these ordinances, and considers the great and dreadful passages which they set

before him, to say in his heart, I observe on the Altar somewhat very like the Sacrifice of my Saviour! For thus the Bread
of Life was broken: thus the Lamb of God was slain and his
Blood shed. And when I look on the minister, who by special
order from God distributes this bread and this wine, I
conceive that thus God himself hath both given his Son to
die, and gives us still the virtue of his death.[11]

For Wesley, the elements are not seen as the fruits of creation to
be offered to God. There is no offertory procession with its
accompanying theology of creation and industry as has become so
fashionable, though technology and economics alike may make
the latter less realistic. The current vogue in some quarters for
Creation Spirituality has made this dominant in some Eucharists.
For Wesley and Brevint, as the Book of Common Prayer enjoins,
the elements are already on the Altar at the start of the service.
They represent God's hospitality rather than our offering, –
though in his *Missale Romanum*, an attack on the Mass, Brevint
follows Augustine and describes the whole Eucharist as offering
and receiving, stressing that the bread and wine are the people's
offering to be received back when consecrated. 'And really the
whole service was little more than a continued oblation. For
Christians before the Sacrament offered their gifts and after it
offered their prayers, their praises and themselves.[12] In the *Christian
Sacrament and Sacrifice* and the Wesley hymns, the elements are,
above all, signs of Christ's sufferings and death. Our offering of
them is transcended by this.

> In this expressive death I see
> The wheat by man cut down for me,
> And beat, and bruised, and ground:
> The heavy plagues, and pains, and blows,
> Which Jesus suff'd from his foes,
> Are in this emblem found. (2)

Through his sufferings 'both from man and God', 'to reverse our
doom', the Lord becomes the Bread of Life. (It is interesting that,
following Brevint, Wesley in one stanza calls Jesus, 'The Martyr'.)
    This sacrifice is ever new, eternally present. In the Sacrament we

are there at Calvary. We have communion with Christ's death, which we 'mournfully' enjoy, as though we had stood beneath his cross.

> Thy offering still continues new,
> Thy vesture keeps its bloody hue,
> Thou stand'st the ever slaughtered Lamb,
> Thy priesthood still remains the same,
> Thy years, O God, can never fail,
> Thy goodness is unchangeable.

> O that our faith may never move
> But stand unshaken as thy love!
> Sure evidence of things unseen,
> Now let it pass the years between,
> and view thee bleeding on the tree,
> My God, who dies for me, for me! (5)

It is the Holy Spirit who brings the Passion of Christ to mind and exposes 'to all our senses his sufferings as if they were present now'.[13] Wesley has a hymn which echoes the epiclesis of the *Apostolic Constitutions* (c. 375) and calls the Holy Spirit 'the witness of the sufferings of the Lord Jesus'.[14]

> Come, Thou witness of his dying,
> Come, Remembrancer Divine
> Let us feel thy power applying
> Christ to every soul and mine;
> Let us groan thine inward groaning,
> Look on him we pierced and grieve,
> All receive the grace atoning
> All the sprinkled blood receive. (16)

One hymn on the Memorial has but slight influence of Brevint. 'Lamb of God whose bleeding love/We thus recall to mind'. It is derived from the Agnus Dei, the Litany and the Gloria in Excelsis. It places beside our remembrance a plea to Christ to remember his sacrifice.

> O remember Calvary,
> And bid us go in peace.

The final verse expresses reluctance to leave the Sacrament until there is forgiveness written on our hearts and the complete image of God restored. Here is the longing for perfection in holiness, the Wesleys' 'grand depositum' of their teaching.(20) The Sacrament is a means towards this.

There follows another hymn, of which the first three of eight stanzas are outstanding. Calvary is the death of God. We are its spectators in the Sacrament. It is a mystery beyond all knowledge, the incomparable act, before which we prostrate ourselves in wondering love.

> Never love nor sorrow was
> Like that my Jesus show'd
> See him stretched on yonder cross,
> And crushed beneath our load,
> Now discern the Deity,
> Now his heavenly birth declare;
> Faith cries out, 'Tis he, 'tis he,
> My God, tht suffers there. (21)

The Means of Grace

> In his sermon on 'The Means of Grace', John Wesley defined these as Outward signs, words or actions ordained of God and appointed for this end – to be the *ordinary* channels whereby he might convey to men preventing, justifying, sanctifying grace.[15].

For the hymns, as for Brevint, the Eucharist is the means of grace, supreme above all others:

> The prayer, the fast, the word conveys,
> When mix'd with faith, thy life to me
> In all the channels of thy grace
> I still have fellowship with thee:
> But chiefly here my soul is fed
> With fulness of immortal bread. (54)

This is due to the institution of Christ, the imperative, 'Do this in remembrance of me', of which Wesley had no reason to dispute the authenticity.

> If Jesus bids me lick the dust,
> I bow at his command. (86)

At this point, Wesley is attacking the Moravians, some of whom embraced a cult of 'stillness', which disparaged the outward signs and exercises of Christianity, and solitarily waited on God. Not so Wesley:

> Because he saith, *Do this*,
> This I will always do
> Till Jesus comes in glorious bliss,
> I thus his death will *show* (ibid.)

The souls in the wilderness languish for the Bread of life, the hungry for the Banqueting house. Yet here is our life and health and peace, the satisfaction of our desires, the way to Christ's 'special presence'. (81) The means whereby Christ comes in the Eucharist is a mystery:

> Who shall say how bread and wine
> God into man conveys!
> Sure and real is the grace,
> The manner be unknown;
> Only meet us in thy ways,
> And perfect us in one.
> Let us taste the heavenly powers;
> Lord we ask for nothing more:
> Thine to bless, 'tis only ours
> To wonder and adore. (57)

There is, however, an epiclesis among the Wesley hymns, the affirmation as in the Eastern Church that it is the Holy Spirit who effects the mystery when we observe Christ's institution:

> Come Holy Ghost, thine influence shed,
> And realize the sign;
> Thy life infuse into the bread,
> Thy power into the wine.

> Effectual let the tokens prove,
> And made by heavenly art,
> Fit channels to convey thy love
> To every faithful heart.

The sign is not external and dead, even if we may not feel the presence. The hymn 86 against the Moravians and 'stillness' attacks their belief that unless we feel emotion and Divine revelation the Sacrament is vain. The Supper is an objective act and its validity is in Christ's institution. But often there is rapture in a banquet intended for all humankind – no Calvinism here.

> In rapturous bliss
> He bids us do this,
> The joy it imparts
> Hath witnessed his gracious design in our hearts.

> O that all men would haste
> To the spiritual feast,
> At Jesus's word
> *Do this*, and be fed with the love of our Lord.

> Bring near the glad day
> When all shall obey
> The dying request,
> And eat of thy supper and lean on thy breast.

> To all men impart
> One way and one heart,
> Thy people be shown
> All righteous and spotless and perfect in One.

> Then, then let us see
> Thy glory, and be
> Caught up in the air
> This heavenly supper in heaven to share. (92)

As the Methodist 1975 Sunday Service prays, the Supper is a foretaste of the heavenly banquet prepared for all mankind. One of the finest hymns, singable today without alteration, paraphrases Brevint in *Missale Romanum* and echoes also the Leonine and Gregorian Sacramentaries.

Sacraments are veils which conceal God as well as revealing him for no more than Moses could we bear the sight of the Divine glory. But in the fullness of life with Christ, the veil will be removed, sacraments will be done away, and we shall feast in the immediate glory of God.

Author of life Divine,
Who hast a table spread,
Furnish'd with mystic wine
And everlasting bread,
Preserve the life thyself has given,
And feed and train us up for heaven.

Our needy souls sustain
With fresh supplies of love,
Till all thy life we gain,
And all thy fulness prove,
And strengthened by thy perfect grace,
Behold without a veil thy face.

A Pledge of Heaven

It is interesting that Wesley, more than Brevint, uses the word 'taste' with regard to the Eucharist. This, says Geoffrey Wainwright, 'is much rarer in eucharistic liturgies and theologies than one might have expected; but its value as an expression for the relation between the "already" and the "not yet" is undeniable.'[16]

One of the hymns says

Here he gives our souls a taste
Heaven into our hearts he pours (103)

Charles Wesley does use the metaphor of taste elsewhere. In the section 'For Believers Rejoicing' in the 1780 Collection, there is a hymn (197), first published in 1749 in 'Hymns and Sacred Poems', which exults in the possession of Christ and dances to the sound of Jesus' name.

Yet onward I haste, To the heavenly feast;
That, that is the fullness, but this is the taste.

There is no mention of the Eucharist, any more than in the Wesleys' Conversion hymn where forgiveness is called 'this antepast of heaven'. (1780 Collection 29) But, clearly, the metaphor is particularly appropriate to the eating and drinking of the Supper.

How glorious is the life above,
Which in this ordinance we *taste*;
That fulness of celestial love
That joy which shall forever last! (101)

The Saviour himself has *tasted* death (100), has we may say, eaten
the bread of affliction and drunk the cup of God's wrath and
thereby has departed from our sight into heaven, but has left
behind his sacramental pledge, to which we will hold on until his
return in the clouds. This will be our welcome home, received
into the arms of the Friend of sinners, who, when he knew he was
going to die, was offering himself totally to God, pledged himself
to his disciples in the Supper. And this we shall ever recall in
heaven.

The metaphor of the pledge recurs in the hymns as does the
translation of the Greek, *arrabon*, 'earnest', though Brevint points
out that an earnest is a part of a promised payment which will be
received in full later, whereas a pledge is not needed once it is
fulfilled. So the graces God bestows in his Sacraments are an
earnest of what will remain and be completed in the happiness of
heaven, while 'the Sacrament's themselves shall be taken back and
shall no more appear in heaven than the cloudy pillar in Canaan.[17]

The Supper fulfils the prayer of John 17 that Christ's disciples
may be perfected in One, which is the life of heaven. It also unites
the Church on earth and heaven, as we saw earlier.

Lift your eyes of faith, and see
Saints and angels joined in one,
What a countless company
Stands before yon dazzling throne! (105)

The saints begin the heavenly Gloria and the morning stars reply
in an antiphon of praise. The angels pay homage, at first prostrate
in silence, but then they join the hymn in a mighty shout of praise.

The Supper is the place of meeting with the departed. No psychic
sessions or medium's contract are needed. Hymn 106 is a paraphrase of Revelation 7.13–17. 'What are these arrayed in white?'
The Eucharist is not specifically mentioned, but in the Sacrament
we are like the seer listening to the chorus of the innumerable host.

The Lord's coming is not attached to any specific point in the liturgy. The hymns make clear that the Eucharist antedates the final advent. There is an echo of the cherubic hymn of the Orthodox Liturgy of St James:

> Faith ascends the mountain's height,
> Now enjoys the pompous sight,
> Antedates the final doom,
> Sees the Judge in glory come.
>
> Lo, he comes triumphant down,
> Seated on his great white throne!
> Cherubs bear it on their wings,
> Shouting bear the king of kings. (98)

The very first hymn of this section describes the Supper, on which we are nourished with living bread, as an occasion when

> We now are at his table fed
> But wait to see our heavenly King;
> To see the great Invisible
> Without a sacramental veil,
> With all his robes of glory on
> In rapturous joy and love and praise
> Him to behold with open face,
> High on his everlasting throne.

The wine which shows Christ's passion will soon be drunk new in the 'dazzling courts above' at the marriage supper of the Lamb. By faith and hope we are already there. 'Suffering and curse and death are o'er'/and pain afflicts the soul no more'. We are 'habour'd in the Saviour's breast', 'safe in the arms of Jesus' as the later evangelical hymn was to say. The imagery is of tenderest intimacy, not erotic, almost of child and parent. (93)

The Sacrifice

Wesley does not fail to affirm the once-for-allness of Calvary, the death that never can be repeated.

> Thy blood hath paid our utmost price,
> Thine all-sufficient sacrifice
> Remains eternally alone.

> Yet may we celebrate below,
> And daily thus thine offering show
> Exposed before thy Father's eyes;
> In this tremendous mystery
> Present thee bleeding on a tree
> Our everlasting Sacrifice. (124)

The next hymn, 125, is the best-known and most influential and, some would say, the most dangerous of all on this subject. It influenced William Bright, the Oxford Church historian's hymn towards the end of the next century, 'And now, O Father, mindful of the love/That bought us once for all on Calvary's tree'.

> With solemn faith we offer up,
> And spread before thy glorious eyes
> That only ground of all our hope,
> That precious, bleeding Sacrifice
> Which brings thy grace on sinners down,
> And perfects all our souls in one.

Neither Wesley nor Brevint would see this as going beyond St Paul's declaration. 'You show forth the Lord's death until he come' (I Cor. 11.26). Some would say that this is parallel, in Jewish manner to *anamnesis*, 'Do this in remembrance of me.'[18] (Cf. G. D. Kilpatrick, *The Eucharist in Bible and Liturgy* Cambridge 1983 12–27) What we remember, proclaim, is Christ's sacrifice and by so doing we offer it to God, not by repeating Calvary but by re-presenting the One Sacrifice. This could have assonances with Jeremias's interpretation, 'Do this that God may remember me and act.'[19] For Wesley this would mean, 'By the merits of Christ's Sacrifice may God bring to us the fulness of his Grace'.

> Father behold thy dying Son
> And hear his blood that speaks above;
> On us let all thy grace be shown,
> Peace, righteousness, and joy, and love
> Thy kingdom come to every heart
> And all thou hast and all thou art.

Another hymn, still sung in part, both by Anglicans and Methodists, is that with which the section on Sacrifice begins,

'Victim Divine, thy grace we claim/While thus thy precious death we show' (116). This paraphrases Brevint very closely, though the following paragraph is found in Brevint's section on the Means of Grace whereas Wesley's hymn is under the heading, 'The Holy Eucharist as it implies a Sacrifice'.

> This Victim having been offered up in the fulness of time and in the midst of the world which is Christ's great temple and having been thence carried up to heaven, which is his sanctuary; from thence spreads salvation all around as the burnt-offering did its smoke. And thus his body and blood have everywhere but especially at this Sacrament a true and real Presence. When he offered himself up on earth, the vapour of his atonement went up and darkened the very sun; and by rending the great veil, it clearly showed that he had made a way into heaven. And since he is gone up, he sends down to earth the graces that spring continually both from his everlasting sacrifice and from the continual intercession that attends it. So that we need not say, *Who will go up into heaven?* since without either ascending or descending, this sacred Body of Jesus fills with atonement and blessing the remotest part of this temple.[20]

Almost every allusion there, every figure, drawn from the Old Testament, is found in Wesley's hymn, together with others, such as the sweet smell of Noah's sacrifice which was well pleasing to God (Gen. 8.21) and is a type of Christ's, which fills the worship on earth, 'these lower courts', 'with divine perfumes'. There is the universality of Christ's sacrifice, offered not in the temple of the Jews but in the whole earth. The atonement reaches all humankind. It rends the veil between heaven and earth. Wesley describes Jesus Christ as 'standing' before the throne of God, his once for all sacrifice not an event of the past, but as though it were offered now as he pleads for helpless human beings. And so,

> We need not now go up to heaven
> To bring the long-sought Saviour down;
> Thou art to all already given,
> Thou doest e'en now thy banquet crown
> To every faithful soul appear,
> And show thy real presence here.

The Orthodox believe that the Eucharist, the Liturgy, is our entrance into heaven. Brevint and Wesley rather suggest that because Christ's Sacrifice rends the veil which separates earth from heaven, its representation brings heaven to us and and we are joined with it without doing any more than obeying Christ's command. There is a distinction without a difference.

This Sacrifice is the great objective act of God in Christ in which is all our hope of that union with God which is 'pardon and holiness and heaven' (111), perfect love, but Brevint says 'Too many who are called Christians live as if under the Gospel there were no sacrifice but that of Christ on the Cross'.[21] His argument is well summed up by Henry H. Knight III:

> The effect of Christ's atonement was not to make our own sacrifice unnecessary but to make it acceptable to God; 'though the sacrifice of ourselves cannot *produce* salvation, yet it is altogether needful to our *receiving* it'. Faithful participants in the Lord's Supper are thus at one and the same time 'faithful disciples', of Christ their Master, 'true members of Christ their Head, and 'penitent sinners' saved by Christ alone. The necessity of a response counters antinomian complacency; the insistence that participants remain penitent sinners counters the illusions of perfectionism'.[22]

The whole Church is a sacrifice, offered with Christ. 'Christ and his Church are one'. (129)

> Would the Saviour of mankind
> Without his people die?
> No, to hm we are all join'd
> As more than standers by,
> Freely as the Victim came
> To the altar of his cross,
> We attend the slaughtered Lamb,
> And suffer for his cause. (131)

As Knight also says, 'There is an interplay of the necessity of suffering love and the joy of our salvation running through this collection of hymns.'[23]

There is also individual consecration, for instance in a hymn to the Trinity, which may have influenced Frances Ridley Havergal's more widely sung, 'Take my life and let it be'. Here is Wesley,

> Take my soul and body's powers,
> Take my memory, mind, and will,
> All my goods, and all my hours,
> All I know and all I feel,
> All I think, and speak, and do;
> Take my heart – but make it new.

> Now, O God, thine own I am,
> Now I give thee back thine own.
> Freedom, friends, and health, and fame,
> Consecrate to thee alone;
> Thine I live, thrice happy I,
> Happier still if thine I die. (155)

Post-Communion

These are hymns of thanksgiving, one a paraphrase of the Gloria with the Book of Common Prayer Eucharist in mind. There is no dismissal into the world as in the Roman Mass or modern liturgies, which some would think should be open-ended, though the Sacrament is clearly related to the whole of life and its relationships. But all revolves around Christ and what God has done in him. The final hymn is a long poem celebrating the early Christians who first obeyed the Lord's command. The Wesleys are convinced that they 'every joyful day received/The tokens of expiring love' and beg God to restore the daily sacrifice, which in this mood, Wesley believes is the secret of the world's salvation.

A modern liturgist would criticise both Brevint and Wesley for the Western medievalism which concentrates the Eucharist on the cross. It is strange that Wesley in one hymn bids us think of Peter and John racing to the tomb on Easter Day:

> Swift, as their rising Lord to find
> The two disciples ran,
> I seek the Saviour of mankind,
> Nor shall I seek in vain.

> Come all who long his face to see
> That did our burden bear,
> Hasten to *Calvary* with me,
> And we shall find him there. (55)

The strength of this position is not only that St Paul and the Synoptists focus the institution on the death of Jesus, but also in the fact that there is no Resurrection without the Cross and that we may not find the empty tomb until we are aware of the crucified body which it had contained. There is one Easter hymn, which recalls the bread broken in Emmaus, preceded by the opening of the Scriptures and prays that our hearts may burn, our zeal enkindled, so that we 'feel/That God and love are one'. (29)

It may be argued that the triumphant, eschatological note implies the Resurrection. Though the hymns have a awesome realism in describing Christ's sufferings so that we return to Golgotha and watch the sacred blood drip to the ground, we are not thereby left with a corpse but rather with the glorified body of him who waits, interceding for us in the company of saints and angels and whose victory we already share in the eucharistic feast.

The frequent mention of blood may repel some, but one detects that it is not repellent in every context and perhaps less in our time when we see it flowing on our screens and transfusions are everyday and there are earnest appeals for donors. Some feminists feel that women's experience should make society more aware of the effect their cycle should have on their understanding of human life and their religious experience. Even so, some of the hymns are not suitable for public singing today. Both John and Charles Wesley referred to the Eucharist as 'the unbloody sacrifice', but, as Kenneth Stevenson has written, the emphasis on 'the bleeding love and mercy' of the crucified Christ is so powerful in the hymns that there is little room for another motif.[24]

For different reasons, some hymns were an embarrassment to Methodists from the first, 'O God of our forefathers hear' has never been included in the Holy Communion section of any Methodist hymnbook even the 1983 *Hymns and Psalms*. I suppose it has been thought suitable as a prayer for general grace and the intercession of Christ apart from the eucharistic reference. And the

Hymns on the Lord's Supper tended to be ignored by nineteenth-century Methodists because of the Catholic revival which thrust Methodists into the Free Church camp, and their discovery by Anglo-Catholic controversialists, who gave them a Roman Catholic interpretation.

It is doubtful if many of the early Methodists who sang them so lustily at crowded communions would absorb their doctrines. The services themselves may have been chiefly rallies of enthusiasts and occasions of fellowship. An intense and central eucharistic piety was not possible for eighteenth-century Methodists.[25]

Even Charles Wesley was not wholly consistent, as we have implied, in his use of the metaphor of 'taste', nor always with regard to the Eucharist. As. W. F. Lofthouse wrote,

> His passion and jealousy for the Lord's Supper were lifelong. If he thought that it, or the Church that administered it, were threatened, he took up arms in its defence as if it were the very citadel of the Christian life. But if he were dealing with the real evangelical doctrine of justification by faith, the Sacrament might be unmentioned.[26]

There are hymns in the 1745 Wesley collection as in Brevint's *The Christian Sacrifice and Sacrament* which could feed modern sacramental devotion and bring healing to our divisions. Geoffrey Wainwright in *Doxology* (1979), a treatment of 'the liturgical way of doing theology', has shown how there is a two-way current from worship to doctrine and back again. He uses the Wesley hymns to illustrate that, like creeds, hymns may be 'first-order' expressions of religious faith. They go beyond the purely rational and logical, use figures and images which would be too daring for prose, and celebrate paradox (op.cit. 191ff). The mystery of the Eucharist demands poetry. Prose – except the poetic prose of a Hooker or a Dix – has caused contention through literalism, persecution, even war. Poetry, especially when sung, lifts our hearts from the Holy Table to the Heavenly Altar and to those things which angels long to see into.

NOTES

1. A Collection of Psalms and Hymns 1743.
2. Bonhoeffer *Life Together* Eng. trans. (London, 1954) pp. 48–51; cf John Wesley's *Directions* for Singing 1761, in F. Hildebrandt and O. A. Beckerlegge eds. *A Collection of Hymns for the People called Methodists* (Oxford, 1983) p. 761; *Hymns on the Lord's Supper* 96.
3. J. H. Arnold and G. P. Wyatt eds. *Walter Howard Frere: A Collection of His Papers on Liturgical and Historical Subjects* (Alcuin Club Collections No. 35 London, 1940) p. 134f.
4. John C. Bowmer, *The Sacrament of the Lord's Supper in Early Methodism* (Westminster, 1951) p. 84.
5. There is a study of him in Kenneth Stevenson *The Covenant of Grace Renewed* (London, 1994), pp. 98–107. Cf. the same author's *Eucharist and Offering* (Collegeville, 1986), p. 259, n. 74; 260 n. 98 where, however, the main treatment in the text is of the Wesleys, p.167–70.
6. *op.cit.* Section IV. See J. Ernest Rattenbury, *The Eucharistic Hymns of John and Charles Wesley* (London, 1948) p. 182.
7. *ibid.*
8. *ibid.* VI, Rattenbury 186f.
9. Stevenson *op.cit.* 105.
10. Cf. Henry H. Knight III, *The Presence of God in the Christian Life: John Wesley and the Means of Grace* (Metchen NJ & London, 1992) p. 136ff.
11. *ibid* II 5. Rattenbury 177.
12. Quoted Stevenson *op.cit.* 100.
13. Brevint II 4; Rattenbury 177.
14. Jasper and Cuming eds. *Prayers of the Eucharist: Early and Reformed* (New York, 1980), p. 75.
15. *The Works of John Wesley ed. Thomas Jackson* 1829–1831 1 381.
16. G. Wainwright *Eucharist and Eschatology* (London, 1971) p. 196.
17. Brevint V:1:Rattenbury 184.
18. I Cor. 11.24.
19. J. Jeremias, *The Eucharstic Words of Jesus* (Oxford revised edn 1966) pp. 237–55.
20. IV; 5: Rattenbury 183.
21. V11:1: Rattenbury 188.
22. *op.cit.* 145. The quotations are Brevint vii/1, Rattenbury 188/Brevint vii/10; Rattenbury 190.
23. *op.cit.* 143.
24. Gerard Austin OP, *Fountain of Life* (Washington D.C., 1991) p. 122: See John Wesley Jackson ed. *Works* x 121.
25. Cf. Henry D. Rack *Reasonable Enthusiast: John Wesley and the Rise of Methodism* 199f.; pp. 417–19.

9

The Oxford Movement and Science: The Word in Scripture and Nature in the Nineteenth-Century Catholic Revival

R. William Franklin

SCIENCE AND CATHOLICISM were both major challenges to the status quo in the Church of England in the nineteenth century; orthodoxy was challenged 'by strange fashions of speech' in science and theology according to Charles Gore in his introduction to the influential series of essays *Lux Mundi* of 1889.[1] In the nineteenth century the popular impression was conveyed that religion itself had been discredited by science and that the substitution of ancient world-views by those of modern science made it unnecessary any longer to trouble about the Christian estimate of the human. And when Gore mentioned 'strange fashions of speech' he was also pointing to the Anglican Catholic revival which began with the Oxford Movement, 1833–1845. A leader of the Oxford Movement to be considered here, E. B. Pusey (1800–1882), and his successors to be considered here, R. W. Church (1815–1890) and Charles Gore (1853–1932), as well as the *Lux Mundi* school, each conveyed the impression that they were upholding the Catholic tradition within the Church of England and reintroducing the people of England to a forgotten heritage. From 1833 two generations of Anglicans argued that the established church in Britain was not the *Protestant* church *of* England, but the *Catholic* church *in* England, and they fashioned their theology into an instrument for a second, and Catholic, reformation. The relation of this resurgence of Catholicism to science is key to understanding the intellectual tradition within which Donald Gray's own work has flourished.

In the nineteenth century the Church of England was faced with a fundamental crisis provoked by the historical criticism of Scripture and the development of a scientific, evolutionary worldview, both of which seemed to undercut two foundations of theistic belief.[2] The first was William Paley's evidential school of natural theology which gained wide popularity after 1794. Paley provided the theological matrix for a mechanistic understanding of direct creation. 'Can you look at the different orders and species which nature presents to you,' Paley asked in a summary question, 'each elaborately designed to fulfill certain functions ... and doubt that they must have been created for the purposes which they fulfill by a designing mind – the almighty Creator of the Universe?'[3] Direct creation was widely questioned after the appearance in 1844 of Robert Chambers' *Vestiges of the Natural History of Creation*, a popular handbook of the sciences defending an evolutionary, more precisely a Lamarckian, theory of human origin that helped prepare the public for the Darwinian theory of evolution of 1859.[4]

A second foundation threatened by science was the Protestant assertion of the preeminence of Scripture as self-authenticating and requiring no further human authority in the church to interpret its meaning. John Ruskin caught the challenge in two sentences: 'If only the Geologists would let me alone, I could do well, but those dreadful hammers. I hear the clink of them at the end of every Bible cadence.'[5] The shadow of science in the first half of the nineteenth century was but one aspect of a general crisis of Protestant identity overtaking the Church of England in this period which served to give an impetus to the revival of Catholic principles within Anglicanism.[6]

In the theological work of the Oxford Movement and in the *Lux Mundi* school, Anglican theologians once again attempted to discover a reasonable ground of authority in matters of faith and to distinguish it from inherited prejudice and uncritical opinion. The Oxford Tractarians and their successors did not wish to give way to what they regarded as the old obscurantism of biblical literalism nor to the emptiness of secular rationalism.[7] They sought to find a way in which the authority of divine revelation could be held in tension with historical and scientific discoveries.

What emerged from their struggle over the course of two generations was a return to the doctrine of the Incarnation as the center around which everything else in Anglicanism should revolve, the Incarnation not simply as a doctrine about the nature of Jesus Christ, but much more importantly as a way of understanding the relationship of time and history to the eternal, and of understanding the relationship of the historic community of the Catholic Church through the ages to the Word of God. What emerged from that struggle was expressed simply and well in a volume which carried the approach of the Oxford Movement into our century, *Essays Catholic and Critical*, first published in 1926. In the preface to its first edition E. G. Selwyn wrote: 'The two terms Catholic and critical represent principles, habits, and tempers of the religious mind which only reach their maturity in combination ... there is no point at which they do not interact; and we are convinced that this interaction is necessary to any presentment of Christianity which is to claim the allegiance of the world today.'[8] What lay behind the achievement of this Anglican Catholic synthesis was two generations of association between theologians and scientists within Oxford and the wider academic community.

An example of this may be found in the career of E. B. Pusey. After John Keble's retirement from Oxford in 1836 and John Henry Newman's migration to the Roman Church in 1845, Edward Bouverie Pusey became the leader of the Oxford Tractarians, who were thereafter sometimes called Puseyites.[9] Keble's relations to science may be described as naive and fearful. When, for example, the British Association met in Oxford in 1832 and the University conferred honorary degrees of D.C.L. upon Brewster, Faraday, Brown, and Dalton, Keble's reaction was to condemn his colleagues who voted to so honor a 'hodge-podge of philosophers' with these words: 'Oxford has truckled sadly to the spirit of the themes.'[10] By contrast, Pusey's attitudes were more open-minded, sympathetic, and informed, yet Pusey also was aware of a clear separation between the disciplines of science and theology.

From 1825 to 1827 Pusey had studied the methods of German

biblical criticism at Göttingen, Berlin, and Bonn, and on his return to England he was appointed Regius Professor of Hebrew at Oxford in 1828 by the Duke of Wellington.[11] Both in Germany and at Oxford Pusey maintained close friendships with scientists. In 1836 Pusey contributed some of the notes to Oxford Professor William Buckland's *Geology and Mineralogy*, and his most eminent friend at Oxford after 1845 was Sir H. W. Acland, the great anatomist and physician.[12] In 1845 Acland was offered the Readership of Anatomy at Christ Church and he went to see Pusey. Acland asked Pusey two questions:

> ' "Am I right in believing that you ... and your friends disapprove of Physical Science as a branch of education at Oxford?" He said, "Yes, we do; and you would not hold up ..." Then I asked him a second question. "Am I to understand that you, who with the Dean and Chapter have appointed me a teacher in a great department of science, will consider me a mischievous and dangerous member of society, when I endeavor to do my duty in my office?" Dr Pusey who was endowed with a sense of humor, threw himself back in his chair and laughed aloud. "The desire to acquire such knowledge, and the power to obtain it, are alike the gift of God, and to be used as such. As long as you discharge your duties in the manner which this implies, count on my support in whatever you do." '[13]

Dr Acland went on to report that Pusey invariably attended the meetings of the Christ Church Chapter in the Oxford University museum and that at such meetings he paid great attention to the reports on the progress of enlarging the biological collections. During one long vacation he lent his stables to Acland to be used as a laboratory. In 1847 the British Association met in Oxford and Pusey lent his house in Christ Church to the scientists and seven of them, including J. H. Green and R. H. van der Hoeven stayed with him. Pusey wrote to A. P. Stanley in 1850 that he did not fear the introduction of more scientific teaching at Oxford: 'In proportion as there is hope that science should be religious, I should be glad to see science established at Oxford ... I have no fears from it. Of course it ought to do good service, if it knows its province.'[14]

Pusey was elected to the Oxford Hebdomadal Council in October 1854, and from that date he provided support for the growth of the biological sciences in the university by his votes in the council. For example, in 1855 the final vote for 30,000 pounds for the construction of the new Oxford University Museum would have been lost without his help.

In the course of this work, Pusey published two statements on science and religion. The first was a paper which he read to the Norwich Church Congress on October 5, 1865. *The Spirit in Which the Researches of Science Should Be Applied to the Study of the Bible* begins with a warning against the fear of science among Churchmen and against defending too zealously matters not connected to the central facts of the Christian faith: 'The right interpretation of God's Word will never be found in contradiction with the right interpretation of His works.' [15] In the second part of the paper Pusey argues that the settlement of the clash between science and religion that had shaken the educated world after the publication of Darwin's *Origin of the Species* would be found in a new realization that faith and science have quite distinct spheres which are not commensurate. In a key passage Pusey encourages Anglican Catholics to take an independent line between Biblical literalists on the one hand and secular rationalists on the other: 'Science relates to causes and effects, the laws by which God upholds His material Creation, or its past history. Faith relates to God, His Revelation, His Word, and is a God-given habit of mind by which a Christian makes conclusions about natural experience and fits them into his philosophy of life ... This then is our attitude toward any researches of any science; entire fearlessness as to the issue; awaiting that issue, whenever it shall unfold itself.' [16]

But Pusey was not able to remain so confident. Darwin's *Descent of Man*, unlike his *Origin of the Species*, distressed the Regius Professor of Hebrew because it seemed to imply that the human mind was derived from the pithecoids without any evolutionary gap. However, as long as the human personality was agreed to be a product of direct divine creation, Pusey could contemplate with a skeptical shudder the possibility of physical descent from ape-like ancestors. In July 1878, while at Ascot, Pusey wrote his final statement on the relation of the faith of the Oxford Movement to science, 'Un-science, not Science, Adverse to Faith,' and in November 1878 the sermon was delivered to a congregation which had jammed the Church of St Mary the Virgin in Oxford to hear what the old Tractarian would have to say on the subject. The sermon was dedicated to the same Dr Acland who had visited Pusey in 1845 and was now Regius Professor of Medicine in Oxford.

Pusey beings in 1878 with the point that he had made at the Norwich Church Congress in 1865: that science and faith have nothing to fear if they keep to their proper spheres. Yet now in 1878 Darwin's theory is labelled a transgressor of the true bounds of science. It is a myth, not certain knowledge based on certain facts about the physical world, Pusey's definition of science. Darwinism has now become a prime example of the unscience which has been adopted by some as a weapon against religion: 'It is of course an invasion of a foreign province, when Darwinism speculates upon man's development in religion and morals. For physical science has obviously nothing to do with either.' [17] Likewise, theology is defined as a discipline dealing only with the spiritual dimension of creation: 'Theology looks with equal impartiality on all geological theories; atomism, plutonism, neptunism, convulsionism, quietism, provided that in whatever way it pleased our Creator to act, that this be laid at the foundation, that the earth was not eternal, but was created.' [18]

The incarnational principles that Pusey adopted while participating in the Oxford Movement prevented him from reacting to scientific discoveries by either rejecting orthodox Christianity because of inadequacies in the biblical record revealed by science, or by damning science as anathema to the believing Christian. Pusey welcomed science as a legitimate part of the university and of the Christian life. What lay behind Pusey' way of thinking was a conscious return to a patristic way of thinking about the Incarnation, particularly a return to the notion expressed dogmatically at the Council of Chalcedon in 451 C.E. that human history and the created order as a whole can be the locus of divine presence, that God is present to humans not by negation but through a long process of perfecting and completing what humanity is. Central to Pusey's understanding of Christianity was a revival in the nineteenth century of this patristic focus on the Incarnation of Jesus, of the church as his abiding incarnation, and the humanism implicit in the Word becoming flesh. The Catholic tradition of understanding the Incarnation with its emphasis on the authority of the worshipping community as in some sense an extension of the Incarnation, allowed Pusey to believe that the rational and scientific investigation of reality may have something to say to us that enables us to understand the Christian faith more profoundly and in its wider implications.[19]

The next generation of Anglican Catholics continued along both aspects of the line of advance laid down by E. B. Pusey. In the career of R. W. Church we see the fruitful collaboration of a Tractarian with a scientist; in Charles Gore we see the flowering of Pusey's incarnational impetus. R. W. Church, who ended his career as Dean of St Paul's Cathedral in London, combined belief in the Catholic nature of the Church of England with a remarkable liberality of outlook and vigorous grasp of the science of his time. Church was a spokesman for the ideals of the Oxford Movement after it had moved from the colleges of Oxford out into the advanced 'ritualistic' parishes of the London slums and docks and into the country villages, yet he was also an amateur scientistic and the frequent correspondent of a great American botanist.

Though he was trained in the humanities from 1833 at Oxford, Church gained a serious respect for science while an undergraduate, and he studied physiological histology while at Christ Church.[20] In 1851 the Harvard botanist Asa Gray (1810–1888) visited Oxford to consult about plants, and he had breakfast with Church in Oriel College. Gray was a long-time friend of Charles Darwin. His botanical work influenced Darwin, and Gray became one of the leading exponents of Darwin's theory of evolution as outlined in *The Origin of the Species*.[21] Asa Gray and R. W. Church at once became friends and Church gave a dinner soon after in Gray's honor for a group of Oxford scientists in the very room in which the Oxford Movement had begun, the Oriel Common Room. This was the beginning of a close association and exchange of letters of many years with the botanist which opened Church's eyes to the continuing discoveries of science and guided him through the era of troubled scientific controversy. Asa Gray helped Church, while yet a true son of the old principles of the Oxford Movement, to recognize the implications of a whole world of new truths to which the Tractarian fathers were oblivious.

In January 1846 Church helped to found *The Guardian*, a paper dedicated to the maintenance of the tenets of Anglican Catholicism, yet a journal ready to report recent developments in many areas of knowledge and to face the theological problems raised by scientific inquiry openly.[22] The bold editorial policy of *The Guardian* was itself a sign of a new positive era of Anglican Catholicism following Newman's secession to Rome. In March 1846 Church reviewed the sequel to Chambers' *Vestiges*, a notice which received the commendation of the British scientist Sir Richard Owen. The book is dismissed by Church as bad science because the facts of Chambers' theory remained unproved. The work, however, is important, the reviewer feels, because it demonstrates the end of the old Paley school of evidential natural theology as a basis of Anglicanism. With the destruction of the Paley synthesis, religion and science must now be separated or they will collide: religion must now find deeper, more Catholic foundations, science must be cut free from theology and allowed complete freedom of investigation:

> 'If science is to advance, it must be cultivated freely ... and if moral truths and religion are not to suffer, it must be not by allying them with the physical sciences ... Keep in view the great principle that belief in God does not depend upon the natural; that nature is not the real basis of religion, and we can safely afford full and free scope to science ... The *Vestiges* warns us ... of the vanity of those boasts which great men used to make, that science naturally led on to religion. It may lead beyond the experiment and the generalization to vast theories – visions and histories for the imagination – to a substitute for religion.'[23]

When he became Rector of Whatley Parish, a small community of 200 parishioners which allowed the priest time to pursue his own interests, Church had a small laboratory fitted up so that he could continue chemical and astronomical experiments. He followed scientific developments by means of journals sent to him from Harvard by Asa Gray, where for thirty years Gray provided the total curriculum in botany. Church sent Gray five pounds to contribute toward a house for Gray's beloved herbarium in Cambridge which led on to the Arnold Arboretum, which still exists today, and the American botanist noted the surprise of his Harvard colleagues at this evidence of a lively interest in science, of 'a country parson far away in England.'[24] If Gray travelled to England to work at Kew Gardens, he usually also visited two people, R. W. Church and Charles Darwin, and sometimes included Church in the Darwinian circle.

At the time the evolutionary theory storm broke over Darwin, the Anglican priest profited from his acquaintance with an eminent scientist who was on familiar terms both with the theory and its author. Thanks to his association with Asa Gray and his own critical reading of Darwin, Church quickly acclimated the readers of *The Guardian* to *The Origin of the Species*. He wrote to Gray that there was disquiet in England about *Origin*, but that he was not troubled, and he had this to say about Darwin's work in March 1860: 'I should think that it is *the* book of science, which has produced the most impression here of any that has appeared for many years. But it is shortness of thought to treat the theory itself as incompatible with the ideas of a higher order.'[25]

Yet science to Church, as to Pusey, ultimately had limits. His faith conceived God to be at work in a world that requires more than empirical methods for knowledge. As he studied both science and theology, Church came to a conclusion, not unlike that of Pusey, that an understanding of the workings of the universe is to be gained through knowledge of the incarnate logos. That in Jesus 'the Word was made flesh' meant to Church that:

> 'we know much, but what we know is out of proportion to the immensity of what do not know, or what we cannot know. Our knowledge of God's kingdom, of its working and ways, is like all our knowledge of the highest kind, a combination of light and certainty on some great points, with ignorance and darkness on others equally great.'[26]

But Church was confident that because of the Incarnation mortals are not groping toward the light, the light is an assured possession. All questions of origin are not answered for mortals, but to Church because of the Incarnation of God in Jesus Christ there is one veil the less on the unfathomable mysteries of the unseen. The way was opened for the combination of evolution with the Incarnation to produce *Lux Mundi*.

In the seventies and the eighties of the nineteenth century there was a change in the perceived battlefield of science and religion. Whereas during Pusey's time belief or unbelief had been a matter of extreme earnestness, Samuel Butler and others in the last decades of the century were now bringing to their rejection of Christianity the first breaths of that flippancy that would be consummated in the work of Lytton Stratchey. Faith began to have to reckon with fun. Browning could breezily write in 'Gold Hair' that:

> 'The candid incline to surmise of late
> that the Christian faith proves false, I find
> For our 'Essays and Review' debate
> Begins to tell on the public mind
> And Colenso's words have weight.'[27]

Disraeli reportedly told Queen Victoria that he was the blank page between the Old and New Testaments.

For survivors and heirs of the Oxford Movement, the mood also changed. The party that was born in the 1830's out of the academic disputes of dons, tracts, and heresy hunts, had spread, armed with new theological and liturgical weapons, out into the slums and country parishes, there to struggle for Catholic truth. There were two streams of Tractarianism that emanated from Oxford. One channel bearing the old traditions of Pusey and the early leaders flowed through college chapels, quadrangles, and cathedral chapters, carrying R. W. Church, Charles Gore, and Aubrey Moore. It is with this more precisely theological branch that the remainder of this paper will be concerned. The other more ritualistic and socially radical channel ran through the advanced parish churches bearing Lowder, Dolling, Mackonochie and Stanton, creating religious hysteria in places like the parish of St George's in-the-East in London.

Two years after Dr Pusey's death in 1882, his ecclesiastical heirs erected Pusey House, a library, as a memorial. The Oxford Puseum was operated by Anglican Catholic priests who were called librarians, but who were also expected to bear witness to a Catholic understanding of Anglicanism within the university. The first librarian to be named was Charles Gore. Gore recognized that in the new atmosphere of the times there were two possible ways that orthodox Christians could engage in apologetics. One was to encounter the flippant attitude of the new disbelief with what would later be referred to as the Chestertonian style – confident, paradoxical, smart at repartee, and very much on the offensive. Gore decided that, on the other hand, he would be utterly serious and treat what he felt to be contemporary man and woman's complicated predicament of faith in the light of science with gravity. Yet, he perceived that if the principles of Tractarianism were to be saved for a new generation, it heirs must adopt a radically sympathetic attitude toward science and biblical criticism. Out of Gore's new stance and his work at Pusey House sprang the *Lux Mundi* school of liberal Anglican Catholicism, which in some ways may be regarded as a second Oxford Movement. Its object was 'to try to put the Catholic faith into its right relation to modern intellectual and moral problems.'[28]

In the theology of Gore we see a positive rather than a negative and destructive aspect of the impact of science upon religion in the nineteenth century. The Catholic revival had allowed some Anglicans to admit the factual inadequacies of the Bible and of the Paley school and yet remain orthodox. The unfear of science in some Tractarians had allowed a second generation to embrace evolution and combine it with a Catholic understanding of the Incarnation, Christ's continuing presence on earth at worship and in the life of the church, joined to a deemphasis on the importance of the Hebrew Bible for Christian faith. To Gore and his friends, Darwin's theory showed not only how God had worked naturally in creation, it also disclosed how God worked theologically – that God gradually disclosed revelation to mortals, and the climax of the evolving revelation had been Christ's Incarnation. Therefore

Jesus Christ, the Lux Mundi, is the consummation of both the evolution of nature and the evolution of revelation. All that comes before Christ in the plan of salvation and in the record of God's dealing with the Hebrew people is therefore understandably imperfect. The church which comes after Christ is the continuation of this incarnate body on earth and has been given divine authority to interpret the eternal truth of the Incarnation in the light of the new knowledge of each age.

Charles Gore soon found like-minded Anglican Catholics at Oxford. Aubrey Moore, Arthur Lyttleton, H. S. Holland, J. R. Illingworth, E. S. Talbot, R. C. Moberly, William Locke and others in 1889 published a collection of essays entitled *Lux Mundi – A Series of Studies in the Religion of the Incarnation*. In his introduction to the work Gore states that its object is to bring the Christian creed 'into its right relation to the modern growth of knowledge,'[29] and he argues that Anglicans ought not to be content to recognize science's legitimacy in its own realm, but moving beyond the boundaries that Pusey had set, an atmosphere should be created 'in which religion interprets and is interpreted by science, in which faith and inquiry subsist together and reinforce one another.'[30] Thus for Gore *Lux Mundi* is part of the process 'in which the Church, standing firm in her old truths, enters into the apprehension of the new social and intellectual movements of each age: and because 'the truth makes her free,' is able to assimilate all new material, to welcome and give its place to all new knowledge.'[31]

One of the essays in *Lux Mundi* was written by Aubrey Moore, a priest regarded by contemporaries as a distinguished botanist who to Charles Gore was a symbol of 'how two lives of faith and of science can be met in one.'[32] Moore was a canon of Christ Church, select preacher to the university in 1885–1886, Whitehall preacher in 1887–1888, and at the same time during these years he was also actively engaged in university botanical research projects. Unfortunately Moore died in 1890, and he has left behind to us only a few collections of essays and sermons. Moore's essay on 'The Christian Doctrine of God' in *Lux Mundi* is typical of these writings in its argument that the theory of evolution has restored the truth of Divine immanence in the Incarnation which the deism of the eighteenth century had denied.

In the essay Moore seeks to answer the question: 'What fuller realization of God's revelation of Himself is He giving us through the contradictions and struggles of today?'[33] The answer is that God is leading Christians to a truer knowledge of God, that every new truth from science 'is designed by God's providence to make his revelation real, by bringing out hidden truths.'[34] Since the dawn of the scientific revolution, God had tended to be regarded as being more and more separate from the world, throned in magnificent inactivity, remote from the physical universe, a cold and silent maker: 'Science had pushed the deist's God farther and farther away, and at the moment when it seemed as if he would be thrust out altogether Darwin appeared, and under the guise of a foe, did the work of a friend.'[35] Moore came to the positive conclusion that Darwin's discoveries had forced moderns to make two choices: either God is everywhere present in nature, or nowhere present. There must be a return to the Catholic view of a direct divine agent immanent in nature, worship, and the church, or acceptance of a complete atheism. Darwin has forced a choice between the Catholic conception of Christianity or atheism: 'It seems as if, in the providence of God, the mission of modern science was to bring home to our unmetaphysical ways of thinking the great truth of the Divine immanence in Creation which is ... essential to the Christian idea of God.'[36]

So what is the significance of this pattern within the longer history of Anglican thought: that Pusey would lend his stables and house to scientists, vote for money for biological collections, and welcome science if it were true science; that Church could write articles about planets and theories of geology and condemn the 'shortness of thought' of Christians who vilified Darwin; and that Gore and Moore could use science as a tool for theological understanding and incorporate evolutionary theory into their construction of a progressive Catholicism. It means that the leaders of one conservative school of nineteenth-century Anglicanism did not condemn science and thereby rupture the relationship which had existed between Christianity and science in the university since the medieval period and during the great advances of the seventeenth century.

The Tractarians and their successors were able to do this

because, despite all their talk of Catholicism, they continued to hold in fruitful tension the old Hookerian balance of reason, Scripture, and tradition which had been present within Anglicanism from the end of the reign of Elizabeth I. The nineteenth-century recovery of an incarnational focus in Christianity enabled the Tractarians to perceive human reasonableness as a reflection and a participation in the rationality of God. They came to understand that the Word of God has authority and can be appropriated only in the course of a rational human interpretation of it. Such a conclusion was in fact no radical departure from Richard Hooker's defense of human reason in matters of faith and in opposition to Puritans who judged everything by the explicit words of Scripture, and it is significant that both John Keble and R. W. Church published editions of Hooker.[37] At the end of the sixteenth century Hooker was not far from the nineteenth century when he wrote these words in the *Laws*:

> 'the selfsame Spirit, which revealeth the things that God hath set down in His law, may also be thought to aid and direct men in finding out by the light of reason what laws are expedient to be made for the guiding of His Church, over and besides them that are in Scripture.'[38]

What nineteen-century Anglican Catholics intended to do about the questions of science which faced them was to hold a particular balance, a particular tension, in which the primary authority of Scripture could be recognized, but always as that was interpreted within the historical teaching and public practice of the church. Some things in Scripture have authority and some do not; the determination is made by the guidance of the Holy Spirit within the historic continuity of the church. Charles Gore, in his 1891 Bampton Lectures, summed up well the significance of this strain in Anglicanism for our consideration of the relation of science and faith, of the Word in Nature and in Scripture. Here Gore said that what the Church of England had always striven for, albeit not always successfully, is the authority which Christ himself shows us in Scripture. It is not that He speaks infallibly; it is rather an authority which exists 'to develop sonship'. To develop sonship meant to Gore that Christ enables those who hear Him to use the gifts of reason and science in order that they might respond to the best kind of authority which 'refuses to do too much for men, refuses to be too explicit, too complete, too clear, lest it should dwarf instead of stimulating their higher faculties.'[39]

In the ashes of a movement which seems destined for failure with the secession of John Henry Newman to Rome in 1845, Pusey, Church, Gore, and Moore found classical principles upon which an Anglicanism could be reconstructed which was at once Catholic, critical, and humane. Donald Gray can best be understood against this background, which is far larger than his generation, before which he, with resources of faith and hope, beckons us forward to see a Christian *consummatio* of word and science as part of the fulfillment of humanity destined for the future.

NOTES

1. Charles Gore, ed., *Lux Mundi* (New York, 1944) 4.

2. The pre-nineteenth-century context is set in Amos Funkenstein, *Theology and the Scientific Imagination: From the Middle Ages to the Seventeenth Century* (Princeton, 1986); the nineteenth-century context is set in Adrian Desmond and James Moore, *Darwin* (New York, 1991), Jon H. Roberts, *Darwinism and the Divine in America: Protestant Intellectuals and Organic Evolution, 1859–1900* (Madison, 1988), and Marshall D. Saplins, *Evolution and Culture* (Ann Arbor, 1960); the twentieth-century context is set in Robert Russell, William Stoeger, George Coyne, *Physics, Philosophy, and Theology* (Vatican City, 1988).

3. William Paley (1743–1805) in Charles Gore, *The Reconstruction of Belief* (London, 1926) 6; editions of Paley's *Works* with a *Life* by A. Chalmers (5 vols., London, 1819); most recent study of Paley is M. L. Clark, *Paley: Evidences for the Man* (London, 1974).

4. Chambers (1802–1871) is discussed most recently in M. Millhauser, *Just Before Darwin* (Middleton, 1959).

5. Ruskin quoted in L. E. Elliott-Binns, *English Thought 1860–1900: The Theological Aspect* (Greenwich, 1956), 175. For an account of the relationship between biblical criticism, science and faith see Rudolf Bultmann, 'Humanism and Christianity', *The Journal of Religion*, 32 (1952) 77.

6. I have previously discussed industrial revolution and political revolution as part of the challenge to the Protestant identity of the Church of England in this period in the following publications: *Nineteenth-Century Churches: The History of New Catholicism in Württemberg, England, and France* (New York and London, 1987); in 'Pusey and Worship in Industrial Society', *Worship* (September, 1983) 386–412, and most recently in *The Case for Christian Humanism* (Grand Rapids, 1991).

7. In his incisive *Tracts*, which came out from 1833 to 1841 and earned the appellation Tractarian for the movement, John Henry Newman upheld the Church of England as a 'divine' or 'ecclesial' institution with a social mission.

8. E. G. Selwyn, ed., *Essays Catholic and Critical* (London, 1926) xxviii.

9. To Victorians generally, 'Puseyism' was, in the words of John Wolffe, 'an unfocused term of abuse,' suggesting troglodytic crankiness and unpatriotic oddity, as in Thomas Carlyle's phrase, 'to procreate a spectral Puseyism.' Typical of negative nineteenth-century use of the term is 'Puseyism and the Church of England,' *The London Quarterly Review* (January, 1895).

10. Geoffrey Faber, *Oxford Apostles* (London, 1954) 254. Any description of Keble's attitude toward science must be gleaned from remarks made here and there in his works about the problems posed for religion by the scientific investigation of nature. In no treatise does Keble address himself specifically to the issues raised by science. I have not considered Newman in this article, but by February 1840 Newman has this to say on the impending clash between science and religion: 'Everything is miserable ... I expect a great attack upon the Bible – indeed, I have long expected it. At the present moment indications of what is coming gather. You have geologists giving up parts of the Old Testament. All these and many more spirits seem uniting and forming into something shocking.'

11. I discuss Pusey's German relations in my article, 'The Impact of Germany on the Anglican Catholic Revival in Nineteenth-Century Britain,' *Anglican and Episcopal History* (December, 1992) 433–448 and in my *Nineteenth-Century Churches*, 224–271.

12. William Buckland, *Geology and Mineralogy* (London, 1836, 2 vols.). Buckland went from Oxford to be Dean of Westminster Abbey and there continued to combine his career as priest and scientist, being seen invariably in the Abbey with a blue bag with bones and fossils sticking out of it.

13. H. P. Liddon, *The Life of E. B. Pusey*, Vol. 4 (London, 1897) 331. The friendship is documented in a collection of manusript letters, MS Sir H. W. Acland to E. B. Pusey, 1838–1847, Pusey House, Oxford.

14. Liddon, *Life of Pusey*, Vol. 3, 391. Two articles serve as guides to further reading on Pusey, science, and university matters: Leighton Frappell, ' "Science in the Service of Orthodoxy:" The Early Intellectual Development of E. B. Pusey,' and Jean Ellis, 'Pusey and University Reform,' both in Perry Butler, ed., *Pusey Rediscovered* (Oxford, 1983) 1–33, 298–331.

15. Maria Trench, *The Story of Dr Pusey's Life* (London, 1900) 417. The full text and title is E. B. Pusey, *The Spirit in Which the Researchers of Learning and Science Should Be Applied to the Study of the Bible*. A Norwich Church Congress Paper: it occupies pp. 181–190 of the *Report of the Proceedings* (London, 1866). The paper was also privately printed in an edition of 24 pages.

16. Leonard Prestige, *Pusey* (London, 1933) 102–103.

17. E. B. Pusey, *Un-science, not Science, Adverse to Faith* (London, 1879) 10. The sermon was preached on the Twentieth Sunday after Trinity, 1878, two editions, and about 5,000 copies of the sermon were printed.

18. *Idem.* Pusey also published a letter to the *Church of England Pulpit and Ecclesiastical Review*, dated February 7, 1879, in reply to a review of *Un-Science Not Science*.

19. Pusey himself defined 'Puseyism' as 'in a word, reference to the Ancient Church, instead of the Reformers, as the ultimate expounder of our Church.' E. B. Pusey, 'What Is Puseyism?' reprinted in H. P. Liddon. *Life of Pusey*, Vol 2 (London, 1898) 140–141. The main resource for this return is *Library of Fathers of the Holy Catholic Church*, in 48 volumes, 1838–1885, the translations supervised by E. B. Pusey.

20. Here we should not forget the following book: R. W. Church, *The Oxford Movement: Twelve Years* (New York and London, 1891). Two articles of the last thirty years credit Church's book with fixing 'Oxford Movement' as the name of the Anglican Catholic revival and 1833–1845 as the standard dates. They are R. W. Hunt, 'Newman's Notes on Dean Church's "Oxford Movement," ' *Bodleian Library Record* (Feburary, 1969) 135–137; and Owen Chadwick, 'The Oxford Movement and Its Historian,' in *The*

Anglican Tradition (Wilton, 1984) 99–124. Church was elected a Fellow or Oriel College Oxford in 1838 and during this period worked with Pusey on a translation of Cyril of Alexandria's catechetical lectures for Pusey's *Library of the Fathers*.

21. From 1842 Gray served as Fisher Professor of Natural History at Harvard and he directed the Harvard Botanical Garden and developed a herbarium which became the most valuable one in the United States.

22. Church's article in *The Guardian* on Le Verrier's discovery of the planet Neptune drew an appreciative letter from the astronomer himself. These and other articles on scientific matters being for the most part original studies on the questions treated, they were collected as *Occasional Papers* (2 vols., London, 1897).

23. R. W. Church, *Occasional Papers* (London, 1897) 64–65.

24. B. A. Smith, *Dean Church* (London, 1958) 134. The point here is that Americans were surprised at Gray's close friendship with an English priest because Gray was best known after 1859 as the leading advocate of Darwin in America, who in opposition to many American Protestant clerical voices sought a fair hearing among Christians for Darwin's theory, so that a just theological appraisal could follow.

25. Mary Church, *Life and Letters of Dean Church* (New York, 1874) 104.

26. Smith, 269. It is of interest that Church also wrote a life of *Bacon* (London, 1884).

27. Elliott-Binns, *English Thought*, 6. The context of this is described well in two books of G. W. E. Russell, *The Household of Faith* (London, 1902) and *Portrait of the Seventies* (New York, 1916).

28. J. G. Lockhart, *Viscount Halifax*, Vol. 2 (London, 1936) 27.

29. Charles Gore et al, *Lux Mundi* (New York, 1944) viii. Gore also discusses science during this period here: 'On the Theory of Evolution and Christian Doctrine,' *The Report of the Church Congress of 1896* (London, 1896) 140–145; and 'The Theory of Evolution and the Christian Doctrine of the Fall,' *The Church Times* (February, 1897) 208–209.

30. *Ibid.*, ix. For more on this see: James Carpenter, *Gore: A Study in Liberal Catholic Thought* (London, 1960); and Gordon Crosse, *Charles Gore: A Biographical Sketch* (London, 1932).

31. *Ibid.*, xliii. For more on this: A. M. Ramsey, *From Gore to Temple* (London, 1960).

32. *Ibid.*, ix. Aubrey Moore is the author of two books published after his death: *Science and Faith* (London, 1892) and *From Advent to Advent* (London, 1901).

33. *Ibid.*, 47.

34. *Ibid.*, 48.

35. *Ibid.*, 82.

36. *Idem.*

37. R. W. Church published an edition of the first book of Hooker's *Laws of Ecclesiastical Polity* in 1868. In 1836 John Keble issued a learned edition of Hooker's *Works* in three volumes. For more on the tradition of reason in Hooker see H. F. McAdoo, *The Spirit of Anglicanism* (New York, 1965).

38. Richard Hooker, *Laws of Ecclesiastical Polity* (Oxford, 1890) III, viii, 18.

39. Charles Gore, *The Incarnation of the Son of God* (London, 1891) 198. In the twentieth-century Gore addressed the themes of this article in the following works: *The Anglo-Catholic Movement Today* (London, 1925); *The Doctrine of the Infallible Book* (London, 1924); *The Reconstruction of Belief* (London, 1945).

10

'Liturgical Laboratories of the Church': The role of English cathedrals in Anglican worship today

❀ *Michael Perham* ❀

It is *Heritage and Renewal*,[1] the Report of the Archbishops' Commission on Cathedrals, that describes cathedrals as 'the liturgical laboratories of the Church'. This essay explores the part that cathedrals have played in the liturgical development of the Church of England this century and the opportunities that now present themselves for the coming century. It begins with some description of what has happened over the last decades, and analyses the reasons why, in recent years, cathedrals have not been able to grasp the liturgical initiative. It then looks at two recent reports, *In Tune with Heaven*, and *Heritage and Renewal*. It reproduces what I hope to be useful thinking by PRAXIS in evidence to the Cathedrals' Commission, and ends by working through some of the issues that the paper and, more particularly, the propositions, raise in relation to two important areas: the ministry of the bishop in his cathedral and the place of the laity in the liturgy.

Heritage and Renewal asserts

> Cathedrals are the liturgical laboratories of the Church; they have the freedom and the potential flexibility to meet the spiritual needs of many who may not be even on the edge of formal Church who may encounter the divine presence when they attend cathedral worship as members of a secular group for a special service.[2]

179

The original idea in the title of this essay, cathedrals as liturgical laboratories, will surprise many, for their reputation is often as places where yesterday's liturgy is celebrated and guarded as nowhere else (and the reputation is not always undeserved) and the more developed argument, set out in the paragraph above, comes as a disappointment, as if a liturgical laboratory should operate only on the frontiers, where the Church is engaging with those on its fringe and outside its usual influence. That cathedrals should be at work there is clear, but surely the role of the cathedral as 'liturgical laboratory' applies equally to the mainstream of its liturgical life, in relation to its immediate community, to its regular congregation, and to that wider group of church people within a diocese for whom it is a 'mother church'?

It is well placed to be a liturgical laboratory for two immediate reasons. Firstly because it is a religious community. Cathedrals will vary in the extent to which they do feel like that; it will perhaps be strongest in the foundations that were originally monastic and in the places where the majority of those who work together live close to one another. This community of priests, musicians, vergers, as well, nowadays, as Administrators, Visitors' Officers and the like, because it has the opportunity to worship so often and to reflect together quite easily, has an almost unique opportunity to be a liturgical laboratory where lessons may be learned. That it fails to be that so often is no excuse for abandoning the ideal and the possibility.

The potential is there also because the resources are present for intelligent and theological reflection. If a college of canons and their lay staff cannot bring theological insights and the other kindred disciplines to bear on issues of worship, where else is it to happen in a way that can stand back from the immediacy of parish life and bring a different perspective into play?

But the fact is that, despite the potential, few have looked to the cathedrals for model and inspiration in liturgy through recent decades, perhaps through centuries, save in the unhappy imitation of the nineteenth century cathedral music tradition adopted ill-advisedly in too many parish churches until quite recently. And this has been true through a period where cathedrals have in many different ways recovered a sense of purpose and of mission, have prospered, and probably today contribute more to the life of the Church than they have ever done before.[3] Cathedrals have regained a very significant place in the Church's mission, but it has not been principally because of their worship, and certainly not because they have been liturgical laboratories.

There have, of course, been exceptions. When Dean Bennett brought about a new style of cathedral life at Chester in the 1920s, a style taken up and adopted surprisingly speedily in cathedrals all over the land, at the heart of his reforms were a Sunday eucharist devised and celebrated with a concern for detail and for beauty, a cathedral chapter committed to a daily pattern of shared worship that included Eucharist and compline, and the use of the building as a series of holy spaces regularly used for worship.[4] The new cathedrals have also shown a liturgical creativity not often found in the older ones. Dean Dwelly's initiatives in Liverpool may now seem eccentric in some respects, but they were an honest and creative attempt to find to develop a new liturgical style for a new building and a new age.[5] Joseph Poole was Precentor at Coventry when that new cathedral was consecrated in 1962 and there developed there a strong liturgical style, innovative in days before the Church of England began to revise its liturgy, and which took seriously both its new building and also the new era for which it was devised, drawing very much on the thinking of Bishop John Robinson in his *Liturgy Coming to Life*.[6] It has now needed very definite change and development thirty years on, but at the time it made its impact on liturgical thinking in the wider Church, and even now gives to Coventry worship a rationale and an integrity that is not always found elsewhere.[7] It is difficult to find examples more recently, save for the liturgical thinking and practice that has gone hand in hand with the completion of the cathedral building at Portsmouth under the leadership of Provost Stancliffe, though it is early to judge how this will be retained and developed.[8] Dean Jasper at York in the 1980s made the minster to some extent the exemplar of his liturgical work for the Church of England, but only by a new layer that sat somewhat uncomfortably on the work done by Dean Milner-White thirty years before.

Why has there been this comparative failure in the last couple of generations to develop the liturgical role of the cathedrals alongside the other ways in which they have moved forward? I detect seven factors at least.

The first has been the reluctance of cathedrals to adopt the revised rites that spread through the Church of England in the 1960s and 1970s and were enshrined in *The Alternative Service Book 1980*. The Book of Common Prayer still has a major place in the life of most cathedrals in a way that has been lost in parish churches. The Sunday Eucharist in quite a few follows the compromise Rite B order, retaining the Prayer Book language if not its structure. This may reflect the conservatism of cathedral clergy, but more often the reluctance of the musicians to engage with the new texts, and also the nature of cathedral regular congregations. It would be easy to over-simplify, but there is truth in the picture of the cathedral as 'liturgical refuge', a place for people alienated by the liturgy of their parish churches. As such the Sunday congregation may be reluctant to be in the forefront of innovation.

The second factor, and one that grows out of the first, has been the growing musical divergence between cathedrals and many churches, not just in the choice of music for choirs, but even in hymns and the singing of psalms. It is not simply that a number of parishes of a more evangelical kind have moved to charismatic and 'renewal' music, but that almost every parish church has been influenced by such music, and a hymn book like *Mission Praise* has established itself as the principal hymn book in many parishes across the churchmanship spectrum.

Thirdly, perhaps more fundamentally, has been cathedral tradition, custom and, crucially, statute. In cathedrals things have often been set down in writing that in parishes would never have gone beyond an oral communication of how things are done. Head vergers and minor canons in more leisured days created sets of instructions not far short of customaries and lawyers wrote into statutes what services should be held, and who should celebrate them and who preach the sermon at them. Such tradition, custom and statute is jealously guarded in an unthinking and untheological way, and gets in the way of proper creativity and innovation. Statute and laboratory do not easily go together.

A fourth contributor has been the reduction in the clergy

staffing of cathedrals. In the past there was often a canon (whether styled 'precentor' or not), or even a dean, with a broad feel for liturgy, often for its architectural setting, sometimes for its words, sometimes for its movements, supported by minor canons with musical expertise to sing the service. Deans with this kind of priority and over-view have become rare (as the managers have taken over). Some cathedrals have had a canon precentor, but he has nearly always been without a succentor to do the singing and therefore the skills most needed of the precentor himself are musical. Broader liturgical skills have tended to take second place. In other cathedrals the only liturgist has been a non-canon precentor, not a member of chapter, sometimes not present when the dean and canons discuss the worship in their cathedral, and therefore not in a position to give liturgy its proper place in cathedral life and mission. *Heritage and Renewal* identifies the need for one member of chapter to have overall responsibility for the liturgy[9] and there is evidence of a move in this direction. But while one person is required to carry the full range of liturgical and musical skills, suitable candidates will always be in short supply.

The bishop has also been a factor. Bishops have, to some extent, reclaimed their liturgical role in the life of the Church. They are out and about in the parishes as never before (and there are more of them to be out and about). When they go to a church, they no longer sit idly in their chair, stirring only to absolve and preach and bless, but take hold of the liturgy, as is their duty, and use it as an important part of their ministry. But it tends to be out in the parishes that they are doing this, not in the church of their *cathedra*, because they are either uncomfortable or unwelcome there. The sense of not being welcome is more often about what they are welcome to do, rather than whether they should be there are all, but there are places where the only place where the bishop cannot be the bishop liturgically in his own cathedral. And so the episcopal influence on liturgy, and in some cases the bishop's liturgical laboratory, is away from the cathedral church.

Then there is the challenge of the building. The trend of the liturgy, especially of eucharistic worship, in the last two generations, has been towards the intimate and the informal, towards fellowship and worship 'in the round'. Cathedrals are not often

designed to go in that direction. Good liturgy can never fight its
architectural setting, and cathedral buildings nearly always draw
the eye to the distance, flourish more on pilgrimage models than
commune models, and resist the informal and relaxed. It has been
difficult to make the cathedral a laboratory without redesigning the
laboratory first. Some years on, some cathedrals are boldly and
imaginatively doing just that, while others can feel relieved that, as
one fashion gives way to another, it is easier now to make the case
for taking the building seriously and going with it, rather than
fighting it.

The final factor is the failure to recognise the quite different
kinds of 'congregation' that a cathedral serves and the tendency to
provide for one what is appropriate for another. In most cathedrals
there are four quite distinct varieties of congregation.

The first is the *foundation* and those who so attach themselves to
it day by day that they become part of it in reality if not in law.
These are the people, clergy and a variety of holy souls, who gather
every day, sharing in the divine office and often in the Eucharist
also, joined when the service is sung by members of the choir,
nearly always men and boys, who are themselves members of this
foundation. This is the base community, where liturgical experiment, alongside reverence for a received tradition, ought to be
possible within a secure common life.

The second is the *Sunday congregation*. In most cathedrals the
foundation is so swamped by lay people treating the cathedral
almost as a parish church that it is a quite different assembly. A
significant proportion of this congregation changes from week to
week, drawing in visitors and tourists, but in the majority of cathedrals there is regular congregation, in some cathedrals of several
hundred, who come week by week and regard the cathedral as
'their church' and are looking for a eucharist that relates the
strengths of cathedral worship, not least its music, to the mainstream liturgical life of the Church. Some, as has been said, are
looking for a liturgical refuge, but others are happy to be drawn
into new things, or the rediscovery of lost things, providing all is
well explained and well done.

The third congregation is the *diocesan gathering*, the assembly of
faithful Christian people, who worship week by week in their

parish churches, and come to the cathedral, whether it be for an ordination, or a synod, on an installation, or a centenary, wanting to be swept off their feet by the splendour and the glory, but also wanting to be reassured by a family likeness with what they experience back at home.

The fourth is the *frontier congregation* for whom cathedral worship is not mirrored in regular parish worship, people who come, perhaps once a year, because they belong to the British Legion, or the Young Farmers, or the Girl Guides, or else on a once off occasion for VE Day or for a Service to remember a relative killed in a car crash. If they bring any expectations, they are very different ones from all three of the other groups.

The failure of the cathedral has sometimes been the failure to ask for which of these categories a service is designed and how different their needs may be.

For all these reasons it has been difficult for the cathedrals to take the lead in liturgical formation and exploration through the last two decades. It is, nevertheless, important not to exaggerate their failure. Some cathedrals have developed Sunday Eucharists that attract growing congregations and that reflect the best of liturgical thinking and practice. Some cathedrals know how to uplift a congregation from county or city or diocese that fills the building and to send them away genuinely inspired. And, in any case, there are signs of change and that cathedrals are beginning to regain the initiative and to develop a role that makes them liturgical laboratories, and much more, for the worship of the wider church.

Two recent reports have pointed in this direction. The first of them was *In Tune with Heaven*,[10] the report of the Archbishops' Commission on Church Music, published in 1992. This commission also spoke of the cathedral as a 'laboratory for the community',[11] and spelt out the liturgical role of the cathedral in these paragraphs:

> We belong to a generation which has grown up knowing little of the language of religion, or of the basic doctrines and faith of Christianity. Our culture is fragmented and secular, and for most people Choral Evensong, for example, has little to offer except beautiful music. This is true even for many

younger Christians. The cathedral tradition is an undoubted musical gem. But a more truly popular liturgy is also required which will combine the demand of St Teresa of Avila for something 'plain and homely' with that which has majesty, poetry, otherness and the power to communicate. A cathedral is in a particularly good situation to give the Church a lead in this area, and to offer an inspiring vision for the future. It has few constraints and more resources than the average parish, and as the mother church of the diocese and the focus of the Bishops' ministry, it should be expected to show the way.

The cathedral's greatest advantage is in its recognition that worship is the well-spring of all else. This is expressed by the daily services said or sung, morning and evening, every day of the year. From so solid a base it should not be difficult or daunting to make experiments ...

The sheer scale of most cathedral buildings,with their different parts and open spaces which allow considerable flexibility, is another great asset. It invites exploration both of movement and of sound, and a lone instrument or the calling of one voice to another, as if from nowhere, can create a most powerful effect, as can a procession up the full length of a large building.[12]

If *In Tune with Heaven* prepared the way for a more positive assessment of the cathedral's liturgical role, the Cathedral's Commission report, *Heritage and Renewal*, endorsed the earlier recommendations, took them further and pressed the case for fresh initiatives. It noted the national role of the cathedral at times like a memorial service after a disaster, 'great symbolic acts of worship, in which the affairs of men and women are raised to God and sanctified by him'.[13] It recognised the growing divergence between cathedrals and parishes, but added that 'the acceptance of such a dichotomy between "cathedral" and "parish" styles of worship does not prevent some hard work being done to build bridges between the different approaches'.[14] It pleads for 'bridge services', the equivalent of the old preaching services in the nave on a Sunday evening when the cathedral adopted a more popular style. There is food for thought in its recommendations, and certainly the direction that it indicates is one to encourage cathedrals in the liturgical enterprise. In the end its analysis of this area is, perhaps, a little thin, and even its proposals somewhat disappointing. But the direction is right.

Among the submissions drawn up for the Commission was one from PRAXIS,[15] which set out ten propositions on the liturgical role of the cathedral. These are here reproduced for a wider readership and the remainder of this essay is a reflection on some of these propositions.

1 Cathedral liturgy provides a model for parish liturgy, not in the sense that parishes should imitate the 'style' of cathedral worship, but in the sense of being prayerful worship, thought through theologically, showing a sensitivity both to the building and to the pastoral needs of the particular congregation, well presented. Every diocesan occasion is an occasion of liturgical formation.

2 Cathedral liturgy provides the principal setting for the bishop to exercise his liturgical ministry. In the cathedral people are able to see him working out his ministry in a liturgical, sacramental and pastoral context. His own liturgical ministry is part of the liturgical formation of his clergy and people. It is the duty of those responsible for cathedral worship to assist him in this ministry and to allow him to undertake it.

3 Cathedral liturgy can often be creative and exploratory in a way not often possible in parishes, especially in worship provided for, and worked out with, groups outside the Church, or on the fringe of its life, who come for special services.

4 Cathedrals can be a resource to their Diocesan Liturgical Committees, in providing both hospitality and expertise, for diocesan liturgical courses, and the cathedral's own liturgist (and sometimes its master of music) should be involved in the DLC's work.

5 Cathedrals are well placed to create new texts and to commission new music to broaden their own worship experience and to add to the liturgical resources of the whole Church, and this facility needs encouragement.

6 The cathedral's effective liturgical ministry is dependent on one of its senior clergy being responsible for a liturgical department. Where liturgical leadership is 'shared' among the dean/provost, the canon in residence and a junior post 'precentor', the liturgy will inevitably lack direction. In making this appointment, the need for a priest with liturgical skills is more fundamental than the need for a musician or a singer.

7 Cathedrals are places where liturgical activity is well thought through theologically. People must know *why* they are doing what they are. 'Our custom', 'our tradition' or even 'our statutes' are not sufficient justification.

8 Fine liturgy is one of the principal ways in which a cathedral may engage in the work of mission and evangelism. There needs to be the right balance of, on the one hand, worship that leaves people spellbound, and, on the other, a sense of welcome and of accessibility, expressed in practical ways like the provision of a user-friendly service book.

9 Cathedral buildings need to be adapted to meet the liturgical needs of the day. Without being philistine or anti-heritage, cathedrals must look to ensure that the furnishings and the spaces of the cathedral allow for the preaching of the word and the celebration of both baptism and eucharist in a way that draws the whole worshipping community into active participation.

10 The dominant style of cathedral worship, with its restrained catholic order and ceremonial, is to be treasured. Nevertheless cathedrals need to be bold in discovering how other styles of worship can be used successfully within the building.

Much of what these propositions assert is confirmed both by *Heritage and Renewal* and by the evidence of this essay. One area that the report neglects, however, and which calls for further clarification, is the cathedral as the setting of the Bishop's liturgical ministry. It often brings into sharpest focus the conflict between liturgical theology and custom, tradition and statute.

The Bishop is the normative president of the Christian sacraments. He delegates that presidency, over both baptism and eucharist, to his presbyters in their parishes from week to week, but their ministry derives from his, and when he is among them in worship they would not expect to preside, though they might share in his liturgical ministry in an appropriate way. 'When the Bishop is present, it is appropriate that he should act as president',[16] declares a note in the Alternative Service Book, and that is unnecessarily cautious, and liturgical practice has already made it look so. Wherever the Bishop goes in his diocese, he is the president of the liturgy. If it is not always so, the exceptions are now very rare. The *Book of Alternative Services* of the Anglican Church in Canada puts it more strongly: 'As chief officer it is the bishop's prerogative to preside at the Lord's table and to preach the gospel.'[17] Because the cathedral is the bishop's church, here of all places one would expect his ministry to be fully exercised. Yet sometimes the only church where the Bishop is not the eucharistic president is his own cathedral.

Custom and even statute intervene. Sometimes, not envisaging the bishop wanting to be in his cathedral, or not envisaging that the principal service of a festival day will be the eucharist, custom or even statute lay down that the dean or the canon in residence, or even a minor canon shall be the president, whoever may be present. Sometimes it is not simply a matter of not envisaging the Bishop's presence, but the use of custom or statute to assert the chapter's independence of the Bishop. The Bishop is left high and dry on his throne, while the dean or provost presides at the altar. How can that be justified theologically? The truth is that this kind of theological question is never asked in some cathedrals, though others have worked this through and adopted a style that affirms the collegial nature of ordained ministry, with the Bishop as president, and the chapter, or a more inclusive body of his priests, gathered around him. Where theology and ecclesiology are brought to bear, liturgical principles soon emerge. They emerge not only for the cathedral community, but for the diocese as clergy and lay people, coming to the cathedral on a variety of occasions, see the relationship between bishop and priests expressed liturgically.

An ordination provides a particular example of how this

relationship is expressed, and of how the liturgical ordering of a cathedral sometimes makes it difficult. Ordination is by the prayer of the whole assembly with the laying on of hands by the Bishop and *his presbyters*. That is the theory and the theology. The reality tends to be the laying on of hands by the Bishop and the candidate's chosen friends, or by the Bishop and his senior staff, other priests often some way distant from the liturgical sitting in the quire or out in a transept. The picture of ministry, and of the relationship of the new minister to bishop and college of priests, in such arrangements cannot help to form people liturgically or theologically. A sanctuary full of choir stalls and Victorian furnishings, or a temporary altar on a small dais, will never allow the liturgy to express ecclesial relationships. Liturgical re-ordering may address the issue, but even with liturgical re-ordering, the issue seems sometimes not be faced.

The Bishop's presidency over initiation raises another set of problems, addressed by the English House of Bishops in 1995 in *On the Way*.[18] Although people may learn to look to the cathedral to see the Bishop presiding over the Eucharist, and to see their parish celebrations as derived, in some sense, from that, there is little enough in most dioceses to enable them to look to the cathedral to see the Bishop presiding over the rites of Christian initiation that are equally his ministry and to which their own parish baptism services relate in a parallel way. Bishops have very often allowed candidates whom they are to confirm to be privately baptized in advance of the confirmation, and this has built up a quite false view of the relationship between the two rites, Baptism appearing to be a kind preliminary to a full membership of the Church conferred by episcopal Confirmation. Few cathedrals can claim to be, or bother in their self-description for visitors to claim to be, the principal church where the Bishop admits new Christians through Baptism. And yet even a notice to that effect near the cathedral font would say something about a church geared up to mission and evangelism in a post-christian society.

'Near the cathedral font': but therein lies another of the problems. In many cathedrals the font is so placed that, if the Bishop did wish to make Baptism a focus of his liturgical ministry in the cathedral, he could not do so. The font is in a corner, or a chapel or an

ambulatory. Perhaps a parish church can be forgiven for some of
the odd things that go on: semi-private baptisms where the font in
the corner will do, or baptism in water from a bowl on a table on
the chancel step, or borrowing the tank at the local Baptist Church
because there is nothing suitable in the parish church for the adult
who, very reasonably, wants to be dipped in the water as the
Prayer Book urges. But a cathedral, a place that sets standards,
thinks things through theologically, and needs to work by clear
liturgical principles, must help the Bishop in his baptismal ministry
by giving him a church in which he can baptize within a great
liturgy with all his people gathered around him.

One more example of how the cathedral can help the bishop
and the diocese to get the liturgy right must suffice. Each year in
an increasing number of dioceses the clergy, and some lay people
too, come to the cathedral on or near Maundy Thursday for the
'Chrism Eucharist', at which the Bishop blesses the holy oils.
Clergy, in growing numbers, take the oils back to their parishes.
But that is then the end of the matter. The Bishop is not sure when
to use the oil he has blessed, not even sure sometimes whether to
allow its use, and his cathedral will often keep a supply locked up
for those who come back for more, but will never use it in cathedral liturgy. The use of oil has ceased to be a mark of a particular
churchmanship. Thoroughly biblical, whether in the anointing of
priests and kings, or in the provision for the sick, it is an area of
liturgical ministry where people want to learn from seeing and
experiencing sound practice. They ought to be able to come to the
cathedral to baptisms, to ordinations, to services of healing and
discover a confident Bishop exercising his ministry with the holy
oils generously and effectively. Oil locked up in an aumbry will get
neither theology nor liturgy anywhere.

Here then are a whole cluster of issues related to the Bishop and
his liturgical ministry where a cathedral can ensure that custom and
statute give way to clear thinking, principle and the desire to see
principle worked out in satisfactory pastoral practice. In that way
people will see the bishop 'working out his ministry in a liturgical,
sacramental and pastoral context' and this ministry as 'part of the
liturgical formation of his clergy and people'.[19]

There is, however, another area of ministry that needs to be expressed liturgically in the cathedral even more than the bishop's ministry. It is the ministry of the laity. It is another area where theological clarity will challenge custom and statute. For cathedrals more than any other aspect of church life live by hierarchy. It is a highly developed hierarchy, seen at its most potent in the line up for ecclesiastical processions, where the comparitive order of residentiary canons, suffragan bishops and bishop's chaplains can occupy many pages of cathedral memoranda. But, worse, it is a priestly hierarchy, and lay people simply do not feature. There are cathedrals still where at the principal eucharist clergy alone read the lections, clergy alone lead the prayers of the people, clergy alone distribute the sacrament, or, if lay people do any of these things, it is only because of clergy shortage, and so, on any great occasion, the laity will not be needed, for there will be sufficient priests. This hierarchical principle is expressed most tellingly at the ordinations of bishops, usually in London at Westminster Abbey, Southwark Cathedral and St Paul's. Who shall read the gospel? Not a deacon from the new bishop's diocese, but the senior prelate present, usually the Bishop of London. Who shall read the epistle? Not a lay person from the bishop's new diocese, but the second senior prelate present, usually the Bishop of Winchester. Who shall read the Old Testament Reading? Probably the Dean or the Provost. This extraordinary 'jobs for the senior boys' approach to liturgy needs to be challenged, for it can have its equivalent on special occasions in parish life too. It is the cathedral where it can be challenged, where role and ministry have been thought through with theological care and given appropriate liturgical expression, lay people, deacons, priests and bishops each playing their part and revealing together the nature of the Church.

To be a 'liturgical laboratory' is more than to be a place that gets it right and sends out clear signals. Providing a proper model is part of the cathedral's ministry, but finding the model, especially the model that can work within the constraints of a particular building, will require something of the laboratory approach, whether it be experiment with the daily prayer of the foundation, or the eucharist of the cathedral's Sunday congregation, or the great occasion when the building is packed out with people unused to being there. In the laboratory there are of course some disasters and some failures. And, in any case, the laboratory image, for all its importance, is only one side of a picture that needs to recognise also the cathedral's role as conservator, historic monument and shrine, and the utmost sensitivity is needed if the right balance is to be struck. Nevertheless, it is the laboratory mentality that the cathedrals, with only a few notable exceptions, have failed to master in relation to liturgy, and it is not only the report of an Archbishops' commission, but a whole Church crying out for help with liturgical formation, that needs that mentality to be mastered now.

NOTES

1. *Heritage and Renewal,* The Report of the Archbishops' Commission on Cathedrals (London, 1994).
2. *Heritage and Renewal,* p. 19.
3. The story is well told in Roger Lloyd, *The Church of England 1900–1965* (London, 1966), chapters 18 and 28.
4. See *The Church of England 1900–1965,* pp. 392–399.
5. For a description of Dwellys' work, see Stanley Morison, *English Prayer Books: An Introduction to the Literature of Christian Public Worship* (Cambridge, 1943) pp. 118–132.
6. John Robinson, *Liturgy Coming to Life* (London, 1960).
7. H. C. N. Williams, *Coventry Cathedral in Action* (Oxford, 1968).
8. David Stancliffe, 'A Pilgrimage from West to East' in Christopher Crooks (Ed) *The Guiders' Guide to The Cathedral Church of St Thomas of Canterbury, Portsmouth* (Portsmouth, 1993).
9. *Heritage and Renewal,* p. 54.
10. *In Tune with Heaven,* The Report of the Archbishops' Commission on Church Music (London, 1992).
11. *In Tune with Heaven,* p. 226.
12. *In Tune with Heaven,* p. 216.
13. *Heritage and Renewal,* p. 18.
14. *Heritage and Renewal,* p. 20.
15. PRAXIS is sponsored by The Church of England Liturgical Commission, the Alcuin Club and the Group for the Renewal of Worship. These propositions were drawn up for PRAXIS by the prsent author.
16. *The Alternative Service Book 1980,* London, 1980, p. 2.
17. *The Book of Alternative Services of The Anglican Church of Canada,* Torono, 1985, p. 183.
18. *On the Way* (London, 1995).
19. Proposition 2 of the PRAXIS document quoted above.

11

Preaching and Lectionary

Horace T. Allen, Jr.

IT IS REPORTED that John Calvin of Geneva once said that he would be willing to cross seven seas in quest of the unity of Christ's Church. This contributor to this volume of essays in honour of Donald Gray can testify to the fact that Donald has in fact crossed the same sea, the Atlantic, more than seven times in such a quest. This he did as a representative from the Joint Liturgical Group of Great Britain between the years of 1990 and 1993 in order to participate in the (North American) Consultation on Common Texts' work of refining its *Common Lectionary*.[1] The fruit of that work and of Donald's ecumenical and trans-Atlantic journeying has now been published as *Revised Common Lectionary*.[2] That work is rapidly finding its way across yet more seas, East and West, and is in this way becoming a means whereby John Calvin's own vision is being realized.

This is not to simply convert Canon Gray into a dedicated Calvinist however, since ecumenism is also the professed vocation of his own ecclesial home, the Anglican Communion. His extraordinary efforts in this ecumenical development of a lectionary system which has its origins in the Roman *Ordo lectionum Missae* (herinafter OLM) of 1969[3] and which, as already noted, is rapidly becoming normative for many Anglican Provinces and national Protestant churches, some of which have heretofore never make available to their clergy such a system, have borne witness to this noteworthy Anglican inclusiveness. Thus it was possible for this writer, in reporting on these developments to point out to the Episcopal Board and Advisory Committee of the (Roman Catholic) International Commission on English in the Liturgy (hereinafter ICEL) on May 2–3, 1991[4] that by virtue of the wide-spread use of *Common Lectionary*. Protestants, Anglicans and Catholics were already experiencing a profound unity around 'the table of God's Word', as paragraph 51 of *Sacrosanctum Concilium* puts it.[5] In response to this report, that venerable liturgical scholar and reformer, Fr. Godfrey Diekmann, OSB, quickly underlined the significance of this lectionary convergence by reminding the Board and Committee that this is exactly what the post-Conciliar framers of *OLM* (Study Group 11) had in mind, *at his own suggestion*. His biographer, Sr. Kathleen Hughes cites his diary from that time to the effect that 'I gave a brief report on Montreal, and urged contact with Protestants, especially in three year cycle of readings'.[6] He also reminded the ICEL Bishops and their advisors that *already* a large measure of unity *has been achieved* at the table of the Word even if such is not the case with regard to the table of the Eucharist. It was a dear and aged Jesuit friend of this writer who pointed out that this formulation of 'two tables' is perhaps first to be found in Thomas a Kempis's *Imitatio Christi*, Book 4, Chapter 11:

> For in this life I find there are two things especially necessary for me, without which this miserable life would be insupportable ... for the word of God is the light of my soul and thy sacrament is the bread of life. These also may be called the two tables set on either side, in the storehouse of thy holy church. One is the table of the holy altar having the holy bread, that is the precious Body of Christ. The other is that of the divine law, containing thy holy doctrine, teaching the right faith, and firmly leading even within the veil, where is the holy of holies.[7]

It is in pursuit of this ecumenical unity around the table of the Word that Canon Gray has in more recent years made his way, in the company of the English Language Liturgical Consultation (hereinafter ELLC) to meetings with the Faith and Order Commission of the World Council of Churches in Geneva (1993) and with two dicasteries of the Holy See in Rome (1994), the Pontifial Council on Promoting Christian Unity and the Congregation of Divine Worship and the Discipline of the Sacraments, in order to encourage the Holy See to enter into active engagement with the ELLC so as to make possible the use in Roman Catholic Provinces of the English-speaking world, if only on a trial basis, of *Revised Common Lectionary*. Thus has Donald Gray moved mightily on the ecumenical scene, and crossed his 'seven seas' in pursuit of a unity at the table of the Word which may yet prove more powerful and convincing for the average worshipping Christian than all the schemes for demoninational integration or interchurch cooperation in social or secular efforts.

It is not surprising that a Donald Gray should become so deeply involved in this enterprise of fashioning a Sunday, eucharistic lectionary system for ecumenical use. One has only to remember his years of service as a parish priest and preacher. Preaching for him is clearly one of the great delights of priesthood. To hear him preach is to experience an amazing unity of voice intonation and pacing, of the subtle and graceful use of his body (even as he walks to and from the pulpit), a rich sense of the drama in the words and the Word, an ease in public address and above all, an earnest yearning to engage his hearers in his own hearing and experiencing of the biblical message as embodied in the particular pericopes at hand. All this he now carries off in the vast spaces of Westminster Abbey as though he were in the simplest parish church with a scattering of more or less attentive faithful worshippers.

It is this relationship between preaching and lectionary formulation that provides this essay with its agenda. The question to be addressed here is that of the particular impact of *Revised Common Lectionary* upon Christian preaching, especially in those ecclesial communities where it is now most widely in use, that is, the Protestant and Anglican churches of the English-speaking world. To be sure that impact will take different forms among these different churches particularly in terms of their several traditions of preaching. That will be taken into account. But the thesis of this survey is that the principles inherent both in the Roman *Ordo* '69 and *Revised Common Lectionary* (hereinafter RCL), if faithfully heeded by preachers, will radically re-shape the face of preaching in these communities. Already in the United States for instance, in churches which never imposed or even suggested any kind of lectionary, one hears rumblings of resentment from older clerics about this 'new lectionary preaching' as though it were some kind of straight-jacket from which escape becomes impossible (on the one hand) or a lazyman's (sic) approach to preaching (on the other hand). At the same time, it is suggested that a pastoral integrity or spiritual freedom of the preacher is now being threatened. The sheer fact of such deeply felt opposition, among what might be called 'Free churches', and in the Unite States this probably includes Prebyterians, indicates that use of RCL does in fact imply a new or different kind of preaching. Nor is the resistance solely on that side of the ecclesiastical divide. Throughout the years since 1969 and the various denominational attempts at revision of OLM, there has been a running battle of sorts concerning the use of the Old Testament in Ordinary Time for instance. Churches which have used a version of the 1570 Roman Lectionary have had some difficult in getting used to an Old Testament reading and have tended, understandably, to prefer the OLM 'typological' or 'linked' (with the Gospel) hermeneutic. Thus RCL has had to accommodate this concern by listing an alternate table of Old Testament lessons for Ordinary Time after Pentecost which utilizes this 'linked' principle, in addition to its own semi-continuous pattern for Old Testament reading on those post-Pentcost Sundays. And lurking behind this discussion is that larger question of whether thematic linkage should characterize the entirety of the lectionary's readings, Sunday by Sunday. This of course is the outstanding difference between OLM/RCL on the one hand and the Joint Liturgical Group's two- or four-year plan on the other hand. Throughout this discussion Donald Gray has been a most evenhanded and knowledgeable sage, especially since few of the North American framers of RCL have had any experience whatever of the British scheme.

As all lectionary framers quickly discover, such a process is one of seemingly endless choices: books to be used when? versification? which parallel passage? how to 'cut' lengthy narratives? what to do with controversial ethical issues? how to take into account ancient customs? and on and on. But as all lectionary framers hope, presumably the choices made will make for more responsible handling of the scriptures in the context of liturgy, that is, better preaching, even though this is certainly not the only reason for reading the scriptures during public worship. For a discussion of this issue, the reader may refer to two of the addresses given at the Toronto Congress of *Societas Liturgica* in 1989, one by Paul Bradshaw and one by this writer.[8]

In order to amplify the thesis of this essay that OLM/RCL might already be having a significant effect on contemporary preaching (as if the sheer volume of publishing efforts by way of commentary and homiletical helps didn't prove the point *prima facie*) the following implications of using these systems may be identified: (1) Sunday as sequential, making possible narrative preaching rather than disconnected oracular 'hits or misses'.(2) Scripture as its own context due to the *lectio continua* principle and the respect for various literary genre as found in the Bible, (3) Scripture as governing the liturgical calendar especially in the festal seasons of Advent/Christmas and Lent/Easter, (4) the preacher as 'obedient' to the text rather than choosing it for his/her own purposes, and (5) preaching as a more participatory experience, within the parish and ecumenically and in terms of a richer integration of musical and educational parish programs, than has been possible heretofore.

Before turning to an elaboration of these five points, this writer should enter a caveat about the perspective which he brings to these matters. Being from North America the experience of the churches there will form the principal data base for these reflections. Further, being a Presbyterian teaching in a seminary of the United Methodist Church the primary consideration will be the effect of using a lectionary system in the first place. Attention will also be paid, of course, to the experience of preachers in other churches for whom RCL is, as lectionary, not a new experience, but rather as a different kind of lectionary using different principles of selection from those which have for decades been used, as in the Episcopal, Lutheran and older continental Reformed churches.

1. *Sunday as Sequence – Narrative Preaching*

Perhaps the single most revolutionary result of using RCL, for churches which have never used a lectionary *and* for churches whose lectionaries were based in the Western, Latin tradition, will be the experience of Sunday as the occasion for a sequence of biblical passages. It could be said that the history of lectionaries in the Western church has been a gradual shift from *lectio continua* (as in the Syngagogue and the early Roman church) to *lectio selecta*. The continuing occasion for this shift was calendrical, in that the Sunday calendar came to include more annual dates, in contrast to the earlier pattern wherein the Pascha was the only annual festival (and that, only after the Council of Nicaea) with perhaps Epiphany in the East (also a fixed date) and then Christmas in the West (a fixed date). Thus, as the 16th century Reformers perceived, the principle recurring festival of the Church was in fact, the Lord's Day. Hence there was no reason to interrupt the course reading of 'the memoirs of the apostles or the writings of the prophets'.[9] It was only as the annual calendar became more elaborate in the cycles of Sundays around Christmas and Pascha that the *continua* pattern was interrupted by a *selecta* principle. This of course had probably been done even in the Synagogue on Sabbaths proximate to the Pascha and the High Holy Days.

At the same time, as the first Milennium drew to its close other calendrical cycles imposed their own 'selected' periscopes on the Sunday sequence such as the sanctoral and Marian festivals. Thus, by the time of the Reformation of the 16th century continuous reading had disappeared altogether, and even had it not, the linguistic barrier would have rendered it unintelligible. Further, the celebration of Mass, which might have secured the uniqueness of the Lord's Day festival, having become a daily event, was insufficient to suggest to the faithful that the Lord's Day, as a recurring weekly event, formed its own calendar with a combination of proper and ordinary elements having to do with the regular *anamnesis* of the death and resurrection of the Lord. The increasing secularization of the Lord's Day and the increase in number of holy Days only reinforced the loss of that day as a continuing sequence of celebrations.

It was probably John Calvin, with his extensive knowledge of the early Fathers, who most clearly understood the symmetry between the Lord's Day as the primary Christian festival, the Lord's Supper, and the course reading of scripture on that day. Thus his reading and preaching of the scriptures on the Lord's Day reverted to *lectio continua*, being interrupted only by the annual festivals of Christmas, Easter and Pentecost. Indeed, when thwarted in his attempts to recover a weekly eucharistic celebration or even a monthly schedule he turned to those great festivals as the eucharist days, a strategy which even his own ecclesial descendants in Scotland and North America, have never understood with their strict 'quarterly' pattern, even though the Puritan anti-Prayer Book *Directory for Worship* of the Westminster Assembly (1645) recommended course reading from the Old and New Testaments.

With the publication by the Holy See of OLM in 1969 the Western rite at last returned to this principle in large measure. Thus the Synoptic Gospels are read in their entirety, week by week, year by year, resorting to a *selecta* pattern only for Lent/Easter and Advent/Christmas. Thus also the Pauline, Johannine and Pastoral epistles are read the same way during Ordinary Time, post-Pentecost. And with RCL (and its immediate predecessor, *Common Lectionary*)[10] the *continua* principle was applied to the First Reading in Ordinary Time post-Pentecost. As Donald Gray can testify, this departure from OLM has created the greatest controversy both within and without the consultative process. That is why, as noted above, RCL provides an alternative set of Old Testament pericopes for this period in the Year which more nearly accords with the Roman typlogical system as found also in the *Lutheran Book of Worship* (1978)[11] and the Episcopal *Book of Common Prayer* (1979)[12]. It can be reported however that as of this writing it has been announced in the Consultation on Common Tests (North America) that both the Evangelical Lutheran Church in America and the Episcopal Church in the United States have officially approved RCL as an option to the tables now printed in their own books, although the Lutheran Church recommended the typological option for the Sundays post-Pentecost.

But what does this recovery of *lectio continua* mean for preaching? Interestingly the most important points apply equally to traditional lectionary-using churches and to those which have not done so until this past decade. And one suspects that the significance of this recovery is only now becoming clear. This recovery requires that the preacher, and the hearers, need to think about a Sunday to Sunday sequence of pericopes. Put another way, the scriptural context for Sunday's sermon is 'horizontally' determined rather than 'vertically'. The consonance of lessons is week to week rather than lesson to lesson on a given Sunday, at least in Ordinary Time post-Pentecost. This makes the often heard complaint that lectionary preaching doesn't provide opportunity for 'series' sermons quite ironic since the *continua* principle builds that possibility into the heart of the proclamation. The difference from the popular assumption is that the 'series' is embedded in the scriptures themselves rather than some artificial construct such as 'Great Personages in the Bible'.[6] The Apostles' Creed in Paul's Letters', etc.

This places the preacher and people in a new relationship to the recurring Lord's Day. It assumes a fairly stable and regular congregation and means that preacher and people must undertake the kind of preparation for the Lord's Day through the week which may well, as a side effect, bring back to Protestant homes the daily scrutiny of the scriptures. For the preacher it certainly means that there will have to be a more careful study of biblical books in use than was ever the case when one went skipping about one's favourite books week to week. This professor's students are counseled each year in Advent, or shortly before, to purchase and familiarize themselves with the latest and best commentaries on the Gospel for the year. The same could be said for the epistles to be read after Pentecost. Further, it is to be hoped that by the end of each of the three year cycles the congregation itself will have a fairly clear picture of the unique characteristics of the synoptic Gospel for that year.

This is emphatically not to turn the Lord's Day celebration into a liturgical 'bible study' session, as some have charged. It is simply to include in one's preaching the sort of contextualization which is essential to understanding the pericopes as the bases for sermons and homilies.

What is equally difficult for many preachers to accept is the above-mentioned fact that for fully half the calendar year the three readings for the day may well have no thematic coherence. Even the most sophisticated series of lectionary commentaries find it hard not to find some sort of interrelationship among the three (and some would say, four, since they fail to grasp the unique function of the Psalm for the day as a sung response to the First

Reading). Worse, whether guided by these commentaries or their own traditional concept of preaching, some preachers, realizing that there is no inner relationship thematically, will simply preach three rather brief and simplistic sermonettes! Evidence of this sort of assumption often surfaces with the question as to why, if one is not going to use all three lessons in the homily, does not read them at all. That is to say, in certain traditions the assumption has been that the one only reads from the scriptures for the purpose of preaching. The corollary of this assumption is its undoing (certainly in a Protestant context), namely, that what once was called 'dumb reading', that is, reading without commentary, cannot possibly be edifying for the people of God. Surely this evidence a kind of Protestant 'priestcraft' which is thoroughly inappropriate precisely in that tradition. One recalls a line from a much-loved hymn of William Cowper: 'God is His own inter-preter, and He will make it plain'.

There is however a way to counter this sort of challenge and also to respect the *continua* principle. That is to preface all readings by the briefest kind of *incipit* whereby the community is reminded of the textual context of each lesson, whether or not it is to be used homiletically. Indeed, it well might be a worthy project for some parish preacher to produce a full three-year set for liturgical use as one doctoral candidate of this Professor of Worship has already done.

In conclusion then we can posit the proposition that RCL, properly used, will require of the preacher a new level of biblical background and of the people a new level of concentration that will carry over from one Sunday to the next. One needn't belabour the deeper implications of this exercise for a theological description of the character of the liturgical assembly as the princi-ple place for continuing catechesis and deeping in faith wherein the ever-changing biblical material, in sequence, is paired with the ever-the-same eucharistic celebration.

2 Scripture as its own context
This point is obviously closely related to the previous paragraphs. The particular matter which needs attention here has to do with the questions of literary genre and the formation of the various

books of the Bible in relation to their communities and the canon-
ization process. Here we are taking aboard at least two fairly recent
schools of biblical study: on the one hand the 'canon criticism'
school which addresses the historical process by which given
Christian communities formed and canonized their books, and on
the other hand the 'literary historical' school with reads the scriptures in terms of their relationship to known literary forms of their
times.

One might observe that these two schools of thought are actually describing the formation of the canonical books as 'lectionaries in the making'. The goal of these two schools of study is to
provide us with a sensitivity as to how given books were formed,
in the context of their particular communities and of literary
conventions of their own times. Just as the goal of OLM/RCL is
to provide contemporary communities with a form of proclamation which takes account, on a weekly basis, of these factors in
order to re-form those historic communities in the present day, the
homily being the operative literary form. In this regard one thinks
of the suggestive small book of Raymond E. Brown, *The Churches
the Apostles Left Behind*[13] or James A. Sanders' *Torah and Canon*[14],
Canon and Community[15] and *God Has a Story Too*.[16]

These schools of biblical criticism return the study and proclamation of the scriptures to their original communal, ecclesial
context in prospect just as the use of a lectionary whose basis is
largely continua and whose selecta Sundays relate to the community's recurring annual festivals, do the same in retrospect.
Moreover, with scripture as its own context ('interpreter') the
liturgical assembly is constantly being introduced to what the late
Karl Barth called 'The Strange New World within the Bible'.[17] As
he puts it: 'within the Bible there is a strange, new world, the
world of God …'[18] And again, 'There is a river in the Bible that
carries us away, once we have entrusted our destiny to it – away
from ourselves to the sea'.[19] Here too we discover a powerful
symmetry between the Liturgy of the Word and the Liturgy of the
Table, between the spoken language of scripture and sermon and
the prayed and gestured language of the Table, the 'two tables'.

In this regard it is possible to think of the homily itself as a
particular literary form, particularly closely related to the commu-

nity within which it occurs. A sermon needn't always be hortatory, or didactic, or narrative, though it well may be, depending on the scriptural material for the day. A sermon might be lyrical, poetic, hymnic, eucological, meditative, as well. One has only to dip into the homilies of the ancient Fathers to discover this, and how interesting that they were often, if not always, working with a *continua* principle. That of course is the reason that RCL reads books such as epistles, synoptic Gospels, Acts and Old Testament history in a continuous or semi-continuous way, whereas the Fourth Gospel is used in a 'selected' way in relationship to the Christian calendar just as it seems to be organized in relationship to the Jewish calendar.

At a time when the world of the Bible is increasingly 'strange', both because of increasing biblical illiteracy and because of the increasingly secular and even violent character of contemporary society, the preacher must be able to find a way for the people of God into the world of God. And a preacher, Catholic or Protestant, who works carefully with such a lectionary system as we now have, will find that that 'world of God' just might make more sense than the 'worlds in collision' of our times which seem always to be either exploding or impoding. As Luther's hymn proclaims, 'That word above all earthly powers, no thanks to them, abideth ... God's truth abideth still: His kingdom is forever'.

3 Lectionary and Calendar

We now turn our attention to the guidance RCL provides for the preacher in those festal seasons wherein the principle of selection is not *continua* but *selecta*: Advent/Christmas (incl. Epiphany and 1st Epiphany) and Lent/Easter (including Pentecost/Trinity). Once again we must take note of the different 'directions' from which preachers in various traditions will come to RCL. Clerics of the so-called 'liturgical churches', such as Roman Catholic, Lutheran and Anglican, will be quite used to the consonance of season and lectionary, even though (as we will note shortly) the lections chosen may well require certain changes in their traditional understanding of these seasons. On the other hand, clerics of the so-called 'Free churches' have either paid no attention to the classic annual calendar or, and this is of considerable importance, have begun to celebrate these cycles of Christmas and Easter, simply as seasons, without regard to the regulatory authority of a lectionary. Curiously, this has been the pattern in many North American Protestant communities. Thus these seasons of Advent, Christmas/Epiphany and Lent/Easter/Pentecost have come to be observed without proper attention to the way in which classical Western lectionaries have *defined their meaning*. On the face of it, this is a strange and even contradictory way for Protestants to shape their worship, that is, by reference to a set of seasons without regard to the way in which biblical selections for those seasons define them. This has resulted in all manner of anomalies such as the Fourth Sunday of Advent being designated 'Christmas Sunday', and in one church's Ministers' Daily Diary the Sunday after Christmas being designated 'The Fifth Sunday in Advent'. At Epiphany, the Magi would often displace the Baptism of the Lord depending on where in the week January 6th occurred. In the Paschal cycle a penitential mood has pervaded all the Lenten Sundays without noticing that those Sundays are not even counted as part of Lent in that they anticipate Easter, not Good Friday (a misunderstanding which was not altogether absent from the more liturgical churches and which has only been corrected even there by the Gospels and related pericopes for Lent in OLM/RCL). Also, among the Free churches there was little sense for the *season* of Easter, the Great Fifty Days and as a result Pentecost was a detached, free-standing festival which became 'the Birthday of the Church' (as though Christ had not called his church into being at the moment of the calling of the Twelve!).

With the emerging use of RCL however, preachers were jolted into a re-definition of much of the festal times *on the basis* of the biblical pericopes. A curious twist, in that a Catholic-derived, biblical system was needed to call Protestant preaching to a more evangelical use of the classic calendar! Thus it suddenly became clear that Advent had to do not with the First Coming but the Second, and this at precisely the moment North American Protestantism began what has become a near universal practice of lighting candles each Sunday of Advent in anticipation of ... Christmas! Thus the service on First Advent begins with the solemn declaration, by lighting the first of the Advent candles, that Christmas is only four weeks away, but then at the reading of the Gospel for the day the congregation hears quite another message: 'Watch and pray, for *no one knows* the day or the hour' of the advent of Messiah. This confusion is further compounded by the cultural pressure to being singing Christmas carols as early as that First Sunday in Advent, such that one even hears references to 'this Christmas season'. And of course when the Twelve Days of Christmas are begun on December 25th, the worshipping community, like its surrounding culture, is tired of the whole thing and has little interest in further festivity, except for welcoming the Magi at Epiphany. As already mentioned, the same corrective has been administered concerning the Sundays in Lent by virtue of the biblical plan of OLM/RCL which anticipates Easter rather than Good Friday. A further revision of (Protestant) homiletical tradition is administered by these lectionary systems at the newly-designated Passion/Palm Sunday moment which in much of Free church practice was devoted exclusively to the Triumphal Entry, the Passion being left to the days of Holy Week (which are increasingly poorly attended, and celebrated in sometimes embarrassingly literalistic and dramatic fashion) so that the preacher never has an opportunity to 'preach the Passion'. Finally, the pericopes for the Sundays after Easter now remind the most careless preacher that the Resurrection celebration does not end with Easter Day but in fact *begins* with it.

Thus it has come about that this ecumenical lectionary system has at last reminded the universal Church that it is the Bible that shapes the calendar and preaching, and not the calendar that shapes the preaching. For those who have eyes to see and ears to hear, this is the clear message of Prof. Thomas Talley's magisterial study *The Origins of the Liturgical Year*.[20] It is precisely this mix of continuous and selected biblical pericopes that give the calendar of the Christian community whatever shape and evangelical significance it is to have.

4. Preacher and Text

For preachers from ecclesial traditions which have never prescribed a lectionary the current situation requires a totally new way of thinking of their relation to the biblical texts. Oddly, this new way is in a direction which would seem to be axiomatic for Protestants but which in fact has certainly not been. Thus the preacher now no longer chooses the preaching texts; they choose the preacher. The way this is most often expressed is the complaint that 'There's nothing about these texts that "turns me on" '. To express this situation in a more sophisticated way, one might observe that for the preacher to live with the luxury of choosing the weekly preaching texts is to run the grave risk of reducing the Canon of Holy Scripture to those books and pericopes which are congenial with the preacher's own theological preoccupations, or, worse, with the limitations of the preacher's seminary study of the Bible. Most preachers who take on the responsibility of working consistently with the lectionary soon became painfully aware of how little of the Canon they were using when the principle of selection was entirely their own interests and favorite passages. This of course was precisely the intent expressed in Vatican II's *Sacrosanctum Concilium* in its often-quoted paragraph 51:

> The treasures of the Bible are to be opened up more lavishly so that a richer fare may be provided for the faithful at the table of God's word. In this way a more representative part of the sacred scriptures will be read to the people in the course of a prescribed number of years.[21]

Underlying this reality of course is the larger and more significant issue of the inspiration of Holy Scripture. In Calvinism this has been expressed by the doctrinal affirmation that the scriptures only become 'the Word of God' by virtue of the 'inward testimony of the Holy Spirit'.

There is of course a more probematic side to this laudable practice of placing oneself, as preacher, at the disposal of the lectionary table. That is the danger that one abandons altogether any creative energy in making the lectionary's choices one's own. This can result either in a careless and forced attempt to define a 'a common theme', even when such does not exist as in the Sundays after Pentecost, or, as mentioned above, a lifeless and perfunctory series of three (or four!) brief comments on the texts of the day. This is why lectionary preaching requires that the preacher plan well ahead as to which of the biblical sequences are to be followed, after

Pentecost, for instance. It is also doubly important that the preacher have a minimal understanding of the lectionary's own principles and plan in order that the selections made by the lectionary be clear to the preacher well before the sermon is planned, and, perhaps more importantly, that the preacher then bring his or her own critical facilities to bear on any given Sunday's selections as to whether the lectionary's choices might have to be amended or edited. Thus, although the use of a lectionary can be of vital assistance to the preacher, one must guard against a certain homiletical laziness since the principal choices for the sermon have already been made. It could be said that the preacher is only using the lectionary well when the sermonic work is *harder* than when the preacher was choosing the texts week by week.

5 *Preaching as Participatory*

Perhaps one of the most important possibilities at the parish level which the use of RCL provides, and this is not altogether different from using any other lectionary system, is that it becomes possible to invite the parish community to enter into a regular discipline, along with their preacher, of study and preparation for Sunday's Liturgy of the Word. As was not possible in a time when the preacher choose the texts on a week by week basis, often sometime during the week just before their use, it is now possible to alert the congregation in advance (at least at the previous week's assembly) as to what the lessons will be on the following Sunday. This in turn suggests that regular lectionary study groups might be convened wherein the pastor can work in advance, *with the faithful*, to prepare the homily. This could also be conjoined with training sessions for lay readers, for it is often the case that only when one takes the time to proclaim the pericopes out loud that certain subtleties and nuances begin to appear.

Another aspect of parish participation has to do with the proper intergration of various elements of the parish liturgy and life, such as music and Christian education. Use of RCL makes possible what churches which have long had their own systems have always known, namely, that it is possible for the parish musician(s) to plan ahead regarding choral and instrumental music which will relate to the biblical texts for the day. With the publication of RCL a vast publishing activity has developed to point the way for such integration on a weekly basis. The same may be said of curricula now being produced for use in the parish's Church School and adult education programs. These programs need no longer be tangential or even totally unrelated to the liturgical and homiletical life of the community, but rather supportive thereof.

Another way in which preaching may become more participatory has to do with the particular way in which RCL has been so widely accepted already, ecumenically. The English Language Liturgical Consultation, upon whose Steering Committee Canon Gray sits, continues to hear of wider and wider use of this system, not only in the English-speaking world of Great Britain, North America, Australia, New Zealand and South Africa, but also in other language groups as in Scandanavia, Korea and in many mission situations in the Third World. This use in all these places is by Anglicans and quite a few Protestant bodies. Further, the close relationship between RCL and the Roman Lectionary (OLM) means that throughout the world many churches in hundreds of thousand local situations are reading the scriptures together on the Lord's Day. This has already resulted in the formation of clerical lectionary study groups throughout the world and especially in those places where ecumenical cooperation is an accepted and acceptable experience. This represents a fulfillment of the fondest hopes of the framers first of *Common Lectionary* and now of *Revised Common Lectionary*. One might be allowed the vision that as separated ecclesial communities begin to participate *together* in the weekly, homiletical study of the Holy Scriptures, the Lord's priestly prayer is coming to fruition: 'I have given them your word ... Sanctify them in the truth; your word is truth' (John 17.14, 17).

Donald Gray has not sailed his seven seas in vain. The realities and visions here recounted represent an impressive ministry, biblically and ecumenically. One of Canon Gray's Roman Catholic colleagues in these efforts, the renowned liturgical pioneer and canonist, the Rt Rev. Msgr Frederick R. McManus, reflected some years ago that these developments are 'by far the most successful and practical ecumenical progress in Christian worship since the Second Vatican Council ...'[22] Nor need we fear that our colleague of Westminster Abbey will take the occasion of his sixty-fifth year to rest on his many laurels. As one hymn puts it, a hymn which is much beloved for its use in the precincts of another Abbey, that of Iona:

> I feel the winds of God today;
> Today my sail I lift,
> Though heavy oft with drenching spray,
> And torn with many a rift;
> If hope but light the water's crest,
> And Christ my bark will use,
> I'll seek the seas as His behest,
> And brave another cruise.[23]

NOTES

1. Consultation on Common Texts, *Common Lectionary: The Lectionary Proposed by the Consultation on Common Texts* (New York, 1983).
2. Consultation on Common Texts, *The Revised Common Lectionary* (Nashville, 1992).
3. Congregation for Divine Worship, *Ordo lectionum Missae*. (Rome, Vatican Polyglot Press, 1969).
4. ICEL is the Secretariat for the Conference of Catholic Bishops for whom English is either the principal language used in worship or at least is used in a substantial number of dioceses. It is governed by its Episcopal Board to which each Conference sends one bishop. They in turn are advised by a panel of liturgical scholars.
5. Vatican Council II, Constitution on the Liturgy, *Sacrosanctum Concilium* (4 December 1963) no. 51, tr. International Commission on English in the Liturgy, *Documents on the Liturgy, 1963–1979: Conciliar, Papal, and Curial Texts* (Collegeville, 1982).
6. Kathleen Hughes, R.S.C.J., *The Monk's Tale – A Biography of Godfrey Diekmann, O.S.B.* (Collegeville, 1991) p. 232.
7. Thomas a Kempis, *The Imitation of Christ*, tr. Rt. Rev Richard Challoner, D.D., (New York, 1871) pp. 441–442.
8. Horace T. Allen, Jr., 'Lectionaries – Principles and Problems: A Comparitive Analysis', and Paul F. Bradshaw, 'The Use of the Bible in the Liturgy: Some Historical Perspectives' in *Studia Liturgica*, publ. by *Societas Liturgica*, 22/1, pp. 68–83 and 35–52.
9. Lucien Deiss, C.S.Sp., tr. Matthew J. O'Connell, *Springtime of the Liturgy – Liturgical Texts of the First Four Centuries* (Collegeville, 1979) p. 93.
10. Consultation on Common Texts (1983).
11. Inter-Lutheran Commission on Worship, *Lutheran Book of Worship* (Minneapolis/Philadelphia, 1978).
12. The Episcopal Church in the United States, *The Book of Common Prayer* (New York, 1979).
13. Raymond E. Brown, *The Churches the Apostles Left Behind* (New York, 1984).
14. James A. Sanders, *Torah and Canon* (Philadelphia, 1972).
15. James A. Sanders, *Canon and Community* (Philadelphia, 1984).

16. James A. Sanders, *God Has A Story Too – Sermons in Context* (Philadelphia, 1979).
17. Karl Barth, *The Word of God and the Word of Man* tr. Douglas Horton (London) n.d., pp. 28–50.
18. *Ibid.*, p. 33.
19. *Ibid.*, p. 34.
20. Thomas J. Talley, *The Origins of the Liturgical Year* (New York, 1986).
21. Austin Flannery, O.P., ed., *Vatican Council II – The Conciliar and Post Conciliar Documents* (Collegeville, 1975) p. 17.
22. Frederick R. McManus, 'Report on the Consultation on Common Text to the Episcopal Board of the International Commission on English in the Liturgy' (Washington, D.C.: 6 March 1982).
23. *Scottish Psalter and Church Hymnary* (Revised Edition) (London, Oxford University Press, 1929) no. 528.

12

Liberating Word

 *Sehon Goodridge*

IN AN integral approach to the Liturgy the distinction between ministry of the word and ministry of the sacrament cannot be maintained. The word read and expounded liberates the people of God for corporate offering and thankful celebration. This experience is especially true for a people who have been powerless and voiceless. We recall how Moses proclaimed the word of God to the Israelites in their wilderness experience: The God who liberated would initiate and keep covenant with them, fashioning them as a people. Those who were previously regarded as non-persons, oppressed and deprived, heard God's liberating word, affirming their person-hood and summoning them to participate in his gracious and good purpose for them and for all humankind. This was also the experience of Black slaves who for the most part could not read nor write, but who heard the word of God in the galleries of the master's Churches, and interpreted it in their life situation and projected the hope of liberation. Like the Israelites, they rose up and sacrificed with joyful celebration. This indissoluble link between liberation and celebration has been emphatically made in Liberation Theologies to which we shall refer later.

Of course, we have the foundational witness of Jesus within the worship of the Synagogue, as he read the Isaianic scroll and interpreted it:

'The Spirit of the Lord is upon me,
because he has anointed me to bring good news to the poor.
He has sent me to proclaim release to the captives
and recovery of sight to the blind,

213

to let the oppressed go free,
to proclaim the year of the Lord's favour.'
And he rolled up the scroll, gave it back to the attendant,
and sat down. The eyes of all in the Synagogue were
fixed on him. Then he began to say to them, 'Today this
scripture has been fulfilled in your hearing'.[1]

Jesus's ministry was characterized by the way in which he consistently brought the poor, the disabled, the oppressed and marginalized into the proclamation of the Kingdom of God by word and deed. This was not good news for the powerful and privileged who religiously, socially and politically benefited from the status quo. For them he was too dangerous, too subversive. He was pushed out of the world, handed over, crucified and buried. But God had the last word; he raised him up. What an act of liberation and vindication! 'Christ has died, Christ is risen, Christ will come again.' In a real sense God's word has not returned to him void, but has accomplished his good purpose.

God's strange and surprising way of liberation is marked by subversive narratives which run counter to the prevailing hegemonic narratives. Our attention has been called to the former:

These stories are placed in the midst of the royal recital, which is where narratives of transformation must always survive. Elijah must always live his faith in a world where decree goes out from Ahab (or Caesar Augustus); Elisha is always one who suffers under Jezebel (or Pontius Pilate). When the prophet acts, Ahab (or Herod) is sent into a furious rage. The narratives, however, concede nothing to Ahab nor Jezebel (nor to Caesar, Pilate nor Herod) because they are alternative accounts of history to which those royal figures have no access and in which they have no important roles to play. Indeed, one of the purposes of such narratives is precisely to delegitimise the kings, who are taken much too seriously in the main narrative and who take themselves much too seriously. By being given minor parts of these old narratives, the kings are made marginal.[2]

The prophetic narratives woven into dominant recitals of power
and control are indeed strange idioms; they protest against, and
undermine, hegemony which is shown to lead only to hostility and
death. These narratives offer an alternative way of breaking the
circle of violence and dissolution. In the same way the proclaimed
and enacted narrative of the liturgy signifies liberation, reconciliation, new life and hope.

The prophetic counter-prevailing narratives help to perceive
the world according to the reality of God's reign, and not according to conventional notions of reality which are constructed by the
powerful. These narratives point to shift of power in the world;
they point to God's action in help of the weak and down-trodden.
The marginal ones are the ones who summoned to perceive the
world differently, and to live and act according to this new vision.
This is liberation: to see, judge and act differently. It is this different way of perceiving and knowing that is the hallmark of the
liberating word:

> To be drawn into this new and different way of knowing the
> real world around us involves a radical re-education that
> reaches us:
> *... to watch, expect, and participate in the shift of power* toward
> women, blacks, the poor, and all other marginal ones whom
> royal modes of life have declared to be non-existent;
> *... to be present, as we are able, with the communities from* below
> who treasure such subversive narratives, who know differ-
> ently, who are special recipients of God's gift of power for life
> in the world ...[3]

The distinction has been made between the conversation 'on
the wall' and that 'behind the wall' (using the narrative of 2 Kings
18.19ff): the former is according to imperial rationality, with little
space for memory, vision and hope; the latter is according to a
rationality born of struggle and suffering, but also of imagination
and hope.[4] It is the story 'behind the walls', in our churches as
moral communities, that we must tell and recite, lest we end up
only with the story on the wall, with knowledge of what to do, but
with no will, courage or enthusiasm to act. It is this story 'behind
the walls' that liberates from our egoism and vested interests, to

realize the glorious liberty of the sons and daughters of God.[5] There is a clear connection between liberating word, liberating liturgy and liberated discipleship.

In liberation Theologies there is a definite epistemological shift: the experience of the poor is integral to the very process of knowledge. The preferential option for the poor compels us to take seriously the experiences of poor people. Through this process of learning from the poor, those who are in a more dominant position within society can be re-evangelized, and their values and perspectives raised. The powerful need to her the word through the voices they have rejected in their own society – the socially, culturally and economically deprived in the third world, and the 'new poor', the 'left-behind', in more affluent countries. The other shift is that in the very act of evangelising: it is not the gospel and culturally despised, but the gospel and non-persons. The good news is liberating when it enables people to feel like persons made in the image of God, for whom Christ died, and are alive in the Spirit. It is this new quality of life, with all its possibilities, that must be proclaimed. The powerless seem to have a quicker access to an understanding of the gospel than do the powerful. It has been observed that 'liberation theology is an understanding of the gospel arising precisely in the midst of such traditionally rejected voices'.[6]

Proclamation that over-emphasizes the need for self-abasement may not be liberating. Humility is indeed a virtue and the pride is the root of much sin. But if people are made to grovel in self-pity, carry a poor self-image and cringe before a judgmental God, they are denied the liberating word, that they are children of God and heirs/heiresses of the Kingdom. One recalls statements from parishioners like these: 'the parson really gave it to us this morning'; 'the parson gave us a ticking-off'. Such people may go home feeling miserable, but the sermon may not help then to change their behaviour. The primary purpose of preaching is to allow the Gospel to be heard, known and appropriated as good news – as liberation from bondage to sin and death.

> ... where our preaching can go beyond the survival aims of therapeutic theory to salvation from the bondage of sin and death, maintaining and building upon the inherent worth of

the individual, then we have a basis for preaching as the very architecture of a moral world.[7]

Proclamation that easily equates 'sin' with an inner attitude, with merely private frailties and faults, ignoring social and structural injustice, may arouse the suspicion of Liberation Theologians. Total salvation commits us to an examination, and denunciation, of unjust social structures and relationships. I have made this point elsewhere:

> Salvation includes Liberation from all those forces that frustrate and dominate. When such forces incarnate and manifest themselves in the structures of society, then the Kingdoms of this world need to be restored to their servant-nature, and become the Kingdom of our Lord and his Christ. Jesus' enactment of this unwordly Kingdom is of political significance in the world. Its enactment is a challenge and a rebuke to all wordly power systems. He therefore makes the firm political assertion, 'My kingdom is not of this world' (John 18.36). Those who follow him and face the demands of the kingdom must learn to distance themselves from the false security of wealth, the insatiable quest for power and the debilitating preoccupation with wordly care. The politics of the Kingdom is a distinctive type of politics, the politics of the cross, the power of suffering and service on behalf of human liberation and reconciliation ...[8]

We are challenged to rediscover the place of justice within our christian tradition. There is a tendency to avoid the use of the word 'justice' less we be branded socialists or Marxists. But we must remember that justice is embedded in our tradition. Justice and love bear a dialectical relationship; we cannot have one without the other. The revered Brazilian ecclesiastic and theologian, Dom Helder Camara, has stated: 'My socialism is a special one which respects the human person and turns to the gospel. My socialism is justice'.[9] Camara is convinced that we do not need to flirt with Marxism, but only be faithful to the foundational Judaeo-Christian tradition. The prophets of the Eighth Century BCE were perhaps more radical than Marx. For example let us take the following from Amos and Micah:

'I hate, I despise your festivals
and I take no delight in your
Solemn assemblies.
Even though you offer me your
burnt offerings and grain offerings,
I will not accept them;
and the offerings of well-being of your fatted animals
I will not look upon.
Take away from me the noise of your songs;
I will not listen to the melody of our harps.
But let justice roll down like waters,
and righteousness like an ever-flowing stream.' [10]

'With what shall I come before the Lord,
and bow myself before God on high?
Shall I come before him with burnt offerings,
with calves a year old?
Will the Lord be pleased with thousands of rams,
with ten thousands of rivers of oil?
Shall I give my firstborn for my transgression,
the fruit of my body for the sin of my soul?
He has told you, O mortal, what is good;
and what does the Lord require of you
but to do justice, and to love kindness?
and to walk humbly with your God?' [11]

We have noted earlier that Jesus' understanding of his ministry included the inauguration of God's reign of justice, bringing release and liberation. We may also note that the *Magnificat* which we sing to various magnificent chants is very subversive and liberative. God indeed lifts up the lowly and down-trodden and vindicates the meek of the earth. The Liberation Theologian Jose Miranda has aptly affirmed:

'When God intervenes, his principal activity is directed to the conscience. And through people's consciences he achieves his true intervention ... The God of the Exodus is the God of conscience. The Liberation of the slaves from Egypt was principally a work of the imperative of liberty and justice inculcated into the Israelites.' [12]
Miranda also affirms the gospel as salvation, because it reveals

God's justice which has been realized through the death and resurrection of Christ, and gives faith its capacity to make men just.[13]

In our tradition justice is seen as the condition of peace and love.
Justice is the essence of the covenant relationship which commits
us to the mutual respect and responsibility. The covenant community all belong and participate. All have rights and duties. The
poor, the outcast ('sinners' and 'tax-collectors'), women and children are accepted. There are 'Diveses' and 'Lazaruses'. Racial,
ethnic, religious, social and gender barriers are broken down.[14]

We are at a point where we can consider what would happen if
we reassigned the cast of characters in our narratives and messages.
This challenges has been well put to us:

> A Liberation preacher soon comes to ask the question of the
> cast of characters almost automatically, and then comes to the
> realization that this sort of question must be asked, not only
> of particular texts, but also of the entire thrust of biblical
> history. Why is it that in Christian communities even the
> most powerful think that they stand with the children of Israel
> and do not see that in many ways they are closer to Pharaoh
> than to Moses and his host? Why is it that so many preachers,
> when approaching the prophetic text, take for granted that
> they are the prophets, and the congregation is the disobedi-
> ent Israel that must be chastised? Why is it that so many
> secure, prosperous congregations can read the Psalms that
> deal with powerlessness or with political persecution as if they
> were the powerless and the persecuted? Why is it that so
> many religious folk can listen to the teachings of Jesus as if
> they were the despised publicans and harlots that will go first
> into the Kingdom? If the question of power and powerless-
> ness is fundamental in order to understand the message of
> scripture, the manner in which that question may be brought
> home to us is through the way in which we assign the char-
> acters in the biblical account.[15]

What the liberation preacher seeks to do is to restore the text to
its original socio-economic and political setting and allow it to
interface with similar contexts today. He/she dares to recast the
characters, and allow the poor, the powerless, the disadvantaged

and the disabled to be the *personae* of the narrative and message. Imagine Psalm 23 being read by the poor in deprived areas. They are struck not only by 'the valley of the shadow of death' but also by the 'table prepared in the presence of the enemies' (hardly appropriate at a funeral!). The 'table' is the assurance that God will fill a concrete need for food. They also know that they are hungry because they have 'enemies' who are destroying them, denying them access to resources. Let us examine also passages dealing with 'household laws' (Ephesians 5.21–6.9; Colossians 3.18–4.1; 1 Peter 2.18–3.7). If taken out of their original context they are very oppressive. Women feel hard done by. What about hearing simultaneously the limitation of their husbands' power? Similarly, are slaves to hear words directed at them and not the words directed at the masters? Are slaves to be obedient and submissive, while their masters remain arrogant and oppressive? This has been precisely the burden of the message to slaves seated in the galleries of churches, with a prime view of pulpits and altars, but not of their masters in the naves. These words of the New Testament which were intended to be read and applied to socially mixed gatherings, assumed different meaning when read insituations of segregation between masters and slaves. We must therefore be vigilant less than socio-political setting in which a text is being interpreted does not legitimize oppression, rather than signal liberation.

If recasting the characters in our narratives and message is important the use of context – life stories is equally important. The lived experiences of people are an effective starting point for reflection, and the biblical stories became open invitations to further exploration. A vital model is therefore to enter into dialogue with people about concrete community situations and offer them tools with which they may make their own discoveries. Jesus' use of parables remains the model for our adoption. The way of the parabolic is the way to discovery and participation. Parables in a real sense empower people, and this is a lesson that the liberation preacher has learnt. A daring to reflect and read the text in different circumstances and from different perspectives, has been well demonstrated.[16] In the specific context of people's struggle for human liberation and community development stories invite them to be subjects and participants, relinquishing the disposition of passive submission and dependence. Someone may wonder where is the theological under pinning for such a process. This question has been well addressed:

> In theological terms, what this means is that we are speaking of the Kingdom. A theology of liberation is a theology of Kingdom. The goal toward which we move is the fulfillment of the promises of the Kingdom. As citizens of the Kingdom, we must renounce service to the present order. We are Christ's not Caesar's, and for that reason we refuse to give ourselves to Caesar. Since in Christ the Kingdom has come, we can now live out of the new order. But since he is also still to come we are not yet fully liberated, but in the process of being liberated – or, in more familiar terms, of working out of our own salvation with fear and trembling, for God is at work in us (Phil. 2.12). To attempt to preach this liberation in our churches may be a very costly thing. But then, the gate is narrow, and the way is hard that leads to life.[17]

During my five years of pioneering work as Principal of the Simon of Cyrne Theological Institute in London (1989–1994), I was deeply committed to the Black experience and perspective as an interpretative grip in theological exploration. I was most appreciative of the encouragement given me by people like Donald Gray whom we are honouring by this publication. The experience of struggle and suffering, from slavery to emancipation, from colonization to decolonization, has been peculiarly that of Black people. We rejoice that the demonic system of apartheid in South Africa has been dismantled and we support our brothers and sisters in their growth into freedom. We can recite this saga of liberation like the children of Israel for it is formative of our faith, spirituality and worship. We have kept faith in God who liberated and will liberate, a God whom we meet, and praise and adore in the struggle. God's word has been heard in all its liberating power and we respond in celebration and thanksgiving. It is amazing how Black people, despite the odds, sing, dance and shout for joy. Our liturgy is truly liberative for at its heart is the liberating word, interfacing with our life-story, our history, our projected hope, and our confidence that we shall overcome.

This is the perspective and focus of Black preaching. The preacher has a solemn responsibility and a trusted authority. The importance of the oral tradition and story-telling in the biblical tradition is emphasized. Dialogic preaching keeps worship alive as the preacher's call goes out: 'Praise God!' or 'Let's praise him'![18]

The Mystery of black suffering and divine liberation have shaped the convictions and perspectives of Black Christians. James Cones, a Black Professor, and one of the pioneers of Black Theology in the United States of America has called our attention to this fact:

> On the one hand, the faith of the black people as disclosed in the sermons, songs and prayers, revealed that they faced the reality of black suffering. Faith in Jesus did not cancel out the pain of slavery. Sometimes I'm up, sometimes I, down, Oh, yes, Lord! But on the other hand, Jesus' presence in the experience of suffering liberated black people from being dependent upon the historical limitation of servitude for a definition of their humanity. Thus they began to project this new knowledge of themselves with future apocalyptic imagination. They began to sing and preach about a 'home in glory' where they would 'sit at the welcome table'. Heaven thus was not so much an opiate as it was a revolutionary judgement that black people made about American society on the basis of Jesus' presence in their lives. It was the 'age to come' that had broken into the present age, giving black people a vision of freedom enabled them to struggle now for the liberation of the little ones ...[19]

Such a vision enabled black preachers like Martin Luther King Jr to struggle for human liberation. He had reached 'the mountain top' which enabled him to envision the goal of liberation even though he apparently saw that the path would lead to his death. But he was grasped by the conviction that suffering in the struggle for freedom was liberating. God would have the last word of vindication.

A good study of 'Black Preaching' has been made by, Henry H. Mitchell, a Black Theologian in the United States of America.[20] Mitchell illustrates the variety of styles, the spontaneity, and the dialogic nature of 'Black Preaching'. He also emphasizes the importance of the sermon climaxing in the Black celebration of freedom in Church. Mitchell writes:

> The uniqueness of the Black introduction is the relational role between speaker and audience. The uniqueness of Black climax is similarly more related to feeling tones than to any standard set of elements. This may come as a surprise to some critics of the Black preacher. For these critics, every climax is stereotyped as leading to a graveyard and some tears and shouting. The Black climax, at its best, is a kind of celebration of the goodness of God and the standing of Black people in his Kingdom, as there elements have been expressed in the message.[21]

Of course any claim that the liberating word can only be heard by Black people and not by white people must be avoided. But the opportunity is offered for both groups of Christians to meet and share in the spirit of Christians partnership. Black people will share their experience of the word of God who has met them in the sufferings and struggles of their history. They will tell their stories, share their biblical insights, and demonstrate style, nature and aim of their preaching.

From the richness of our Black experience we have much to share with the whole people of God. To be catholic is to be universal, but to be universal is not to be uniform strictly speaking to be catholic is to belong to the whole with every part, and every group, participating. Black people can play their part in the building up of the whole church. We can share our understanding of the word of God:

> For Black people the story is our story, the Bible promise is our hope. Thus when the word of scripture is proclaimed in the Black community, it is not a new message but a new challenge. Scripture is part of our roots, the Bible has sunk deep into our tradition; and the good news of the gospel has been enmeshed in our past of oppression and pain. Still the message was heard, and we learned to celebrate in the Midst of sorrow, to hope in the depths of despair and to fight for free-

dom in the face of all obstacles. The time has come to take this precious heritage and to go and 'tell it on the mountain'.[22]

We can also share our gift of freedom, we have the memory of dehumanizing slavery, racist prejudice and oppression. Those to whom freedom has been denied can best understand the proclamation that Christ has set us free. Freedom is God's gift and we are accountable to him for it in the lives of others. For this reason all forms of injustice and oppression must be resisted, none are free, unless all are free. The gift of freedom also carries with it the demand of freedom: the task of working for the total liberation of total humankind.

The gift of reconciliation is a further gift we can share. The proclamation of the gospel liberates us from hatred and revenge, and commits us to forgiveness and reconciliation. Reconciliation is indeed the fruit of liberation. The world has marvelled that in the after-math of the dismantling of apartheid Black people have not sought revenge, but have shown a remarkable spirit of forgiveness. They have displayed not the instruments of warfare, but the instruments of peace.

> … This peace is the fruit of justice. We must be a part of those movements for justice that seek to reduce bombs and increase bread, to replace bullets with the printing of books. We must work with all who strive to make available the fruits of creation to all God's children everywhere. It was in chains that our parents were brought to these shores and in violence were we maintained in bondage. Let us who are the children of the pain be now a bridge of reconciliation. Let us who are the offspring of violence become the channels of compassion. Let us, the songs and daughters of bondage, be the bringers of peace.[23]

To this gift of reconciliation is added the gifts of joy and community.

> Joy is a hallmark of Black spirituality. Joy is first of all celebration. Celebration is movement and song, rhythm and feeling, color and sensation, exultation and thanksgiving. We celebrate the presence and the proclamation of the word.

This joy is a sign of our faith and especially our hope. It is never an escape from reality, however harsh it may be. Indeed this joy is often present even in the midst of deep anguish and bitter tears.[24]

The experience of sorrow and joy is shared in community. It is particularly expressed in Black people's liturgy and worship; worship must be a shared experience; worship is largely a celebration of community gathered in the name of the Trinity. Worship must also embrace social justice and social concerns, that all God's children may be free.

We have examined the necessity of an epistemological shift if the word of God is to be truly liberating. The word of God must not solely be interpreted and proclaimed from the point of view of power and control, but from the point of view and perspective of the powerless and marginalized. Christians in the Western churches have been invited to engage in what has been called 'counter-imagination'.

> ... It is not imagination that is at all congenial to dominant intellectual or political modes. It does not easily conform to either the revolutionary or the reactionary advocates of our world. When it comes, it makes no accommodation to the epistemological assumptions or social biases of the congregation. It is, however a nervy offer of a world in and through a radically different perspective. It is my judgement that the low-energy of the church and the fatigue of many clergy come about because we begin by making too many concessions to the dominant epistemology around us. We make these concessions because we know we will not get much of a hearing otherwise, or because we ourselves have this incredulous, sinking feeling about the claims we are about to utter.[25]

The inclusion of the poor, the deprived and the disabled in our analysis, will make a difference to our interpretation and proclamation. We must dare to recast the characters of our narrative and message. We must dare also to use the interpretative grid of suffering and struggle. This grid has proven very liberative and celebrative for Black christian communities whose liturgy and worship overflow with joy. Those who were considered 'no people', are now confident that they are God's people. The right hand of the Lord has been victorious; they have been liberated. They can sing the Lord's song and shout for joy. It is this gift of joyful celebration that Black christians can contribute to the liturgy and worship of the church. They can witness to the experience of God's liberating word and action in the midst of the suffering and struggle, with firm confidence and joyful enthusiasm.

NOTES

1. Luke 4.18–21 *The New Oxford Annotated Bible* – The Revised Standard Version OUP 1991.
2. Walter Brueggemann, *Interpretation and Obedience: From Faithful Reading to Faithful Living* (Augsburg Press Minneapolis, USA, 1991) p. 30.
3. *Ibid*. pp. 38–39.
4. *Ibid*. pp. 60–65.
5. Romans 8.21. cf Galatians 5.1, 13.
6. Justo L. Gonzalez and Catherine G. Gonzalez *Liberation Preaching: The Pulpit and the Oppressed* (Abingdon Press, Nashville, USA 1992) p. 19.
7. John Snow, *The Impossible Vocation: ministry. In the meantime* (Coyly Publications, Cambridge, Massachusetts, 1988) pp. 90–91.
8. Sehon Goodridge, 'Salvation and Political Justice' in *Windows on Salvation*, Donald English (ed.), (Dorton, Longman and Todd Ltd) 1994 (p. 136).
9. Sen J. de Broucher, *Dom Helder Camara: The Violence of a Peacemaker* (Maryknoll, New York, Orbis, 1970).
10. Amos 5.21–24.
11. Micah 6.6–8.
12. Jose Miranda, *Being and the Messiah* (Maryknoll, New York, Orbis, 1977) pp. 34–5.
13. Jose Miranda, *Marx and the Bible* (Maryknoll, New York, Orbis, 1974) pp. 62–3; 189–92.
14. Galatians 3.28. Cf. Colossians 3.11; Ephesians 2.11–22.
15. Justo L. Gonzalez and Catherine G. Gonzalez Op. Cit. p. 78.
16. Cardenal, Ernesto, *The Gospel in Solentiname* 3 vols. (Maryknoll, N.Y. Orbis books, 1976–79), see also Sam Amirtham (ed) *Stories Make People* (WCC, Geneon, 1989).
17. Justo Gonzalez and Catherine Gonzalez Op. Cit pp. 112–113.
18. See Joel Edwards (ed.) *Let's Praise Him Again: An African-Caribbean Perspective on Worship* (Kingsway Publications, 1992).
19. James H. Cone, *God of the Oppressed* (S.P.C.K. London, 1977), p. 193.
20. Henry H. Mitchell, *Black Preaching* (J. B. Lippincott Co., Philadelphia and New York, 1970).
21. *Ibid*. p. 188.
22. David T. Shannon and Gayraud S. Wilmore (ed.) *Black witness to the Apostolic Faith* (Faith & Order, U.S.A., 1985) p. 47.
23. *Ibid*. p. 76.
24. *Ibid*. p. 78. Cf John 15.11; 16.20.
25. Brueggemann, *The Bible and Post-modern Imagination. Texts Under Negotation* (SCM London, 1993) p. 20.